The CQ Press Writing Guide for Public Policy

*This book is dedicated to my four sons, Sam, Abe, Daniel, and Luke.
I hope it helps make the world in which you're growing up a better place for you,
and for others, to live, one little bit at a time.*

Sara Miller McCune founded SAGE Publishing in 1965 to support the dissemination of usable knowledge and educate a global community. SAGE publishes more than 1000 journals and over 800 new books each year, spanning a wide range of subject areas. Our growing selection of library products includes archives, data, case studies and video. SAGE remains majority owned by our founder and after her lifetime will become owned by a charitable trust that secures the company's continued independence.

Los Angeles | London | New Delhi | Singapore | Washington DC | Melbourne

The CQ Press
Writing Guide for
Public Policy

Andrew Pennock

University of Virginia

FOR INFORMATION:

CQ Press

An imprint of SAGE Publications, Inc.

2455 Teller Road

Thousand Oaks, California 91320

E-mail: order@sagepub.com

SAGE Publications Ltd.

1 Oliver's Yard

55 City Road

London EC1Y 1SP

United Kingdom

SAGE Publications India Pvt. Ltd.

B 1/I 1 Mohan Cooperative Industrial Area

Mathura Road, New Delhi 110 044

India

SAGE Publications Asia-Pacific Pte. Ltd.

3 Church Street

#10-04 Samsung Hub

Singapore 049483

Library of Congress Cataloging-in-Publication Data

Names: Pennock, Andrew.

Title: The CQ Press writing guide for public policy / Andrew Pennock.

Other titles: Writing guide for public policy

Description: Washington, D.C. : CQ Press, a division of SAGE, 2019. | Includes bibliographical references and index.

Identifiers: LCCN 2018013137 | ISBN 9781506348780 (pbk.)

Subjects: LCSH: Communication in public administration. | Communication in politics. | Written communication. | Policy sciences. | Persuasion (Rhetoric)—Political aspects.

Classification: LCC JF1525.C59 P46 2019 | DDC 808.06/632—dc23

LC record available at https://lccn.loc.gov/2018013137

Acquisitions Editor: Scott Greenan

Editorial Assistant: Sarah Christensen

Production Editor: Bennie Clark Allen

Copy Editor: Talia Greenberg

Typesetter: C&M Digitals (P) Ltd.

Proofreader: Eleni-Maria Georgiou

Indexer: Molly Hall

Cover Designer: Candice Harman

Marketing Manager: Jennifer Jones

18 19 20 21 22 10 9 8 7 6 5 4 3 2 1

Brief Contents

Detailed Contents

Preface

As a policy maker who has worked in federal, state, and local governments, I have presented in committee meetings and persuaded important people to shift resources to better ends while talking in the hallway afterward. I have lobbied in closed-door advocacy sessions and networked with politicians at events. While these are all essential skills, the ability to write well is the most effective policy skill I possess. The policy documents I have written speak for me when I am not there. They provide an overview of my analysis, delineate the meaty details, document the technical arguments, and explore the results that I can only touch on in an hour-long conversation. My written work can have a life of its own—with any luck, it will go out to audiences I could never have met in person and influence them to make the change I want to see in the world.

I recently cowrote a report to the Rhode Island state legislature on the state's 911 system. It is hard to imagine a public policy that meets a more crucial need—everyone in the country, from the poorest to the richest, calls 911 in emergencies. Our research team witnessed this firsthand at the 911 call center. Dozens of operators fielded calls from people around the state at the most important moments in their lives. The calls ranged from the most joyous ("My wife is in labor and the baby is coming now!") to the most tragic ("He's not breathing!") to the most frightening ("I hear someone moving around downstairs.").

Once the research was finished and the analysis completed, it was time to write the report. As I sat down at my computer, I remembered the call center. As I typed, I was constantly reminded that people's lives depend on how well the 911 system functions. Ultimately, my report recommended changes to the system that could shave as much as 20 seconds off of emergency vehicle response times. This meant that ambulances could be on the scene of car accidents more quickly. More parents would survive terrible wrecks and would live to go to their kids' soccer games. Fewer families would spend money on long hospital stays and instead spend their money on their children's education, on vacations, or on the basics like food and shelter. My writing had to reflect the importance of the lives I was trying to protect.

Writing is a means, not an end. It is unlikely that you picked up this book because writing itself excites you. Instead you picked it up because you have a particular public policy goal and want to persuade decision makers to make it a priority. Perhaps you want to reduce the amount of water pollution in drinking water. Perhaps you want to convince a state legislature to reduce burdensome regulations on the shared economy. Perhaps you want to tell a grant-making agency how successful your nonprofit has been at reducing the dropout rate.

I wrote this book to help you achieve these goals.

Acknowledgments

Like all books, this book owes a great deal to many people whose names do not appear on the cover.

The first thanks go to Valerie Cooley and Ben Sammons, who supported me since the beginning of this endeavor. They immediately saw the value in the book and encouraged me throughout the time it took to write. My University of Virginia colleagues, Ray Scheppach and Eric Patashnik, helped me sharpen much of what I have to say about the particular genres contained in this book. Thank you.

Additionally, I owe many thanks to the students who helped with this book. Rachel Black was an outstanding research assistant; she will probably never know the impact she had on the final product. Numerous students contributed writing samples featured in these pages. Many of them go unnamed (by their preference), but they have my thanks again for helping me develop these ideas and helping shape how I teach writing.

Without the help of the wonderful editors and staff at CQ Press, this book would only be a good idea and not a book you can hold in your hands. As such, I owe many thanks to the various editors and staff at CQ Press who have helped this book along the way, including Scott Greenan, Sarah Christensen, Sarah Calabi, Talia Greenberg, Bennie Allen, and Jerry Higgins. I've been grateful for the CQ Press team since the moment I signed.

The various reviewers who provided feedback and encouragement have also helped to improve it. They helped me hold fast to the idea that this book fills a felt need in students' academic and professional development. Your ideas and feedback helped to shape the book in real ways. Thank you.

Finally, I owe a vast debt of gratitude to my family, particularly to my wife, Charity Pennock. Without her support and endorsement, this book would never have been finished. Thanks to my parents, Steve and Helen Pennock, for their help while I wrote. And finally, thanks to my four sons, Sam, Abe, Daniel, and Luke, for the joyous greetings every time I came home from writing. My certainty about your joy made it easier to write when I was away. I'm very grateful.

SAGE Publishing wishes to thank the following reviewers for their assistance:

Michael Abels	*University of Central Florida*
Jeff Gulati	*Bentley University*
Anna Marie Schuh	*Roosevelt University–Chicago*
Marcus Mauldin	*University of Tennessee–Chattanooga*
Marc Meredith	*University of Pennsylvania*

John Mero   *Campbell University*
Stephen Owen   *Radford University*
Derek Ross   *Auburn University*
Matthew Shapiro   *Illinois Institute of Technology*

About the Author

Andrew Pennock is an assistant professor at the Batten School of Leadership and Public Policy at the University of Virginia. He teaches writing in his courses on leadership, policy analysis, political institutions, and Virginia politics and policy.

Prior to joining the Batten School, he taught at Brown University, where he was the director of graduate studies and of the Applied Social, Economic, and Regulatory Analysis (ASERA) Group, which partnered with government institutions, nonprofit organizations, and other entities to provide technical expertise, policy analysis, and program evaluation. A seasoned instructor, Professor Pennock won multiple teaching awards during his time at Brown and at the University of North Carolina at Chapel Hill.

Before completing his PhD in political science at UNC–Chapel Hill, Professor Pennock was a professional, nonpartisan committee staffer at the North Carolina General Assembly. He has continued his applied work through consulting with the governor of Virginia; the United States Centers for Disease Control; the Rhode Island legislature; local school boards; and Serve Rhode Island, Rhode Island's AmeriCorps home.

Professor Pennock's academic research examines public policy in the global economy as well as the scholarship of teaching and learning. His work has been published in *Perspectives on Politics*, *Economics & Politics*, and *PS: Political Science & Politics*.

Outside of Batten, he is the father of four small boys who wrestle with him all the time. He and his wife, Charity, love to cook, read, garden, travel, and have good conversations with people whenever they can.

Introduction

1

Audiences and Audience-Centered Writing in Public Policy

Policy writing plays an important role in shaping public decisions. Every day, policy analysts, nonprofit leaders, and advocates create documents that inform and influence decisions made by legislators, bureaucrats, and service providers. Their decisions affect some of the biggest aspects of our daily lives: how much money is withheld from our paychecks in taxes, which health care conditions insurance companies must cover, who has to live near environmental hazards, and the quality of the schools children attend. Policy writers write to inform and shape these important decisions.

As a policy writer, you will write to inform and persuade legislators, bureaucrats, and service providers on important issues. These policy audiences have unique needs and expectations that differ systematically from the academic audiences for whom you learned to write in college. To help address policy problems effectively you must first learn to communicate with this audience in a language and format they understand. In this chapter, we will explain how to do this by outlining what an audience-centered approach to writing for policy makers is, explaining how policy audiences are different than other audiences, and teaching you about the broad categories of policy audiences who make important public decisions.

Write & Reflect

What important issues made you want to learn to write effectively to influence public policy? Is there an issue in your state that has impacted your family recently? Is there a global issue that has caught your attention and on which you want to make change? Are there problems you work on professionally that you would like to communicate more clearly? Make a list of three issues that are important to you.

What Is Audience-Centered Writing?

Policy writers can more effectively shape policy decisions by becoming audience-centered writers. Audience-centered writers are concerned first and foremost with communicating with their readers. Rather than thinking,

"What do I know?" and then writing a document, audience-centered writers first try to understand who their audience is and what their audience needs to understand. Audience-centered writers always ask:

1. Who is my audience?

2. What are their needs?

3. What do I need to do to communicate with them?

Audience-centered writing is the foundation of policy writing—if you can anticipate the preferences and needs of your target audience, you can introduce them to new information in an intelligible way. This is no mean feat. First, you have to really understand what your audience does and does not know about a topic. Then you have to understand what their needs are: What is it that they need to know? Finally, you have to pay attention to everything from the document's content and structure to its language and formatting to make sure you can communicate effectively with them. If you can use audience-oriented techniques to make your document feel clear and familiar to policy makers, then they are more likely to create and implement the policy change you are suggesting.

> Essentially style resembles good manners. It comes of endeavoring to understand others, of thinking for them rather than yourself—or thinking, that is, with the heart as well as the head. (Sir Arthur Quiller-Couch, quoted in Williams & Bizup [2014])

Audience-centered writing is hard, but it is the only effective way to write in the public policy world; furthermore, people respect you for taking the time to do it. In many ways, it is like good manners: Going a little bit out of your way to help someone else creates a great impression. Decision makers will begin to realize that you put them first in your writing and that you work hard to save them time. This is exactly the reputation you want to have.

Who Is the Audience in Policy Settings?

The key to audience-centered writing in public policy is to understand policy audiences by understanding the world in which they live. Let's start by considering a few examples of decision makers and looking at their daily schedules, ranging from the president of the United States to the county director of a Department of Public Health.

The president of the United States makes decisions that shape the lives of 300 million Americans and affect the rest of the world. The entire federal bureaucracy produces documents that end up on his desk. As a part of his packed formal schedule of meetings on any given day, the president might be given a dozen policy documents addressing topics as diverse as an Ebola outbreak in Africa, extremist group activity in the Middle East, and reforming the Affordable Care Act (ACA).

Life in a legislature is just as busy for any one of the 7,383 state legislators in the United States. Many of these men and women often work as part-time legislators and have full-time jobs when they are not working in the state capital. When they arrive at the statehouse they switch gears from their private jobs to their public ones. An average day might include four committee hearings, a dozen constituent meetings, and several hours of floor debate. At every event, someone is handing them a new document about a new topic. At the end of the day they might be carrying briefs and memos about the rising swell of prison reform, a new bill concerning LBGTQ rights, voter ID laws, and a bevy of other issues.

Bureaucratic life is scarcely less hectic, even for those at the county or city level. An agency executive, such as the director of a Department of Public Health, might begin her day with a staff meeting about the rising toll of the opioid crisis, then join a conference call with federal officials about Zika control before meeting citizens concerned about vaccination requirements for toddlers. At every turn, she will be given a document making the case for a change in policy, with each group hoping she will be swayed by its arguments and evidence.

While policy makers have limited time in their busy days to focus on any one issue, there is a seemingly infinite amount of policy writing produced for them to read and process. For example, U.S. federal agencies such as the Environmental Protection Agency (EPA) or the Department of Health and Human Services (DHHS) propose and create policy by making rules that have the force of law. That is because Congress has given federal agencies the ability to transform the laws Congress has passed into rules that are backed up by actual fines and prison sentences. These proposed and final rules are recorded in the *Federal Register*, which clocked in at 80,462 pages in 2013. The index alone is 317 pages! In total, that's 27 feet of paper. Behind each of the proposed and enacted rules, hundreds of documents were produced by federal agencies to prepare them for publication.

And the *Federal Register* only reflects one slice of the writing by one of the three federal branches of government. State governments produce fewer documents, but multiply by 50 states and you still get a huge number! There are 39,044 local governments in the United States (National League of Cities, 2014) producing documents that shape local policies. At each level of government there are policy makers, policy analysts, advocates, and citizens trying to influence policy. In other words, policy making involves a *lot* of writing!

As you can see, the policy audiences for whom you are writing are incredibly busy with their responsibilities. At the same time, they are inundated with a flood of policy documents every time they round a corner. If you want to effectively persuade and inform this audience, you have to remember just how busy and deluged with information they are. As an audience-centered approach, writing for policy makers has to keep these realities in mind.

The Different Audiences in Policy Settings

While almost all policy makers are incredibly busy, they all will have different background knowledge, interests, and goals about any given topic. Part of understanding your audience is knowing how much they know and care about your topic and what they want to do with the information you give them. For example, some audiences have limited background knowledge about the issue at hand. You have to draw a tricky balance of not talking down to them and not talking over their heads. If this seems like hard advice to follow, it is! Some audiences may want to know the intricate details of a policy, and others may only want to know the broad strokes. Who wants what? Let's take a look at the three types of audiences in policy writing and see how they differ.

Elected Officials

Policy writing is often targeted at elected officials, many of whom make some of the most important decisions in government. Elected officials, both legislators and executives, want to be reelected and are therefore responsive to the broad contours of what voters want on an issue such as health care or food safety. However, voters often know (and care) less about the details of these policies. When faced with these details, elected officials are usually genuinely interested in making decisions that solve problems in a feasible way. They are often open to being persuaded about which particular solution they should choose. Proposed solutions have to effectively solve the problem, be politically palatable, and fit within the budget.

Elected officials need policy writing to be quickly and easily digestible. They are almost never experts on the topic at hand, nor are they likely to become experts.[1] They need to be able to walk away from policy documents with talking points they can take into meetings with other

---

[1] While elected officials are often relative novices in most issue areas, the most effective elected officials become true experts in two or three issue areas during their career (Volden & Wiseman, 2014). These legislators often have a deeper background on a given issue than many staff and lobbyists.

legislators and constituents. They are also more attuned to the politics of each issue and want policy documents at least to implicitly consider the political aspects of a decision.

For example, Representative Greene may be asked to vote on a bill requiring students to have eye exams before starting kindergarten. Representative Greene isn't a doctor, nor was he elected because he is an expert in health care policy. He was elected because most voters in his district agreed with his politics. Now he has to learn about this policy problem and the proposed solution quickly before making a decision that affects millions of families in his state. He needs a document that explains to him why eye exams are important, what would happen if the law isn't passed, and what the impact of passing will be. Armed with this information, he can vote for or against the bill and explain his decision to others.

Bureaucrats

Like elected officials, bureaucrats are crucial players in policy making. Because elected officials are so busy, they often delegate decision making and information gathering to bureaucrats in government agencies. Bureaucrats can therefore have a lot of control over their area, even while they are held accountable by elected officials. Bureaucrats also want to find solutions that effectively solve problems, are politically palatable, and fit within the budget. They are very concerned with doing so ethically because their effectiveness depends on their reputation for being honest.

However, unlike politicians, who work in multiple issue areas, bureaucrats often work in a particular issue area. They are influenced by business groups, unions, nonprofits, and advocates concerned with their issue area. For example, someone working for the EPA might spend every day entirely on wetlands protection and never on clean air, pesticides, or any of the other major areas the EPA covers. In her work on a particular river delta, she would interact with scientists from the state's environmental agency, the local Sierra Club, farmers and golf course owners whose fertilizers impact the delta, and local citizen groups like fishermen who enjoy recreational fishing. Each of these groups is concerned with balancing the protection of the delta with its interests. The EPA employee is responsible for knowing each of their viewpoints and balancing the costs and benefits between the groups.

Policy documents for bureaucrats can be longer and more detailed than documents for elected officials because, like the EPA employee, bureaucrats have deeper knowledge about the topic at hand. In contrast to legislators or executives, bureaucrats generally want more information on both what the recommendation is and a lot more about *how* you arrived at it. They are less politically concerned but have a high standard of transparency because they are responsible for knowing and understanding the details of a policy.

When most people think about bureaucrats, they picture media portrayals of DMV employees processing their driver's license renewals with a vacant look or, worse, a glare. Thankfully, most government employees who read policy documents are much more engaged with their work. Almost all have college degrees, and many have master's degrees in public policy or a related field. They have a general level of knowledge about the issues and how the system works. That said, even a bureaucrat might not have much information about the decision(s) he is being asked to make, especially if the person oversees a large area of responsibility or if the issue at hand is new or has changed dramatically.

The Media

Reporters and editors are a key audience for policy writing because of the crucial role they play in determining which issues are discussed by the public and in policy circles. Reporters and editors are just as busy as other policy audiences as they scramble to report the news on a daily or weekly basis.

Policy writing for the media needs to be even briefer than writing for politicians. Press releases and op-eds are often less than a page long. The media are interested in newsworthy stories, so it is important that your writing links to a current important news topic. Stories are newsworthy when many people will want to read them because they are important, noteworthy, or trendy.

Like elected officials, members of the media are more interested in understanding the broad outlines of an issue rather than the particular details so they can communicate the main thrusts to the public in a nontechnical way. Unlike politicians or bureaucrats, reporters are not as interested in arriving at solutions as they are in reporting about what has happened in the political process or about a particular policy outcome. We'll explore how to write for this particular audience more in Chapter 10.

What Do These Policy Audiences Need to Know?

Once you have identified your policy audience and have a baseline understanding of them, then your next step to creating audience-centered writing is to figure out what it is they need to know about your topic.

Here are four key questions to ask:

1. *What does your audience already know about the topic?* As you saw in the previous section, this differs from person to person and from group to group. Whether you are writing to a particular person or to a group, you have to gauge how much they know about the

topic. Generally speaking, you can assume that policy audiences are broadly educated. Their particular knowledge depends on their personal background, how long they have engaged with an issue in official settings such as committees or floor debates, and how much their constituents have lobbied them about the issue. You will need to research your audience to find out exactly what they know. Listening to speeches, reading what they have written, knowing where they have worked, and actually talking with your target audience are all great ways to get a handle on this.

2. *What crucial knowledge are they missing?* Once you understand what they do know, you need to identify specific information gap(s) you want to fill. What important evidence are they missing? Are they thinking about the problem incorrectly? Do you want to tell them about a new solution? Sometimes people actually know what they don't know. For example, legislatures and executives often create commissions to explore current or future problems. A coastal city might form a commission asking, "How will our city minimize the impact of climate change?" A rust-belt state might form a commission asking, "How can we stop the opioid crisis?" Other times, people are unaware the problem exists or that it can be solved. Either way, you have a starting point to begin helping them think about solutions.

3. *Why does your audience care about your topic, and how much do they care?* Next, you will need to frame your argument based on the interests of the audience. Now that you know about your audience and what you need them to know, ask, "Why do they care about my topic?" In other words, why are they interested? Are they ideologically opposed to or in favor of it? Do they need to help particular groups of voters or special interests? Their level of interest determines how much time and attention your audience will be able to give your document and how you will need to frame your arguments.

4. *What kind of document will best help your audience process this new information?* Finally, you will need to consider what type of document will best enable your audience to process your information. What genres of policy writing should you use? In what format should you deliver it? You will need to pick a genre that matches your audience's specific needs, as well as the setting in which you are writing. For example, a senator in a committee on a particular topic might want a much longer document (like a 10-page policy memo) than a senator who will only encounter a topic briefly in a floor vote (a one-page issue brief).

Learning the Skills of Audience-Centered Writing

Now that you have identified and begun to understand your audience, you need to learn the practical skills necessary for audience-centered writing in public policy settings. The chapters in Part II of this book walk you through this process step by step. *Chapter 2: Generating and Organizing Your Argument* shows you how to move from an initial assignment to a finished document and organize it in a way that provides clear guideposts for your busy policy audience. *Chapters 3 and 4* teach you how to refine your prose and introduce you to skills that will help readers understand your writing. *Chapters 5 and 6* provide advice about incorporating and translating technical language, statistics, and graphics into policy documents. *Chapter 7: Pulling It All Together: Creating Professional-Quality Work* finishes the instruction on audience-centered writing. Being honest and forthright in your writing is a crucial aspect of respecting and honoring your audience.

The remainder of the book, *Part III: Guidance for Writing in Particular Policy Genres*, gives an overview of how to write in common policy-writing genres. These range from email, the most common policy-writing genre, to official testimony for legislative hearings. You can help policy audiences understand your information quickly by writing in formats with which they are familiar and that meet their needs. While each policy audience is different, all policy audiences demand that you craft the components well using the skills from Part II. Each chapter discusses the strategic considerations you need to consider, offers practical guidance about how to write for that setting, and critiques a real-world example.

CHECKLIST

To communicate with and persuade your audience, make sure you can answer each of the following questions about them:

Who is my audience?

- Are they elected officials, bureaucrats, media, or another actor?
- Why do they care about my topic, and how much do they care?

What are their needs?

- What does my audience already know about the topic?
- What crucial knowledge are they missing?

Why do they care about my topic, and how much do they care?

- Why is my audience interested in this topic? What is motivating them?

- How motivated are they to pay attention to what I write?

What do I need to do to communicate with them?

- What type of document will best help my audience process this new information?

EXERCISES

1.1: Which public policy issues brought you to policy writing?

Jot down three public policy issues that got you interested in public policy. In a brief paragraph, write about one of those issues. What made you interested in it? How are you personally connected to it?

1.2: Identify policy audiences involved in your issue area.

Who are the concrete actors (people or groups) who actively create policy about the policy issue that is important to you? Name them and write briefly about how you identified them as key potential audiences.

1.3: Decide what your audience needs to know.

Pick one of the actors you identified and answer each of the following questions about them with a brief paragraph. How did you go about finding out this information?

- *What does your audience already know about the topic?*

- *What crucial knowledge are they missing?*

- *Why does your audience care about your topic, and how much do they care?*

- *What type of document will best help your audience process this new information?* To answer this question, look ahead to Part III and preview different kinds of policy documents you will learn to produce.

1.4: Reflect on audience-centered writing.

How would you define audience-centered writing? Do you think it is important to be an audience-centered writer in order to influence policy? Why or why not?

BIBLIOGRAPHY

National League of Cities. (2014). *Number of municipal governments & population distribution.* Retrieved August 21, 2014, from http://www.nlc.org/build-skills-and-networks/resources/cities-101/city-structures/number-of-municipal-governments-and-population-distribution

Volden, C., & Wiseman, A. E. (2014). *Legislative effectiveness in the United States Congress: The lawmakers.* New York: Cambridge University Press.

Williams, J. M., & Bizup, J. (2014). *Style: The basics of clarity and grace* (5th ed.). Boston, MA: Longman.

The Skills of Policy Writing

2

Generating and Organizing Your Argument

P olicy writing is usually generated in response to a problem. The good news is that your problem is almost certainly interesting, important, and controversial. It likely has important trade-offs, complex or novel scientific dimensions, sweeping technological innovations, or intense political conflicts. Additionally, many people care about it because it impacts their jobs, health, pocketbooks, or communities in profound ways. The bad news is that the problem has not been solved up to this point; otherwise you would not be writing about it!

To write effectively and incisively about your problem requires defining the problem, creating a first draft outline of your argument, executing the research to back it up, and then creating and redrafting your project into a coherent story for your audience. These steps are the first ones in creating an audience-centered document that helps your audience understand and address your crucial problem.

Example: The Problem of Sharing Economy Businesses

Take, for example, the public policy problems created by the advent of companies like Uber or Airbnb. These "sharing economy" businesses essentially allow individuals to rent out property they own. Uber uses an app to coordinate riders and drivers so that anyone with a car and a smartphone can become an Uber driver, driving passengers around town for a fee. Similarly, Airbnb enables owners (or "hosts") to rent out rooms in their homes and apartments to visitors from around the world. As a result, these companies and their competitors have begun to revolutionize transportation and lodging marketplaces across the country.

Today, when you visit Washington, D.C., you can use Airbnb to rent a funkily decorated walkout of someone's brownstone in a leafy neighborhood instead of staying in a drab hotel in a soulless business district. When you walk out in the morning, you do not have to hope that a grubby cab with a surly driver will come down your street. Instead, you can whip out your phone, open the Uber app, and within minutes your driver will arrive in a spotless car with a smile on his face to whisk you away. This is great!

Right?

But there is another side to this story. When you stay in the brownstone, you are causing problems. You may not be paying hotel lodging taxes, so the desperately underfunded public transit system in D.C. has less money to address its crippling problems. The hotel at which you would have stayed employs fewer people because you (and a lot of other people) do not stay there anymore. When you take an Uber, your driver may be endangering you and others because he is not trained and licensed as a taxi driver.

What should government do when new public policy problems emerge, problems like the ones generated by the sharing economy? Someone has to decide which aspects of the story are important and make written recommendations to policy makers about how to deal with their disruptions. Today, that someone is you!

Writing Is Thinking, *Then* Communicating

Writing about your policy problem consists of two important processes, *thinking* and *communicating*, each of which sharpens the other. Writing is not just typing letters into a computer to create grammatically correct sentences. Rather, it is the process of deciding what to say and then saying it in a way that your audience can understand.

Public policy documents are valuable to clients because of the *thinking* that goes into creating them. *Thinking* about your problem begins in earnest when you create your first draft. Before you sit down to write, you have probably read about the problem, talked to stakeholders, and done other research. Creating a first draft is the process of then collecting what you know about your problem and then organizing your knowledge into an argument. A first draft consists of your initial thoughts, puzzling questions, and helpful insights cobbled together into an order that (hopefully!) creates a coherent story.

> *Creating and revising your drafts is the process of thinking about the problem and then organizing your thinking into an argument that will sway your audience.*

For example, if you were to sit down and write about our example from above, the impact of sharing economy businesses, you would undoubtedly already have some initial thoughts. You might know from riding in a taxi that taxi drivers hate Uber, which would clue you into a major political conflict. You might have some questions: Will Uber become so popular that it affects the number of riders on public transportation? Will it cause more traffic congestion? Finally, you might also have some insights from your public policy training, perhaps insights from economic theories about how Uber might increase competition and reduce prices.

Together, these thoughts, questions, and insights are the building blocks that you assemble into an argument in your first draft. Once it is created, then you will begin to understand where there are holes in your logic, where you do not have enough evidence, or where you do not actually know what is going on. Then you will begin to fill in these gaps with research. As you do this, you can begin to rethink your logic, evidence, and conclusions to create an increasingly more complete and coherent argument in later drafts.

> Clear thinking becomes clear writing; one can't exist without the other.
> (Zinsser, 2016)

Once you have made your argument and revised it in your first few drafts, *then* it will be time to work on *communicating* by revising your sentences and paragraphs into prose that your audience can easily understand. We will work on these communication skills in later chapters, but for now let's focus on the process of creating and revising your drafts.

The Process of Creating a First Draft

Unfortunately, polished and influential documents don't flow from our fingertips as we sit in front of a blank screen listening to Bach and sipping tea. Most public policy problems are far too large, complex, and amorphous for you simply to sit down and write out a complicated and nuanced response in one setting. Instead, you need a process. The first step in this process is creating the first draft of an argument by developing a problem statement, creating an outline, researching the details, and fleshing out the first draft into a coherent, if unpolished, argument. This first draft is the first crucial step in creating a policy document that can effectively communicate with the audience you are working to help.

Learn About the Contours of the Issue

To begin the drafting process, you need to know some of the basic contours of your issue. If you are familiar with the broad contours of your topic you can skip past this step to developing the problem statement. However, you often know relatively little about the public policy problem you are being asked to illustrate. For example, Senate staffers may know little about drones when they are assigned to produce a report about how to regulate them safely. If this is the case, then it is useful to do some exploratory research before you formally begin creating your first draft.

You will need to get an overview of the issue to orient yourself. At the most basic level, you need to know: What is the issue? Why is it a problem? What are the main choices available to people who are advocating to solve the problem? Why do people think government can or should help?

How do you go about doing this? One of the easiest ways to learn about the basics of the issue is to read news coverage about it. Look for newspaper stories about Uber. News articles can tell you who is arguing about your issue and why. Another low-cost way is to ask a friend who is familiar with the issue and get them to tell you about it. When Airbnb became an issue in Rhode Island, one state official I know immediately thought of a friend who rented part of her home on Airbnb. He called her on her cell phone, asked if he could put her on speaker, and she explained how Airbnb worked to his team at the statehouse. At the end

Learning the Contours Example: Understanding SARS

The first public policy project I worked on was part of the U.S. government response to the SARS epidemic in 2003. SARS (severe acute respiratory syndrome) was a pandemic flu that began in China and quickly spread to Canada and then to the United States, killing over 700 people before it was finally contained. Shortly after the epidemic ended, the U.S. government began to look at how it responded and what it could do better.

When I joined the team, I remembered that SARS had been in the news but didn't know much about it. The first thing I did was to go back and read the major news coverage of the event from the previous year. It was sobering to learn how deadly it was, killing 10% of the people infected. Suddenly, I understood why it was on the cover of every paper and magazine in the country the previous year and why my team was working on the problem.

From there I learned the basic outline of what had happened and how the government had responded. Once I realized that SARS came into the United States through airline passengers traveling from Asia, I realized why the government was interested in focusing its response efforts on people coming into the country. After a full day of background reading I was ready to think about an initial problem statement.

of the call he didn't understand everything about Airbnb, but he understood enough to get started with the next step: developing an initial problem statement.

Develop a Problem Statement

The very beginning of writing a policy document begins by writing down a one- or two-sentence version of the problem as you best conceptualize it. At the very basic level, what is wrong with the situation that needs to be addressed? For example, your first version of a problem statement might say, "Uber puts riders at risk because their cars do not undergo safety inspections so riders cannot tell whether the drivers and their cars are safe when they get in them." You are likely to struggle with this first step. Do not be discouraged. *Defining the problem (or framing the problem) is a key part of the writing process and is one of the hardest parts of thinking.*[1]

Once you have written down an initial problem definition, think critically about it. You will have taken a particular angle at the problem. You have explicitly made some aspects of the problem important by mentioning them (rider safety) and implicitly made some others less so by not mentioning them (traffic congestion). Does the problem definition identify the key parts of the problem as you best understand them? If not, how would you revise it?

For example, the problem statement about Uber is not great thinking. Is the problem with the drivers or their cars? It is also a terrible sentence—just try reading it out loud! But it does do several things well. It identifies the major players (Uber, drivers, and passengers). It identifies a key problem (passengers can't tell if they will be safe). Importantly, it starts you off on an initial course of research and thinking toward a finished product.

Be forewarned, however: As we will discuss more below, you will likely need to revisit your problem definition and make adjustments along the way. It is okay not to get it right the first time. *Like sailing a ship, you can always adjust your course once you have started, but you cannot adjust your course unless you have started moving.*

Create an Outline

When you have initially/provisionally defined the problem, you have set the course for the next part of your first draft: your outline. You are now able to focus your time and energy thinking and researching a specific take on the problem. Your outline will become the road map for your journey, detailing all the arguments you need to make.

---

[1] If you want help defining your problem, see Bardach and Patashnik (2015, pp. 1–12) for useful tips and tricks.

Problem → Solved
Fighting Writer's Block

Writers sometimes have "writer's block," where they are unable to get started writing or get stuck. Here are a few tips if you're having trouble getting started.

1. *Remember your audience.* You are trying to help a particular person(s). At its heart, writing is simply having a conversation with them. You are good at talking. Picture your audience across the table and talk to them about the problem.

2. *Be courageous! Write something down.* First drafts are not irreversible commitments. You can always change them if you turn out to be wrong, and as a bonus you will be able to talk with authority about why a particular problem definition is the wrong one!

3. *Remember, you are not writing Shakespeare.* All you need to do is investigate the problem and make a recommendation. No need to produce another addition to the Western canon. All you have to do is communicate clearly.

4. *Ask yourself, am I stuck or am I procrastinating?* Sometimes writer's block is really procrastination. According to Neil Fiore (2007), *procrastination is a rational response to unarticulated fears and emotions:* fears about the consequences of succeeding, fears about being imperfect, or about resentments toward your audience or boss. Procrastinating protects you from having to face angry people when your finished product shows they are wrong. It keeps you from having to show people whose opinions you value that your work is not perfect (and it will not be perfect!). It saves you from doing work that goes against your values.

The problem with procrastination is that while it helps in the short run, it hurts in the long run. You damage your career. Your work products are not as good as they could be. You do not help the people for whom you are working. You do not make the world as good as it could be.

If you are procrastinating, ask yourself why you are procrastinating. Are the reasons why you are procrastinating good ones? Sometimes they are not. You will never be perfect. If you put off work until you are, then you will never help people. Sometimes your reasons are good. If you are procrastinating because you do not agree with the work you have been asked to do, then you should think hard about whether or not you are in the right job or program. *The Now Habit* (Fiore, 2007) is a great resource for answering these questions.

Starting from your initial problem statement, begin to outline what you will need to make your argument. Outlining is your first attempt to organize your knowledge about the topic into an argument. Arguments in policy writing are like arguments in every setting. You must connect with your reader over common knowledge, establish the reason you are writing (the problem), explore alternative courses of action, and clearly recommend one of them.

Outlining your argument is an important step because it makes you focus exclusively on the *thinking* part of writing without being distracted by the *communicating* part of writing. In the harsh light of an outline, a bad argument can't hide behind sexy prose. Writing out an outline makes you think through each step in the logic. Creating an outline is a crucial step in policy writing, so make sure not to give in to the temptation to "just start writing"! While this might seem like tough love, the good news is that you can often draw inspiration from other people's outlines as you get started.

A Standard Policy Outline

Public policy documents have standard formats for making arguments. One easy way to begin outlining is to start with the outline of a standard policy format and begin filling in the particulars of your problem. Almost every policy document, from a 700-word op-ed to a 50-page policy analysis, contains the following parts either implicitly or explicitly. Try beginning with this outline:

Executive summary. Provide for hurried policy makers a synopsis of your document that previews each section. This is, of course, rather difficult to write until you know what your argument and recommendations are, so *write it last*. Still, create a placeholder for it in your outline now.

Problem definition (or framing). Assert the nature of the problem. At the very basic level, what is wrong in the world that needs to be addressed?

Background section. Establish a common understanding of the causes, history, and scope of the problem with the audience.

Alternative(s). Consider the different plausible options that are available. Each alternative should directly address the problem and feasibly be able to solve it.[2]

---

[2] One of the alternatives is always to do nothing and see how current trends affect the problem. This helps you think about whether or not government intervention will make the problem better or worse.

Criteria. Describe how you will decide between the alternatives. Effectiveness? Cost? Fairness?

Trade-offs. Compare your alternatives and lay out the consequences of taking one course of action instead of another.

Recommendation. Clearly and explicitly recommend one alternative over the other(s).

Policy makers are people of action and want to know what to do (or, in some cases, what not to do)!

Try beginning with this outline and filling it in with the particulars of your problem. For now, it is fine just to sketch a few items in as placeholders to help you think about your argument. Maybe you do not know every alternative. That is okay, put a few in. For example, in the alternatives section you could simply make a bulleted list of options (e.g., ban Uber, tax Uber, require background checks of Uber drivers, etc.). It will probably be hard to know what you will recommend at this stage. This is good! Your research

Problem → Solved
What if My Problem Does Not Fit in a Standard Policy Outline?

The example outline in the text is drawn from a *policy analysis,* which tries to predict the impact of a policy, but there are other important types of policy writing. How should you start outlining if you are doing another kind of research? One of the best ways to find outline templates to begin with is to look at how writers with a similar task have organized their outlines.

For example, a *program evaluation* retrospectively evaluates whether a particular program actually solved a problem. Many states, for example, have programs that filter offenders to programs that prepare them for jobs rather than sending them to jail, hoping they will be employed after finishing the program. How would you begin outlining an evaluation of one of these programs? With a little research you would find out that North Carolina has a program where young offenders learn skills working alongside Forestry Department officials and that there has been an evaluation of it (Division of Forest Resources, 2010). You could start with their outline until you catch your feet. Then think critically about whether the outline enables you to include everything you need to make your argument.

should help you come to an unbiased recommendation based on evidence, not on preconceived ideas.

> *If you believe that all you have is bits and pieces, make them (mosaic though they may be) into a story. Then you'll only need to improve the story and fill in the missing pieces.* (Krieger, 1988)

Once you have sketched them out it is important to think about how they all fit together. *Does your argument align all the way through the outline?* For example, do the alternatives connect back to the problem definition? The alternatives should flow from how you have defined the problem. If the problem is that Ubers are unsafe, then your alternatives should be about inspections, regulation, training, etc. It would not be appropriate to have an alternative where the city caps the number of Ubers on the road. This might reduce congestion, but it will not make riders safer. If you think that an important alternative is being left out because it does not align with your problem definition, then you need to redraft your problem definition because it did not encompass a crucial aspect of the problem the first time around.

One of the best ways to make sure your argument is aligned is to turn your rough, initial outline into a sentence outline. A sentence outline consists of the usual parts of an outline, but each point is written out as a full sentence. Ideally, each sentence can become the thesis sentence of a paragraph in your final document. Here is a cheeky example extolling the benefits of a sentence outline adapted from Michael O'Hare:

A Sentence Outline About Sentence Outlines

 I. Introduction *[this is one of only two sections you may title with a word]*

 II. A sentence outline is the framework of a paper.

  A. It is just like the ordinary outline you learned in grade school except that

   1. It accepts only full sentences as entries.

   2. It consequently shows a logical structure.

  B. You might *write* the paper by treating each entry as the topic sentence of a paragraph.

  C. In any case, you should treat the outline as the paper itself at every stage; write the paper by expanding the outline, not in a separate document (see III.C).

  D. Don't get carried away outlining; when it gets to about a seventh of the final paper's length, stop and start expanding it into prose.

III. A sentence outline has three great virtues.

    A. You commit yourself to an argument right away.

        1. You can see if your planned scheme will be persuasive.

        2. Since it's only an outline, you can change it without throwing away lots of prose.

    B. It is useful for collaboration and criticism at any stage.

        1. When deadlines change, you have something to show at any time

            a. to your boss

            b. to a client
               [OK, low-level entries don't always have to be sentences.]

        2. You can get advice from colleagues early, when it's useful.

    C. It guides your work efficiently.

        1. You can easily start writing (expanding sections) in the middle of the outline

            a. because you know what the reader will have seen up to that point.

            b. This is important

                i. because beginnings should be written last and

                ii. they are hard to write and thus slow you down.

        2. You immediately see which assertions are worst supported, so you know where to invest research time (see IV.B.4).

IV. Sentence outlines are hard to write but the obstacles are illusory, or at least tractable.

    A. They take more time and thought than topic outlines, but

        1. You have to do this thinking anyway.

        2. You wind up ahead in the long run; fully XX% of writers who try this technique report it reduced total writing time at least XX%.[3]

---

[3] Use 00 and tk (for "to come") as searchable placeholders for facts, citations, and numbers to be filled in later, so you can keep writing and stay focused on your big ideas and overall argument.

B. It's stressful to write down conclusions and assertions that you aren't able to support yet, but

   1. No one ever said writing was easy.

   2. You know more than you think, even if you can't prove it yet.

   3. Keep telling yourself, "I can always insert the word *not* in this sentence if I find I guessed wrong."

   4. You can mark especially questionable entries and qualifications with special symbols or distinctive typography.

V. Conclusions *[this is the other nonsentence heading]*

A. Always make a sentence outline before you write more than a few pages of anything except a poem or a love letter.

B. Insist that your subordinates do the same.

Source: Courtesy of Michael O'Hare, Professor of Public Policy, University of California, Berkeley.

In making your sentence outline, you will soon realize you need a lot of evidence to support your claims and to decide between the alternatives: the number of Ubers, the impact of Airbnb on tax revenues, etc. *One of the real dangers in this stage of creating your first draft is that you will get sucked into collecting data before thinking about what data you need.* Don't do this! When you are outlining, if you know some evidence or citations off the top of your head, feel free to insert them in the outline. If you do not know them, then do not get lost hunting sources down. Instead, make a note about what you think you will need to make your argument or understand the problem. This will remind you to come back and get this fact. It will also save you time. By the time you finish outlining, you will realize that much of what you initially thought was important is not. Finish outlining the argument first, then it will be time to do research and fill in the content.

Write in Your Outline

Once your sentence outline is in place and you have a good sense of how your argument will be structured, then it is time to start filling in the content of the sections. First, just begin by filling in the outline without worrying about doing additional research you may have. Be informal about it. Add a paragraph here or a few sentences there. If you are looking for a starting place, I suggest the background section or the alternatives section. Writing these sections will help you understand what criteria can be used and what the trade-offs might be. If you feel inadequate and underprepared again at this stage, remember that this is *normal.* If the problem was easy to understand or solve, someone would have already done it. Breaking new ground is hard.

Gather Evidence for Your Argument

Sooner or later you will come to the point where you need to find new evidence and you will have to start the research process in earnest. While thinking is often the hardest part of creating a first draft, finding evidence often takes the most time. The good news is that because you spent so much time thinking in the outlining process, you can now target your search on evidence that you need.

Policy research requires you to find evidence that carefully convinces your audience that you are accurately describing and analyzing the problem. If policy writing is "the art of using evidence to persuade" (Majone, 1992), then policy research is the skill of finding that evidence. This process requires more than simply a Google search, perusing newspapers, or dropping in the library to find journal articles matching your search terms. Public policy evidence comes from both documents and from people. *There are four major domains where you should look for evidence: government, academics, interest groups, and media* (see Table 2.1). Public policy research is a mix of interviewing the people who know about your problem and finding documents from which you can glean insights into it.[4]

> It can be tempting to focus on gathering evidence to the detriment of thinking because running around collecting data looks and feels productive, whereas first-rate thinking is hard and frustrating. (Bardach, 2011, pp. 12–13)

Documents

In most cases, you should begin your research by searching for and reading documents about the problem, rather than by talking to people. In academic settings, this process is called a *literature review*. You look over all of the literature written about a topic and cull what is most useful for your purposes. Once your literature review is done, your questions will be well thought out and you can make the most of your interviews. Each domain has strengths and weaknesses, and you should make sure to be aware of them as you begin.

---

[4] For longer, more detailed advice on the research process, see Weimer and Vining (2011, chap. 14: Gathering Information for Policy Analysis).

Table 2.1 Sources of Evidence and Their Uses

	Government	Academia	Interest Groups	Popular Media
Documents	• Often provide good overviews and histories of a problem. • May have produced reports on specific problems analogous to yours. • Agencies produce documents reflecting their viewpoints, so look for differences. • Can tip you to important data sources.	• Helpful for understanding the broad outlines of a problem but unlikely to address your problem directly. • Can provide helpful evidence about the effectiveness of proposed alternatives. • Seek out peer-reviewed policy journals.	• Can quickly help you understand industry or sector viewpoints. • Provide information in testimony, issue briefs, or regulatory comments, op-eds, and other documents.	• Articles can give the broad outlines of an issue and understand what educated readers likely know about the problem.
People	• Gatekeepers of government information you need. • Can be great background on an issue if you have a relationship. If not, come prepared with questions to make good use of their time.	• Can be a good source of systematic knowledge and broad perspective on a problem. • Seek academics working in public policy schools, applied economists, and other applied settings.	• Consult for specific statistics, as they can have data and information not found elsewhere. • Can provide perspectives on a political conflict. • Helpful for understanding technical aspects of a policy.	• Helpful for background information. • Good source of contacts to interview in other domains. • May tip you off to political landmines about which you don't know.

What do you do when there's more written on a topic than you have the time or ability to process? This will be a problem for all but the newest topics or most specific issues. To succeed, you have to take a strategic approach to what you decide to *look over* and what you don't.

First, you have to make sure you only look over things that help you fill in your outline, not just anything interesting on your topic. There is a cost to reading, so make sure you're reading something that is actually on point, not just about the subject generally or somewhat related to your issue. For example, an academic paper about Uber's impact on traffic problems in London may be interesting, but it probably isn't worth your time if your policy problem is the safety of Uber riders in Washington, D.C.

Second, notice that I said "look over" rather than "read," above. Even on relatively new topics there is too much written to read everything written about a topic from start to finish. Instead, you need to skim documents strategically. Remember why you started the document you are reading: For background? To support a specific point? Then, look at chapters, headings, tables, and figures to decide which sections will help you and read those. Reading policy documents isn't like reading novels. There's no need to read from cover to cover. Decide what you need and then read that.

Government documents can be very helpful sources, particularly for understanding the background of a problem. Many branches of government have research arms that produce insightful reports on problems across the spectrum of public policy. These research organizations can yield valuable analyses that shed light on your problem at the federal level (Congressional Budget Office [CBO], Government Accountability Office [GAO], etc.), state level (legislative or executive branches), or local level (municipal budget or policy, like the mayor's Office of Management and Budget in New York City).

Often, agencies have issued reports that establish the factual basis of a problem. For example, an EPA report on air pollution in the United States might have a table containing the most accurate figures available in your area to establish low air quality. Government documents can also alert you to underlying data, much of which are publicly available either on the web or by request. The EPA report would clue you in that the EPA collects these data, that they are likely available over several years, and that the authors know how to access them.

Academic documents can be uniquely useful as evidence. Peer-reviewed academic publications are written by academics and have been reviewed by a number of other academics for accuracy and quality. They are therefore highly respected as evidence. They can be very useful if they provide evidence about the effectiveness of proposed alternatives. You might be able to find an academic study about whether limiting the number of taxicabs reduced traffic congestion in a particular city. This evidence would help you make the case that limiting the number of Ubers in your city will help control congestion. Peer-reviewed policy journals are a particularly good place to search for this type of evidence.

Unfortunately, academic documents also have drawbacks that can limit their usefulness in policy writing. Academics often study a particular event that is unlikely to be exactly the same type of problem as yours. Additionally, they usually study events that are several years old because they must first get the data about it, then analyze them, and then publish them. This process is time-consuming. Academic articles are therefore unlikely to address your problem exactly (Uber's effect on D.C. traffic today), but they can be helpful for understanding the broad outlines (how more taxis on the road affected traffic in major cities from 2010–2012).

Interest groups often produce uniquely helpful documents. Their issue briefs, legislative testimony, and regulatory comments can establish facts that are known only to them. For example, only Uber lobbyists can tell you how many Ubers are operating in your city. Additionally, interest group documents can sometimes discuss proposed alternatives to problems and discuss why they are good for their particular industry. Sometimes they have perspectives you have not considered. For example, Uber lobbyists

Problem → Solved
I Need Timely Academic Resources About My Issue!

One recent, interesting twist in policy writing has been the emergence of *policy blogs* where academics write about their research into current policy issues in language accessible to most readers without the multiyear delay often required for academic publishing. The *New York Times'* Upshot, the *Washington Post's* WonkBlog, and other policy blogs are excellent sources of academic perspective and information about today's problems. In addition, the academics who publish in them are experts whose previous work could be useful reads. Like all sources, there are trade-offs. These blogs are not peer-reviewed and therefore not as authoritative as peer-reviewed documents and shouldn't be cited as such.

will argue against regulation because drunk-driving deaths fall in cities once Uber comes to town.

Popular media articles can help you understand the broad outlines of an issue at the beginning of the research process. This is particularly helpful in establishing the background sections of your argument, especially to understand the timeline of major events that vaulted the problem into the public eye. Media articles are also helpful in reminding you at what level of detail educated readers are familiar with the problem.

People

Once you have read across these four domains you will come to a point where you are familiar with most of the published evidence on the topic. You will still have questions, but continuing to search for and read documents will not be likely to help you to understand the problem better. At this point, it is time to interview people.

Interviewing people with expertise and experience is an important part of the research process because they can provide information you cannot find in a literature review. Interviewees may be willing to offer extra help by speaking off the record or on background about aspects of your problem. They might alert you to collected but unpublished data that they or others have been gathering. They can make connections and provide perspectives that can tip you off about blind spots in your thinking.

One method of interviewing people is a formal appointment on the phone or in person. Interviewing people is a skill that is developed over time with preparation and practice.[5] Be polite and well dressed. Be prepared. Ask good questions. Always finish with questions about who else you should speak to for good perspectives on the topic. Always send a thank-you note. In addition to intensive preparation, interviewing requires courage and entrepreneurship to interact with people and to network with them. If you struggle with this, practice will help!

The other interview method is to have informal conversations during a *site visit*. Instead of talking to someone while sitting in an office, you tour a facility or location and see what the problem looks like in person and how it is being addressed. It can be very helpful to meet the people and see the places you are describing. These visits can be especially helpful in understanding technical details about a problem or proposed alternatives. For example, an EPA official might be willing to take you to the data collection stations that measure air pollution. You will meet the people who collect it. You never know what you will learn.

---

[5] Overviews in Bardach and Patashnik (2015, pp. 12–18); Weimer and Vining (2011, chap. 14).

Gathering Primary Evidence

Sometimes you will have the opportunity to gather primary evidence about your topic through surveys, experiments, or other forms of data collection. While these can be extremely useful, they are also very costly in both dollars and time, making them impractical for most policy settings. If you can gather primary evidence, make sure it is worth the time and effort you expend to get it. Is there a strong reason why you can't use someone else's findings as evidence? Also, make sure you have enough expertise to gather it correctly. Running a survey is expensive but not nearly as expensive as running it twice when you realize you worded the key question in such a way that invalidated the findings.[6]

Think Critically About People's Perspectives and Incentives

Once you have completed your research you will need to think critically about the perspectives and credibility of your sources. Each person you interviewed has a particular set of incentives, and each document does as well. For example, government officials should ostensibly be objective, but you have to think critically about whether or not they are. Often, government documents are biased toward the solutions the agency writing the document can provide. The Department of Transportation will define the problems created by Uber very differently than the Taxicab Commission. Similarly, interest groups only represent one side of an issue. They are not paid to explain the drawbacks of their ideas or the merits of ideas that harm their industry. Academics are usually more objective, but even they may have conflicts of interest or be more interested in publishing than publishing relevant work. Media reports tend to err on the side of being splashy and overly simplified to sell copies. As you begin to fit the evidence you have found into your argument, *think critically about the incentives of your sources and make sure you understand their biases.* With the information you gather, you can credibly write your document.

As you incorporate what you learned from your reading and interviews into your first draft you will soon realize that you need to alter the argument that you first laid out in your sentence outline. These realizations are the beginning of the redrafting process that will help you refine your document into a final product.

---

[6] Collecting and analyzing data is its own field of study. If you are not an expert, make sure to consult one.

Revise Your Draft

Many people believe that writing is best done from start to finish. Begin at the beginning and then write until you are done. Define the problem, outline, research, write, done! This is incorrect. The reality is that for good work to occur, these stages must move in a cycle.

When you started, you really did not know what you wanted to say. You may not have understood how the physical components of the problem worked, how the current policies affected the problem, or how the politics constrained the solutions well enough to write clearly until after you outlined, researched, and wrote about them. Once you go back to your sources you may realize that your outline was missing key sections or included material that does not actually help communicate your points. Revising your first draft is the time to make these adjustments.

> *Writing is thinking. To write well is to think clearly. That's why it's so hard.* (David McCullough)

Missing points or understanding the problem isn't a problem in the outlining and first draft stages, but not fixing them is! Don't view having to fix problems as a sign of failure. Instead of thinking of writing as a line where you move from start to finish without ever circling back, think of it as a spiral staircase that raises your writing closer and closer to an excellent product by passing over the same part of the process again and again.

Redrafting, then, is the process of rethinking your argument and rewriting your first draft in the light of the new evidence that you found in your literature review and interviews. At the end of a first draft, the connections between the ideas may still be unclear until you draft and redraft. Redrafting—or creating second, third, and later drafts—is a valuable process for the writer. *Your document must go through multiple drafts to be useful for the reader.* The writing process forces us to synthesize all of the knowledge we have about a topic and to create meaning. Much like a connect-the-dots picture, all of the parts are there, and it is the writing that allows us to draw a picture to show your audience what they need to see.

Solicit Feedback on Your Drafts

One way to improve your drafts is to have someone else give you feedback. Make sure to ask for feedback at the right times. You should ask for feedback if you are stuck (e.g., you cannot think which criteria should be used) or if you are at a point where the argument is as polished as you can make it on your own. Two groups of people are particularly helpful for providing feedback. For feedback early in the drafting process, it is helpful to ask peers for feedback. They can help you know whether or not your argument is logical and convincing. This could be as informal as having them look over your sentence outline and giving you feedback over coffee. Later, when you have a polished full draft, you should garner feedback from whoever commissioned your work. Their feedback will help you know if you are addressing the problem as they understand it and if your argument is convincing. In many policy workplaces, multiple bosses and groups will review a document before it is published. Their feedback can be enormously helpful in making sure you are communicating with the audiences you are trying to reach.

Project Management: The Backward Timeline

If you want other people to read a draft of your project and give comments, then you have to give them enough time to do so. You also need to give yourself enough time to find new information when you need it. A *backward timeline* is particularly important for creating these spaces when working on a big project. To create one, figure out when the final document is due. Then list all the project benchmarks backward on a timeline, starting with the due date on the right and ending with today's date on the left.

Asking for feedback from others has the additional benefit of giving you time away from the project or from particular sections. When you are writing in the middle of a large document you can forget why you are writing, what you have already said, and how it is all meant to fit together. After a break, you can return with a clear head to see connections that felt muddled last week. A midday walk helps, but taking time overnight or over the weekend is the best way to come back with a fresh pair of eyes.

Unfortunately, taking time away may be an impractical luxury in some policy settings. Often, "deadlines are set by other bureaucratic and political agendas, and a document that is good enough and on time is valuable. Late is worthless. Hence there is finite time to do the work. There may be no extensions, and surely no incompletes" (Krieger, 1988).

Conclusion

Policy documents are exciting to write. The problems are interesting, and thinking through them systematically can change people's lives for the better. It is hard work to think carefully using a sentence outline, to do all the research necessary for having a credible and correct analysis, and to write and rewrite your drafts. In the end, you will have a document with excellent thinking and evidence. Once you have done all of this *thinking*, then it will be time to redraft yet again, this time with an eye toward *communicating* with excellent writing skills. It is to this task that we now turn.

CHECKLIST

1. Create a first draft

- Define the problem.

- Generate an outline.

  o Connect with your reader by establishing common knowledge.
  o Establish the reason you are writing (the problem).
  o Explore alternative courses of action.
  o Recommend one of them.

- Convert the outline into a sentence outline.

- Conduct a literature review and interviews of government, academic, interest group, and media sources you need to support your argument.

- Use your evidence to support your argument.

2. Redraft

- Make sure your argument aligns with the evidence you have found.

- Solicit feedback from peers and clients.

- Take time away if you can and come back with fresh eyes.

EXERCISES

2.1 **Draft and revise a problem definition.** At the very basic level, what is wrong with the situation that needs to be addressed? Write out an initial problem definition that explains what is wrong in the world and gives some sense of how big the problem is.

2.2 **Create an outline.** What do you hope the structure of your final document will look like? Outline the section and any subsection you already know. These sections could be general, like "Alternatives," or they could be specific, like "Alternative 1: Require Uber drivers to pass a road test."

2.3 **Create a sentence outline.** Expand your outline to a sentence outline. Like the example in this chapter, you should be able to read the sentence outline and have a strong sense of what the argument is and what evidence you need to support it.

2.4 **Generate a research plan.** Brainstorm a list of the documents and people you are going to consult for your research. Once you have this list written out, revise the order to be effective and efficient. Which documents you should read first? Why? Will you interview anyone? Who should be first? Why? Which parts of your research plan do you think will be the most difficult?

2.5 **Create a backward timeline.** Start by writing down the date that your project is due. From there work backward through the major steps of the drafting process and set dates for the intermediate steps. You may need to revise your initial timeline to make sure everything has time to get done.

BIBLIOGRAPHY

Bardach, E. (2011). *A practical guide for policy analysis: The eightfold path to more effective problem solving* (4th ed.). Washington, DC: CQ Press.

Bardach, E., & Patashnik, E. M. (2015). *A practical guide for policy analysis: The eightfold path to more effective problem solving* (5th rev. ed.). Washington, DC: CQ Press.

Division of Forest Resources. (2010). *Young Offenders Forest Conservation Program.* Retrieved from http://www.ncleg.net/fiscalresearch/Continuation_Reviews/FY_2009-10_CR_Documents/Final_Report_BRIDGE_CR.pdf

Fiore, N. (2007). *The now habit: A strategic program for overcoming procrastination and enjoying guilt-free play* (rev. ed.). New York: TarcherPerigee.

Krieger, M. H. (1988). The inner game of writing. *Journal of Policy Analysis and Management, 7*(2), 408–416. Retrieved from https://doi.org/10.2307/3323846

Majone, G. (1992). *Evidence, argument, and persuasion in the policy process* (reissue ed.). New Haven: Yale University Press.

Weimer, D., & Vining, A. R. (2011). *Policy analysis: Concepts and practice* (5th ed.). London, UK: Pearson.

Zinsser, W. (2016). *On writing well: The classic guide to writing nonfiction* (30th ann. reprint ed.). New York: Harper Perennial.

CHAPTER 3

Improving Your Writing: Sentences and Words

When you write, you have to *think* about your problem and *communicate* your findings to your audience. Effective writing informs and persuades by communicating your ideas in writing that your audience can understand. On the other hand, if your audience can't understand what you wrote, then your findings and advice are likely to be ignored.

For example, remember back to your research when you were reading various sources. You probably picked up a document that you initially thought would be really helpful but wasn't. For example, if your project was to recommend how your state should address sexting,[1] then you might have been excited to find a report about how Rhode Island addresses the problem. But if the prose read something like this, you might be less enthusiastic:

> With a national average of 20% of teens age 13–19 sexting one another, the act can seem commonplace, even normal. However, if distribution of the pictures in a sext, particularly if such pictures go beyond the person they were intended for, occurs, then it can be consequential, both emotionally and socially, because of actions such as being bullied and creating emotional trauma. Reports of teens committing suicide after photos have been shared with the broader public in high-profile news stories get national attention. In this age of the Internet, photos can also resurface, damaging a person's college, internship, or job prospects.

This report is exactly about your topic, but you might have ended up putting it down after a page or two (or even this paragraph!). Why did it feel so muddled? Is it because you hadn't had your coffee yet, or is it because of something the authors did? Perhaps you really wanted to understand the report and so you read it again and again but still couldn't puzzle out what it meant. Why? Was it because the topic was just too complicated, or could the authors have made things easier to understand?

---

[1] For those born before 2000, sexting is sending sexual pictures via your cell phone. In many states, the law treats sexting between consenting minors as the production, transmission, and/or possession of child pornography. A 16-year-old girl sending a nude picture of herself to her 17-year-old boyfriend both can be convicted of a sex crime and placed on a sex offender registry for life.

What if the authors had revised their paragraph to say the following?

Nationally, 20% of teenagers sext with troubling consequences. Teenagers who sext are sometimes bullied and experience emotional trauma, particularly if their partners forward their sexts to others. Even more tragically, several teens have committed suicide after their sexts were sent to broader social circles. Finally, sexted photos can also resurface later in a teen's life, damaging their college, internship, or job prospects.

Most people find this paragraph easier to read. It communicates the same information but in about half the words and much more directly. You can breeze through the writing and understand the content.

Why is the second paragraph so much easier to read? How can you make sure you write like the second one rather than the first?

Your writing can be easy to read if you revise your drafts using a few key principles.[2] In the previous chapter, you learned the first principle when you learned how to create an argumentative structure (or outline) that is audience centered, logical, and aligned throughout.

Once you had your outline, you filled it in with paragraphs supporting and fleshing out the overall argument. Your paragraphs are now comprised of sentences that are the basic building blocks of your argument. Now that you have a full draft it's time to edit it into sentences that your audience can easily understand by learning the second principle: *Sentences should clearly tell the reader who is doing what.* Remember that writing is both *thinking* and *communicating*. Let's work on creating sentences that *communicate* with your readers.

> *Sentences should clearly tell the reader who is doing what.*

How to Identify and Create Good Sentences

Easy-to-read sentences are the building blocks of easy-to-read documents. *A sentence is easy for your audience to read when they can understand who is doing what.* You can create easy-to-read sentences by following three basic principles:

---

[2] Of course, sentences must also be grammatically correct for readers to understand them. If you need more help understanding basic grammar I recommend you pick up a copy of *The Elements of Style,* by Strunk and White (1999). The first section provides solid advice about the grammatical structure of sentences and the use of commas.

1. Characters Make Good Subjects,

2. Actions Make Good Verbs,

3. Choose Words Wisely.

Armed with these three principles you can identify which of your sentences are difficult for your audience to understand, why they are difficult to understand, and how to fix them. For example, consider the following sentence, which is grammatically correct but painful and confusing:

> The lack of accountability of partners for forwarding sexts to third parties will not protect teens from cyberbullying if legalization happens via the legislature.

If you feel as muddled as I did the first time and second time I read that sentence, then you can begin to understand how confusing a policy maker might find it. Readers are more likely to understand the same information if the sentence is written like this:

> The legislature will not protect teens from cyberbullying by legalizing sexting unless partners are held accountable for distributing sexts to third parties.

What makes the second sentence easier to understand than the first one? At the most basic level, it works better because readers can easily identify the *characters* (the legislature, partners) who are doing *actions* (protect, legalizing, distributing).[3]

Principle 1: Characters Make Good Subjects

Every sentence has both a *character* and a *subject*. A *character* is most often a specific person, institution, or thing performing an action described by a sentence. The *subject* is usually the noun near the beginning of a sentence. In some sentences the character and the subject are the same, and in others they are different. *Audiences prefer sentences where the main characters are the subjects because they can easily understand who is doing the action.*

---

[3] The language of actions and characters is drawn from Williams and Bizup's excellent book *Style: The Basics of Clarity and Grace* (2014). If you need more practice with the principles in this chapter and the next one, you would be well served to buy a copy and work through it.

Let's look back at the original example sentence from above. Here I have underlined the subjects and *italicized* the main characters.

The lack of accountability of *partners* for forwarding sexts to third parties will not protect teens from cyberbullying if the legalization happens via *the legislature*.

Now we can begin to understand why this sentence was so difficult to understand the first time you read it. The subjects in this sentence (the lack and the legalization) are not characters. Characters are usually individuals, groups, or institutions. Senator Elizabeth Warren of Massachusetts, the National Rifle Association (NRA), and the U.S. Congress are all examples of characters in policy writing. Sometimes the characters in policy writing are inanimate. Hurricane Katrina, global warming, and endangered animals are all characters as well. Sometimes characters are common abstractions like the law, education, or the environment. Although these abstractions are not flesh-and-blood people we can still use them as subjects when they are performing an action. Education causes incomes to rise. The law prohibits sending sexts. The subjects in our example sentence are not the characters but instead are vague abstractions, making the sentence harder to understand.

> *Audiences prefer sentences where the main characters are the subjects because they can easily understand who is doing the action.*

When subjects are not characters, readers struggle to understand a sentence because they have to remember a lot of information before they finally understand how it all fits together. They know what actions are (not) being taken but don't know who is doing them until late in the sentence. If they read the sentence a second time they will likely understand it because they will now know who is doing the actions, but that is a lot of work. And you don't want them to do this. If you make them do extra work again and again they will simply stop reading your document, just like you did in the example at the beginning of this chapter.

Now let's look back at the revised version where the subjects are underlined and the characters are *italicized*.

The legislature will not protect teens from cyberbullying by legalizing sexting unless *partners* are held accountable for distributing sexts to third parties.

This sentence is easier to understand because you immediately know who is doing (or not doing) the actions. I rewrote the sentence by finding the characters in the original sentence and making them the subjects of this sentence.

Notice that the revised sentence emphasizes the role of the legislature, rather than focusing on the role of sexting partners. Making characters the subjects of a sentence clearly identifies the important public policy characters who are making the decisions. Putting them front and center ensures that your reader knows who is doing what and that important players are not hidden by murky language. The original sentence makes the legislature almost an afterthought behind the partners. Making sure that your characters align with your subjects helps make who is responsible clearer. In fact, you could make the role of the legislature even clearer by rewriting the sentence again as follows:

> The *legislature* will not protect teens from cyberbullying by legalizing sexting unless *they* hold partners accountable for distributing sexts to third parties.

Example: Put Subjects in Their Places

Now let's work through another example. First, read the following sentence, preferably out loud (but only if you're not in the library!).

> Last year, a debate on a sexting bill was being heard on the part of the Judiciary Committee, when a question by the senator occurred, causing a media firestorm.

Pretty awful. Now let's apply the same process that we used above to understand why this sentence is difficult to read. Take a pen and underline the subjects and circle the characters. Now turn the page to see if you got it right.

Here the subjects are underlined and the characters are *italicized*.

> Last year, a debate on a sexting bill was being heard on the part of *the Judiciary Committee*, when a question by *the senator* occurred, causing a media firestorm.

You can now see that one of the reasons why this sentence is difficult to follow is that the subjects (a debate and a question) and the characters (*the Judiciary Committee* and *the senator*) are not the same. Instead, the characters are buried deep in the sentence.

Try writing a better version of the sentence where you make the characters the subjects and put them near the beginning of the sentence.

_____

_____

_____

A better version of the sentence might look like this one, where the characters and the subjects are the same:

> Last year, as *the Judiciary Committee* debated a sexting bill, *the senator* asked a question that caused a media firestorm.

By making the characters the subjects of the sentences you have made this sentence much easier to read. It now identifies the characters and puts them into the place your reader will naturally look for them. Making characters the subject of the sentence focuses readers on your characters and makes sentences easier to understand. Readers can now easily understand who is doing what.

Missing Characters

Sometimes characters are hidden in sentences. In these cases, you can unearth them and move them to be the subjects as we did in the examples. Unfortunately, in some sentences the character is missing altogether. This makes it particularly difficult for readers to understand. Consider another example about sexting with the subject already underlined:

> Questions of whether or not teens should be charged for sexting under existing child pornography laws present a challenge.

If you try to rewrite this sentence by putting the character first, you will quickly realize that you don't know who the character is. A challenge to whom? To society? To the judicial system? To a specific judge? The readers won't know immediately.

Why would someone write a sentence that omits the character? Two possible reasons. First, it isn't unclear to them who the character is. As the writer, they intuitively know who is being challenged, but they have forgotten that their readers might not. Second, authors are sometimes purposefully unclear about who the characters are. For example, the current sentence doesn't lay the blame on anyone in particular. It just says there are unresolved questions. In contrast, the author could identify the characters by placing them in the subject of the sentence. For example, the author could write the following:

Federal judges have struggled to apply existing child pornography laws to cases involving teen sexting.

Then it would be clear that federal judges are struggling. However, this might be impolitic if the writer knows or works for the federal judges involved and wants to avoid offending them. When characters are missing from key sentences you would do well to think about why that is the case. It could be valuable information about the politics of the situation.

Pro-Tip

Be on the Lookout for Abstract Nouns

One easy way to make sure your subjects are the characters of your sentences is to make sure the subjects aren't abstract nouns. Abstract nouns often embody ideas rather than concrete subjects. Underline the subject and circle the characters in the following sentence:

Environmental ideals have been shown to be diverse in county residents.

This sentence is awkward. "County residents," the main characters in the sentence, are not the subjects of the sentence. Implicitly, we think of subjects as being the actors responsible for doing action. Here, "environmental ideals" is the subject. This sentence is more problematic because it makes the "county residents" seem like passive recipients of these ideals. Where do environmental ideals come from except the people in the county? Now consider this alternative:

County residents have diverse ideas about the environment.

The character in the sentence county residents is now also the subject of the sentence, and they are clearly responsible for their ideas rather than a vague, nebulous force descending on them. Looking for abstract nouns at the beginning of your sentences will help you make sure your characters are your subjects.

Principle 2: Actions Make Good Verbs

Once you have identified who is doing an action by having characters as the subjects of your sentences, the next step is to make sure that the *actions* your characters are taking are the *verbs* in your sentences. Actions are what the characters are actually doing: introducing, lobbying, arguing, serving, releasing, etc. Senator Warren *spoke* on the floor. The NRA *is lobbying* on the bill. The EPA *will choose* which river to clean up.

Just like with subjects and characters, sentences are easy to understand when the verb and the action are in the same spot. Conversely, when the verb and the action are not the same, sentences are more difficult to understand. Consider the sentence we looked at earlier with the verb <u><u>double underlined</u></u> and the actions highlighted:

> The prosecution of sexting cases by district attorneys <u>means</u> the loss of future job opportunities for many American teenagers.

The verb (<u>means</u>) is not an action actively being taken by one of the characters in the sentence. It is an empty verb because it does not contain an action. Where are the actions in this sentence? They are actually hidden in the nouns (prosecution and the loss). This is called nominalization. The author has nominalized the verbs "prosecute" and "lose" by turning them into nouns and making them the subjects of the sentences. Nominalizations are problematic because the actions are now the subjects and the verbs are empty because they don't convey concrete actions.

This sentence can be made easier to read by locating the nominalizations (prosecution and the loss) and transforming them back into verbs (<u>prosecute</u> and <u>lose</u>). The rewritten version fixes this problem:

> Many American teenagers <u>lose</u> future job opportunities when district attorneys <u>prosecute</u> sexting cases.

Now the verbs and the actions align. The characters are taking specific actions that are captured by the verbs. This version of the sentence is clear and easy to read.

Example: Activate Your Verbs

Now let's work through another example and apply the same principle. First, read the following sentence—preferably out loud—to get the full effect:

> The argument put forth by Governor Sammons in regard to the nonpassage of the Sexting Reform Bill by the Rhode Island House of Representatives was based on the tendency of legislatures to avoid controversial topics.

Pretty awful. Now let's apply the same process that we used above to understand why this sentence is difficult to read. Take a pen and highlighter and double underline the verbs and highlight the actions. Are they the same?

Pro-Tip

Identifying Common Nominalizations in Public Policy

If you have a sentence that has weak or empty verbs like some of the example sentences above (was based, means, has been shown, etc.), one of the best places to look for your verb is in a nominalization. Nominalizations are verbs that are turned into nouns. Table 3.1 provides a common set from public policy. When you see one in your writing, strongly consider rewriting your sentence to move the action into the verb.

Table 3.1 Common Nominalizations	
Nominalization	**Verb**
argument	argue
consideration	consider
development	develop
distortion	distorts
election	elect
evaluation	evaluate
expansion	expand
investigation	investigate
intervention	intervenes
passage	pass
prosecution	prosecute
regulation	regulate
review	reviewed

The argument put forth by Governor Sammons in regard to the nonpassage of the Sexting Reform Bill by the Rhode Island House of Representatives was based on the tendency of legislatures to avoid controversial topics.

Highlighting the action in the sentence helps you see why the sentence feels unwieldy to read. The main action (arguing) has been nominalized and made the subject of the sentence (the argument). Instead of having the strong, active verb, "was based" holding the sentence together.

Now that you have identified the action, rewrite the sentence with the action as the verb. A better version of the sentence might look like this one, where the actions and the verbs are the same:

Governor Sammons argued that the Rhode Island House of Representatives did not pass the Sexting Reform Bill because members were afraid to address controversial topics.

This sentence is much clearer. The verb and the action are now the same. Importantly, the subject now also aligns with the character doing the action. The key action in the sentence—"argued"—comes quickly after the subject, and the verb "argued" is more meaningful than "was based."

Notice that it's also easier to attribute the latter half of the sentence to the Rhode Island House of Representatives than it was before. The rewritten sentence clearly attributes thoughts, opinions, and actions to correct characters. This sentence strongly and clearly states that the governor has a poor opinion of the legislature's backbone. Depending on the situation, making this clear may or may not be a wise decision!

When Are Nominalizations Useful?

While you should always be suspicious of having nominalizations or abstract characters as the subjects of your sentences, sometimes it does make sense to use them. Here are two common reasons to use a nominalization.

The first is that some nominalizations or concepts are so familiar that your audience thinks of them as characters. Education, elections, and amendments are all common nominalizations. It is fine to write, "The upcoming election created uncertainty for businesses" because the election is an event that is firmly fixed in everyone's mind.

> *Most readers want subjects to name flesh-and-blood characters. But often, you must write about abstractions. When you do, turn them into virtual characters by making them the subjects of verbs that tell a story. If readers are familiar with your abstractions, no problem. But when they are not, avoid using lots of other abstract nominalization around them.* (Williams & Bizup, 2014)

Second, in the context of a paragraph, nominalizations can help you to refer back to ideas in a previous sentence. For example, both of these sentences appropriately use nominalizations if the decisions and arguments are used previously in context:

Her decision helped the board decide which direction to move.

Their arguments were proven to be unfounded.

Using nominalizations in this context will help you to remind the reader of what you have already discussed without rehashing it in every sentence. We will talk more about this in the next chapter when we discuss how to organize paragraphs that help you communicate best with your readers.

Principle 3: Choose Words Wisely

The final principle to creating easy-to-read sentences is to wisely choose the words in them. The best way to improve the words in your sentences is to follow the first two principles in this chapter. In doing so, the most noxious nominalizations will be weeded out and the sheer number of words in your sentences will decrease. For example, every example we looked at in this chapter was substantially shorter after it was revised. This can easily reduce the length of your document by 20–30%. Policy makers are more likely to read shorter documents. Shortening documents also creates more room to include important arguments and evidence.

That said, having applied the first two principles, you can still help your reader by thinking carefully about your word choice. Here are three rules of thumb that can help you to choose words that help your reader:

1. **Avoid jargon.** Remember that your audience likely knows less about your topic than you do. That is why they are taking the time to read what you wrote. Show them that you are thinking about their needs by not talking over their heads. Eliminate specialized terms that only insiders know. If you

do have to use technical terms, take the time to define them. For example, the terms *characters* and *actions* are jargon, so I took the time to carefully define them before I used them in this chapter.

2. **Consider short words instead of long ones.** Often, our first drafts use language that is more complex than it has to be. Sometimes, we subconsciously choose complex language because we are trying to establish our authority through word choice rather than through careful argument. If complex language or fancy words are needed, then you should use them. But often our sentences will be easier to read and mean the same thing if we use shorter words. Consider this sentence:

> The study seemed duplicative and so we terminated investigation.

"Repetitive" is a more common word than "duplicative" and means the same thing. "Ended" means the same thing as "terminated" and is less wordy. When rewritten, "The study seemed repetitive and so we ended investigation" is quicker and easier to read. Over the course of 10–20 single-spaced pages, using shorter words instead of longer ones can make a big difference in the reader's experience.

While shorter words are often better, longer words do have their place. Sometimes longer words are the everyday language of the field you are discussing, and then you should use them because your audience does. Other times, longer words can helpfully delineate between ambiguous concepts. Finally, a longer word can sometimes save the use of several shorter words and is then language well spent.

Fancy Words and Rhetorical Flourishes

The English language can be beautiful. Choosing right sets of words as you write can bring a smile to people's faces when they read. Unfortunately, policy writing isn't the right place to exercise this skill. Policy writing is a tool that people use to understand the world rather than enjoying the written word itself. Focus on communicating with your policy audience and save your rhetorical flourishes for people who have the time to enjoy them. Perhaps Grandma would enjoy your loquacious sentences in that meandering letter you've been putting off composing for her!

3. **Look for unnecessary repetition.** Sentences in first drafts are often riddled with repetitive phrases and ideas. As we write we struggle to capture everything. We may also be trying out new ways of saying things. That leads us to write things more than once in the same sentence. Take an example from earlier in the chapter:

> With a national average of 20% of teens ages 13–19 sexting one another, the act can seem commonplace, even normal.

Teens are by definition between the ages of 13 and 19. No need to say it twice. Are commonplace and normal really different ideas? The author probably could have conveyed the same ideas by just writing one or the other:

> With the national average of 20% of teens sexting one another, the act can seem commonplace.

Conclusion

Sentences that are easy to read aren't created by luck. Almost no one, not even the best writer, produces good sentences in their initial drafts. The work of *thinking* is simply too difficult to focus on writing good sentences that *communicate* easily at the same time.

Thankfully you can revise your sentences using the principles in this chapter so that they are easy to read. Once the characters are the subjects, the actions the verbs, and your words carefully chosen, your writing will be more concrete, concise, and coherent. Your writing will be easier for your audience to read. You will be more likely to communicate to them what you think is important for them to know about your policy problem, and that is no mean feat!

> *I made this letter longer than usual because I lack the time to make it shorter.* (Pascal, 2004)

Once you have clear sentences, then you can take the next step and join them together into paragraphs that are easy to understand. These paragraphs will then blend into your outline to create a document that communicates with the people you want to persuade. It is to this task that we now turn.

CHECKLIST

Diagnose Your Sentences

1. Are characters the subjects of my sentences?

2. Are actions the verbs of my sentences?

3. Did I choose the simplest words I could to engage my audience?

Rewrite

1. Make the main characters the subjects of the sentences.

2. Make the actions the verbs of the sentences and keep an eye out for nominalizations.

3. Replace jargon or "big" words with common words.

EXERCISES

Characters and Subjects

Practice Sentences: Underline the subject(s) of each sentence and circle the character(s). Then rewrite the sentence with the character as the subject.

1. The CBO's abundance of data enabled evaluation of EPA actions in targeting resources to waterways most in need of cleanup.

   _____

   _____

   _____

2. Testing requirements in many high schools by the school board means the loss of many hours of otherwise productive class time for students.

   _____

   _____

   _____

Applying to Your Own Writing: Identify two sentences in your draft where the subjects are not the same as the characters. Write them down, underline the subject of each sentence, and circle the character(s). Then rewrite them by making the character the subject. Does this make the sentence more easily understood by your audience?

Actions and Verbs

Practice Sentences: Double underline the verb of each sentence and highlight the action. Then rewrite them by making the action the verb:

1. The expansion of universities and hospital properties <u>means</u> that cities will collect less tax revenue.

   _____

   _____

   _____

2. Early experiences have a uniquely powerful influence on the development of cognitive and social skills that are necessary for success later in life.

   _____

   _____

   _____

Applying to Your Own Writing: Identify two sentences (different than the two in Exercise 1) where the actions are not the same as the verbs. Write them down, double underline the verb of each sentence, and highlight the action. Then rewrite them by making the action the verb. Does this make the sentence more easily understood by your audience?

Word Choice

Practice Sentences: Analyze and improve the examples by eliminating unnecessary or repetitive words as well as by fixing the subject/character and verbs/actions:

1. Animosity toward sharing economy companies in the transportation sector like Uber and Lyft on the part of other transportation companies that employ taxi drivers exists not only in our city, but throughout the nation.

   _____

   _____

   _____

2. If distribution of a sexual picture by a smartphone, particularly if such pictures go beyond the person they were intended for, occurs, then it can be consequential, both emotionally and socially because of actions such as being bullied and creating emotional trauma.

   _____

   _____

   _____

Applying to Your Own Writing: Identify two sentences where you can cut down the number of words by eliminating repeated words or choosing words that convey the same information with less text. Write them down, strike through the repetitive language, and suggest new language. Then rewrite them with your suggested changes. Does this make the sentences more easily understood by your audience? Why?

BIBLIOGRAPHY

Pascal, B. (2004). *Selected "pensées" and provincial letters = pensées et provinciales choisies*. Mineola, NY: Dover Publications.

Strunk, W., & White, E. B. (1999). *The elements of style* (4th ed.). Boston: Longman.

Williams, J. M., & Bizup, J. (2014). *Style: The basics of clarity and grace* (5th ed.). Boston: Longman.

ANSWER KEY

Characters and Subjects

1. Analyzed Version: The **CBO's** abundance of <u>data</u> enabled evaluation of **EPA** <u>actions</u> in targeting resources to waterways most in need of cleanup.

Better Version: Because the **CBO** had abundant data, it could evaluate how well the **EPA** targeted resources to waterways cleanup.

2. Analyzed Version: Testing requirements in many high schools by the **school board** means the loss of many hours of otherwise productive class time for **students**.

   Better Version: **Students** lose productive class time because **school boards** require tests in high school.

Actions and Verbs

1. Analyzed Version: The expansion of universities and hospital properties means that cities will collect less tax revenue.

   Better Version: When universities and hospital properties expand, then cities will collect less tax revenue.

   Or

   Cities will collect less tax revenue when universities and hospitals expand.

2. Analyzed Version: Early educational experiences have a uniquely powerful influence on the development of cognitive and social skills that are necessary for success later in life.

   Note that the nominalization "development" is confusing here because the actor "children" is missing from the sentence. Add it back in so that the sentence makes sense.

   Better Version: Children develop cognitive and social skills at an early age, so early educational experiences are a powerful influence on success later in life.

Word Choice

1. Analyzed Version: Animosity toward **sharing economy companies** ~~in the transportation sector like~~ Uber and Lyft on the part of ~~other transportation companies that employ taxi drivers~~ (taxi companies) exists not only in our city, but ~~throughout the nation~~ (nationwide).

   First, make "taxi companies" the subject because they are the actors. Then, realize that "animosity" is a nominalization of strongly disliking someone or something.

   Better Version: **Taxi companies** in our city and nationwide strongly dislike Uber, Lyft, and other sharing economy companies like them.

2. Analyzed Version: If <u>distribution</u> of a ~~sexual picture by a smartphone~~ (sext), particularly if such pictures go beyond **the person** they were intended for, <u>occurs</u>, then it ~~can be consequential~~, both emotionally and socially because of actions such as being bullied and creating emotional trauma. (43 words)

Note that there is one missing actor in this sentence: the sender of the sext. Make sure they play a role in the revised sentence. Also, note that "emotionally" is used twice, and since the consequences already are discussed you can drop calling them "consequences."

Better Version: When a partner who receives sexts distributes it to others, then the sender may be bullied and experience social and emotional trauma. (22 words)

4

Writing Well: Paragraphs and Sections

A s we saw in the last chapter, sentences are the foundation of policy writing. Well-written sentences with characters as subjects and actions as verbs are the first step toward communicating with your audience. But to effectively communicate your thinking, you have to take the next step: building sentences into paragraphs.

Well-constructed paragraphs are made up of sentences that connect together into a story that your audience can understand and remember. They turn the details, nuances, evidence, and examples into an argument that makes your audience nod their heads and say, "I get it." On the flip-side, when a paragraph doesn't work well, the results can be distressing. For example, read the following paragraph and see what you think:[1]

> Within one of the nation's most threatened coastal regions lies the Eastern Shore of Virginia. Storms are intensifying and sea levels are rising at three to four times the global average here. Climate change is linked to both. Tens of millions of dollars have been spent in the past on piecemeal and reactive approaches to address the mounting challenges of climate-related hazards. The area's vulnerability has unfortunately been exacerbated by these efforts.

Ugh.

If you're like me, you were able to understand most of the words and ideas but not how they fit together. Now consider the second, better-constructed version:

> The Eastern Shore of Virginia lies within one of the nation's most threatened coastal regions. Sea levels here are rising at three to four times the global average and storms are expected to intensify. Both of these trends are linked, in part, to climate change. Climate-related hazards are producing mounting challenges that government has often addressed through reactive, expensive, piecemeal approaches. Often, these efforts have exacerbated the area's vulnerability.

---

[1] Example adapted from The Nature Conservancy (2014).

Which did you like better? If you're like most people, you found the second one easier to read. You could follow it straight through without feeling lost. Why? Each paragraph discusses the same topics and uses most of the same words. Each has sentences where the characters are subjects and the actions are verbs. They follow all of the principles from the previous chapter.

What makes the second paragraph so much easier to follow?

The key to understanding the difference lies in understanding two key principles: *cohesion* and *coherence*. These two words may seem similar because they sound similar, but as we'll see, they represent two different aspects of what makes a paragraph communicate with your audience.

Cohesion: Do My Sentences Connect Together?

The reason why most people prefer the second paragraph to the first one is that the second one is *cohesive*. In science, cohesion is the property that describes how molecules hold together with one another. For example, water on a newly waxed car forms droplets because the water is cohesive. The water molecules make tight connections that hold them together, creating surface tension and the beautiful little diamonds on the hood of your car. Similarly, a cohesive paragraph holds together by making tight connections between the various sentences in it. Sentences hold together and paragraphs are cohesive when you

1. begin sentences with ideas that are connected to ideas that your audience is already familiar with and

2. put new information at the end of sentences.

The Importance of Connections

Let's look again at the second example paragraph to see what makes it cohesive. I've numbered each of the sentences to help us work through it.

[1]The Eastern Shore of Virginia lies within one of the nation's most threatened coastal regions. [2]Sea levels here are rising at three to four times the global average and storms are expected to intensify. [3]Both of these trends are linked, in part, to climate change. [4]Climate-related hazards are producing mounting challenges that government has often addressed through reactive, expensive, piecemeal approaches. [5]Often, these efforts have exacerbated the area's vulnerability.

Now let's look to see how the connections are made between the information at the end of one sentence and the subject of the next sentence. Below, I've underlined the information in each sentence that connects to another sentence. The various markings highlight the specific pairings between the sentences.

[1]The Eastern Shore of Virginia lies within one of the nation's most threatened coastal regions. [2]Sea levels here are rising at three to four times the global average and storms are expected to intensify. [3]Both of these trends are linked, in part, to climate change. [4]Climate-related hazards are producing mounting challenges that government has often addressed through reactive, expensive, piecemeal approaches. [5]Often, these efforts have exacerbated the area's vulnerability.

As you can see, the information at the end of each sentence connects to the information at the beginning of the next one. Sometimes the connections between the sentences are explicit. Sentences 2 and 5 both refer directly to information in the previous sentence by saying "these efforts" and "these trends." Other times the connection isn't explicit but the sentences still connect back to the one before because they discuss ideas introduced in the previous sentence. For example, Sentence 4 begins with "climate-related hazards," which is a natural connection to the "climate change" reference at the end of Sentence 3. Both explicit and implicit connections can create cohesion that helps the reader follow the argument. This cohesion is what makes the second paragraph easy to follow.

In contrast, look at the scattered connections between the sentences in the first example paragraph. Again, I've marked the key ideas in each sentence and then used the same marking to highlight the connection elsewhere in the paragraph.

[1]Within one of the nation's most threatened coastal regions lies the Eastern Shore of Virginia. [2]Storms are intensifying and sea levels are rising at three to four times the global average here. [3]Climate change is linked to both. [4]Tens of millions of dollars have been spent in the past on piecemeal and reactive approaches to address the mounting challenges of climate-related hazards. [5]The area's vulnerability has unfortunately been exacerbated by these efforts.

Now you can see why this version was so much harder to follow the first time you read it: It wasn't cohesive. The paragraph is still about all of the same things (rising seas, climate change, government failures), but it's harder to see how they fit together because the idea at the end of one sentence isn't connected to the idea that begins the next sentence. For example, Sentence 4 and Sentence 5 don't connect well. Sentence 4 discusses the "piecemeal and reactive approaches," but these approaches aren't referenced again until Sentence 5 ends with "these efforts." In between the two are 17 words and two other important ideas. It's hard for an audience to make the connection between the ideas with so much in between. By contrast, in the example paragraph, only one word separates the two, making it much easier to follow.

Problem → Solved
How Do I Avoid Sounding Repetitive Again and Again?

When you first begin revising your paragraphs to be more cohesive, you will sometimes find that your writing falls repetitive:

> After my initial work on the project, I gave the draft report to John. John read the draft report over and returned the draft report with comments within a day. The comments that John gave were really helpful.

Yikes.

There are several ways around this.

First, you can use pronouns instead of names. Using pronouns allows this to be less clunky to read:

> After my initial work on the project, I gave the draft report to John. He read it over and returned it with comments within a day. The comments that he gave were really helpful.

Much less repetitive, while still keeping the topics together.

Second, you can refer to previous ideas using *this, these, that, those, another*, etc.

> After my initial work on the project, I gave the draft report to John. He read it over and returned it with comments within a day. These were really helpful.

Of course, no one starts out writing paragraphs that are difficult to understand. Instead, as you write your first draft, what you are really doing is thinking out loud on the page. For better or worse, cohesive paragraphs are rarely the immediate result. We're too busy deciding what we want to say to simultaneously make sure the paragraphs are cohesive. Now that you understand what cohesion is and why it matters, you'll begin to realize when and where your paragraphs aren't cohesive.

The way to make your paragraphs more cohesive is to make sure that your sentences begin with information your audience understands before you introduce new information. This way, you will always make connections back to something you've referenced previously. You will create a chain of connections from one idea to another and will make sure your audience can follow your chain of thought.

One way to make sure your ideas connect together is to make sure your sentences begin with information your audience understands before you introduce new information to them at the end of the sentence.

Additionally, when you begin your sentences with familiar information before complicating or nuancing it at the end of the sentence, you make it easier for your audience to remember what you have to tell them. We don't learn new information in a vacuum. Instead, we learn by connecting new facts and ideas to old facts and ideas that we already understand. You may not have known what cohesion was when we started this chapter, but you did know about water droplets. By giving you an example with which you are familiar, I was able to help you understand and remember the idea of cohesion. Similarly, when you begin with information with which your audience is familiar, you increase your chances that they will remember what you have to say.

For another example, glance back at the example paragraph. Notice how the first sentence establishes common ground with the audience by describing a concrete place most readers know: the Eastern Shore of Virginia. Everyone has heard of Virginia, and mentioning the shore reminds them that Virginia is indeed on the ocean (for those who struggle with geography!). With this common ground established, the audience is ready to learn about everything that is happening there.

Example: Improving a Paragraph

Now, let's work through an example. First, read the following paragraph, preferably out loud (but only if you're not in the library!):

Many coastal areas are inhabited and many will need to be abandoned in coming decades as SLR continues. Tangier Island is the last inhabited island in the Chesapeake Bay. Climate change and associated sea level rise (SLR) are already impacting low-lying coastal areas, including islands, throughout the world. With the predicted SLR, much of the island's remaining landmass is expected to be lost in the next 50 years and it will likely need to be abandoned. Since 1850, 66.75% of Tangier Island's landmass has been lost.

Yikes.

Why was this so hard to follow? Let's analyze this paragraph the same way we did above to understand why it is difficult to follow. Take a pen, pencil, highlighter, or paintbrush and mark up the topics in the paragraph above that connect together.

> Many coastal areas are inhabited and many will need to be abandoned in coming decades as SLR continues. Tangier Island is the last inhabited island in the Chesapeake Bay. Climate change and associated sea level rise (SLR) are already impacting low-lying coastal areas, including islands, throughout the world. With the predicted SLR, much of the island's remaining landmass is expected to be lost in the next 50 years and it will likely need to be abandoned. Since 1850, 66.75% of Tangier Island's landmass has been lost.

As you can see, the sentences in this paragraph are not cohesive. The sentences do not naturally lead from one to the other, and as a result it is hard to follow.

How might you go about fixing this? Which sentence should go at the beginning? First, remember that readers will understand more if you begin with information with which they are familiar. One way to begin is to keep the overview sentence about climate change because it provides the broadest, big-picture introduction with which the reader can connect. With that as your start, rewrite the paragraph, keeping the sentences as whole as you can to make connections fluid.

_____

_____

_____

Here is a better version of the previous paragraph to compare to the one you wrote (try reading both out loud and see if they feel better than the original). Notice how the main topics in each sentence are closer to each other:

> Climate change and associated sea level rise (SLR) are already impacting low-lying coastal areas, including islands, throughout the world. Many of these areas are inhabited and many will need to be abandoned in coming decades as SLR continues. The last inhabited island in the Chesapeake Bay is Tangier Island. Since 1850, 66.75% of the island's landmass has been lost to rising sea levels. With the predicted SLR, much of the island's remaining landmass will be lost in the next 50 years and the island will need to be abandoned.

Much better. This version is easier to read because the ideas at the end of one sentence connect to the ideas near the beginning of the next sentence. Because it's cohesive, it feels less choppy and is easier to read and understand.

Pro-Tip

Using Passive Voice to Improve Cohesion

To create cohesive paragraphs, it is sometime useful to use passive voice. Once you have established ideas and actors early in the paragraph, then you can relax the rules we learned in the previous chapter and use passive voice as a tool to form tighter connections between sentences. Consider the following paragraph, where I have underlined the topics that connect the sentences together:

> [1]Over the last few years, parts of the city that flooded only during major hurricanes have <u>flooded with alarming regularity</u> during small storms. [2]On Friday, the city <u>council discussed</u> the <u>problem of recurrent flooding,</u> which is regularly causing damage to our roads and tunnels. [3]<u>The discussion</u> was intense and tempers quickly flared.

This paragraph feels choppy, and with the topics underlined you can see why. The second sentence is well written, but the topic order is mismatched with the sentences on either side: The ideas don't pair together. Now consider this second version, with the middle sentence rewritten using passive voice:

> [1]Over the last few years, parts of the city that flooded only during major hurricanes have <u>flooded with alarming regularity</u> during small storms. [2]The <u>problem of recurrent flooding</u>, which is regularly causing damage to our roads and tunnels, was the topic of the <u>city council's discussion</u> on Friday. [3]<u>The discussion</u> was intense and tempers quickly flared.

This version flows better because using passive voice reverses the order of the topics in Sentence 2. The topics are now aligned across the paragraph. This increases cohesion and makes the paragraph easier for the audience to follow.

Coherence: Does My Paragraph Make Sense as a Whole?

Cohesion is the first mark of a good paragraph and *coherence* is the second. In a coherent paragraph, all of the sentences talk about the same topics in order to tell a coherent story. The examples we've read above weren't cohesive, but they were coherent. They were consistently discussing the same topics (climate change, sea level rise, flooding). Though they were hard to follow, they weren't riddled with numerous digressions, unhelpful tangents, or (at worst!) non sequiturs.[2] Unfortunately, incoherent paragraphs have these problems.

Incoherent paragraphs don't talk about the same topic the whole time. Instead, they deal with many different topics without explaining how they fit together. Taken to the extreme, a completely incoherent paragraph is as impossible to follow as listening to your hypercaffeinated friend narrate their stream of consciousness. For example, the following paragraph is incoherent to the extreme:

> Subsidence is the natural process of the Earth settling. The Earth settling is like settling for a partner in life: You may not get what you want but it's better than nothing. Nothing is what I wanted from the dining hall after I saw the menu today. But today was sunnier than yesterday, so I was able to get a tan on the quad.

Yikes! Perhaps this author should decrease their coffee intake.

The good news is that you're unlikely to write anything quite so random, but you'd be surprised how often your paragraphs can come across as incoherent to your audience, especially in a first draft and particularly if you haven't established a clear topic sentence to guide you. Consider the following example:

> Struggles with sinking ground in coastal areas are not isolated to Virginia. Cities across the world are struggling with subsidence. In Louisiana, subsidence is caused by compacting sediment left by the Mississippi River. In the fall of 2016, the Geological Society of America released a report from a workgroup of state policy makers and scientists from across the country. The report examined the policy levers that state-level policy makers have at their disposal to slow climate change and recommended a number of potential solutions that fall into two different groups: increased regulation or instituting a national carbon tax. Unfortunately, these ideas are theoretical, as all bills that focus on national-level regulation have died due to pressure from energy companies.

What is this paragraph illustrating? It has a lot of ideas organized (sort of) under two main topics: subsidence (in Virginia, cities across the world, and Louisiana) and a report about solutions to climate change (regulation and a carbon tax). So, which topic is this paragraph illustrating?

---

[2] A non sequitur is something random inserted in the middle of a conversation—much like Doug, the dog in the movie *Up,* who randomly shouts "Squirrel!" in conversation.

As it is currently written, I don't know, either. It is just too incoherent to know. I don't believe the writer meant to be random or disjointed. In their mind, all of the topics are related and the connections are obvious; they are only random to other folks.

How do you know if you've written an incoherent paragraph? In the middle of banging out a draft it's hard to know, so the most important way to check for coherence is to take time away from your writing. When you put down your draft and come back to it a few days later, then you'll have the distance to see a bad paragraph for what it is: incoherent to anyone but the you of three days ago. The other, slightly more embarrassing option is to find a friend or colleague who likes you enough to honestly call B.S. on your paragraph. In my own writing, I've used both because either option helps my audience understand what I need to tell them, but my pride often drives me to make sure I leave enough time to read it over again myself rather than get embarrassed in front of a friend!

Once you know you have an incoherent paragraph on your hands, how do you fix it? First, you need to decide what the point of the paragraph is in the broader structure of your overall argument. Why is it here? What is the topic? Once you've decided why you have this paragraph, then everything that doesn't directly support that point needs to go.

In the example above, if the topic is subsidence, then everything in the paragraph that isn't related to subsidence needs to go, either into another paragraph or out of the document altogether. Perhaps the Geological Society of America report mentioned in the paragraph has a discussion on subsidence, but the author doesn't mention it. If there isn't a connection, then take out the sentences mentioning the report, even though the report is put out by a reputable and prestigious organization.

It's also unclear in the example how preventing climate change is related to subsidence. If there is a connection, then the author needs to make it clear; if not, then that material needs to come out too. All of the sentences that remain need to relate to the topic of the paragraph and help the paragraph make its point in service of the broader structure of your document laid out in your sentence outline.

Consider an improved, more coherent version of the example below that focuses on subsidence around the country that follows the principles above:

> Struggles with sinking ground in coastal areas are not isolated to Virginia. In fact, coastal cities around the country are struggling with subsidence. For example, in Louisiana subsidence is caused by compacting sediment left by the Mississippi River. In Long Beach, California, subsidence has been an issue since the 1940s, when the oil boom caused huge subsidence problems that continue to threaten the city today.

To understand how these sinking areas will interact with climate change and associated sea level rise, the Geological Society of America commissioned a report in 2016. It documented the interaction of the two trends across the country as a part of a larger project on the impact of climate change across the country. The report also focused on informing state-level policy makers about what they can do to adapt to this unique set of challenges created by sinking land and rising seas.

Notice that many of the ideas in the original paragraph are now gone: carbon taxes, regulation, and energy companies. Instead, the focus is clearly on subsidence in the United States. Additionally, what was once one paragraph is now broken into two: one focusing on subsidence and another focusing on the report. With this break, you can understand why the report makes sense to include, as it discusses the interaction of subsidence with climate change. The paragraphs now make sense because they are coherent.

Pro-Tip

Killing Your Darlings (or, Cutting Beloved Sentences)

One common cause of incoherent paragraphs is keeping sentences that you are really proud of writing but that need to come out because they aren't related to the point of the paragraph. Being willing to take out a sentence to which you've gotten attached is perhaps the hardest part of revising paragraphs. Maybe in a flash of inspiration you pounded out a pithy pun or a particularly erudite allusion. Maybe a string of delicious and delectable adjectives made you proud. Maybe your nuanced example reminds you of a cherished childhood memory that makes you smile.

The problem is that when you read that paragraph over again several days later you'll realize that your fun pop culture reference or the big words you delighted in using have distracted you from realizing that the sentence itself doesn't support the point of the paragraph.

As hard as it is in these situations, you have to kill your darling sentences in service of your audience, as many a mournful writer has had to do before you. Take solace, however, for when you read your draft again in a few days the sorrow you feel will be replaced with a feeling of accomplishment when you communicate your point clearly.

If it feels too hard to do in the moment, one intermediate step is to create a second document of sentences (and paragraphs) that no longer fit in your main document. Whenever you cut material you can plop that in the second document and come back to it when (or if) you need it. In the years I've been writing I've never reused the material I've moved to that document, but it does make cutting the initial sentences less painful.

Editing at a Global Level: Making the Document Make Sense as a Whole

....

Once you have your paragraphs that are coherent and cohesive, then it is time to think about how the paragraphs flow together into sections and how the sections fit together to form the whole of your document. This is the global phase of writing. Here you make sure that the big picture makes sense and that your audience can understand what your document as a whole has to say. The same principles that ensured these outcomes at the paragraph level, *coherence* and *cohesion*, will help you achieve these outcomes for the document as a whole. Now it's time to make sure your paragraphs make sense packaged together (*coherence*) and that the audience understands how they fit together (*cohesion*).

Global Coherence: Decide if All the Paragraphs and Sections in Your Draft Should Stay

When you began creating your document, you worked from a sentence outline that gave you a coherent vision for what you were going to illustrate. But chances are that rather than starting at the beginning of the outline and writing the sections and paragraphs sequentially you jumped around. Perhaps you were working on the background for a bit, then working on an alternative, then doing more research, and then writing up a different section. Perhaps you've been writing as a part of a group project and the assembled draft is the first time you've all looked at each other's work. In each section, you or your team have added a lot of value to your project. Now it's time to make sure each of the sections still belong in the document. Each of them has evolved over time. Do they all still speak to the overall point you are trying to make? Is the document coherent?

To check for coherence, make a new sentence outline that reflects what you now have in the document. Depending on the length of the document you may or may not be able to understand the organization at a glance. For shorter documents, you may be able to glance over the two pages you've written and make sure the paragraphs and sections all fit together in order. But for longer documents, it is helpful to write a second sentence outline that represents what you now have. To create this outline read back through your draft and insert headers that represent the biggest sections of your document, then insert subheaders for the subpoints. They will show you the structures of your argument at a glance once you pull them out into a new sentence outline.

Now, look back at the sentence outline you created at the beginning of your project. How closely does your current draft look to the one you

Two Drafts Forward, One Draft Back?

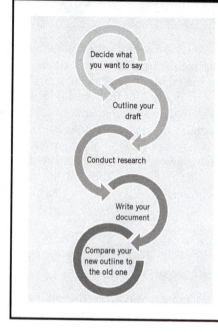

Decide what you want to say

Outline your draft

Conduct research

Write your document

Compare your new outline to the old one

Don't be frustrated if you get to the end of your new outline and you begin to realize that you have to reorder your document. While this might feel like you're starting over (I'm outlining again? Have I not made any progress?! $*#&@!)), the truth is that you have made a lot of progress. You know so much more than you did when you made your initial outline. As you outline, you'll have a better sense of how you need to organize your project so your readers can understand what they need to know.

envisioned at the beginning? Chances are that it looks pretty different than the one with which you started. These changes reflect the nature of writing: Writing is thinking. As you've thought long and hard about your topic you've decided that new things needed to be emphasized and that some things you thought would be very important are less important than you originally considered.

Now that you can see your original sentence outline and your new outline side by side, it's time to ask some hard questions: Do the paragraphs and sections match the sentence outline with which you started? Is the new outline the right way to communicate with your audience? Was the old one better? Does it make sense to reorder your outline? How will you decide?

Without knowing your project, I can't help you make these decisions. But I can tell you that these decisions are some of the most important you'll make in the course of your project. Remember that *thinking*—making hard choices about what to include and what to cut—is the part of the writing process where you add value. At this stage, you'll finally have a complete vision of what it is that you want to say, and—importantly—what you don't want to say.

Surprisingly, knowing what you don't want to include in the final document is just as important as knowing what you do want to include.

Through the writing process you've investigated ideas that sounded promising. But now that you can see the project as a whole you may realize that some of those promising ideas no longer fit. It would have been nice to know that at the beginning, before you did all the work, but sometimes you can't see that reality until you read a full draft and you realize what you have written isn't coherent. Just like with paragraphs, even if sections are well written, informative, and fun to read, if they don't fit into the point of the document, they have to be discarded, no matter how hard you have worked on them.

This might feel like wasted time, but it isn't. When you talk to someone about what you've written, they will inevitably ask you about the parts you

Pro-Tip

Don't Write a Travel Guide About Your Experience Writing Your Document

While there are many reasonable ways to organize your document, the travelogue is almost never one of them. In a travelogue, you organize your document by taking your audience along the voyage of discovery that you embarked upon to reach the conclusions awaiting them at the end of your document. Unfortunately, a travelogue is one of the easiest ways to organize a document because the narrative structure is right in front of you. You just write down everything you did, in the order that you did it, and boom! You have a complete accounting of everything you learned.

While this may be intensely interesting to you (it was your life, after all), it's not the right way to serve your audience. The fatal flaw in the travelogue is that it focuses on you and your journey toward understanding instead of using that journey to give your reader insight into the issue in front of them. If you've written something like this, you may be in trouble:

> When I first was assigned to learn about the increasing intensity of major storms, I was a skeptic, but then, in an interesting turn of events, my mind was changed when I. . . .

Resist the temptation to write about yourself and your journey. Instead, put your audience first by focusing their attention on the issue at hand. Put your conclusions up front and then tell your audience why they should believe you. This will make your document useful, and useful is always interesting. And remember, if your journey of discovery is really interesting you can always write a memoir afterward and reveal how you learned everything you did!

discarded (which sound good to them at first blush, just like they did to you!). But since you have thought hard about why you discarded those parts, you'll be able to explain why they aren't worth considering and why you didn't include them. Even though you won't include these ideas in your final product, chasing down the ideas you end up discarding will be helpful in the end.

One of the primary reasons why you might decide to reorganize your draft is that you'll realize your most important point is made at the end. As you've researched and written you've built an argument from beginning to end, and with all of the logic in place the last section lays out your nuanced, researched, erudite, and important point. For example, now that you understand climate change, subsidence, 100-year floods, and how they all work together, you realize that the city has the ability to make important changes. The last paragraph of your report ends with, "Hence the city can substantially reduce the chances of being submerged in 50 years."

The problem is that this incredibly important information is at the very end of your document, the very spot where a busy policy maker is least likely to see it. If this is the case for you, then it's time to move that information up to the front of your document. As newspaper editors say, "Don't bury the lead," which means don't put the most important information at end of a story or hide it in the middle; instead, put it up front!

Once you know what your most important point is, you should order the remainder of your document to help your audience understand it. Then, with the headline up front, you can reorganize the document so that it helps the audience understand the importance of the information and you can better convince them that what you are saying is true and that they need to take action about it.

Global Cohesion: Help Your Readers Understand How the Sections Fit Together

As you revisit and reorder your document using your new outline, you are creating an increasingly more coherent document focused on informing your audience about your topic. A coherent document is crucial to audiences understanding what you have to say, but it also needs to be cohesive. For your audience to understand your argument you can't simply have crucial facts side by side; instead, you have to show your audience how they fit together into a story.

The most effective way to create cohesion is to utilize the sentences and paragraphs just above and below headings as an opportunity to make big-picture connections between the sections of your document. These are the key spots where your audience looking for connections will see how this particular section connects to the biggest ideas in your document.

Connect to Previous Material

The beginning of a new section is particularly important. For your audience to feel like they know what is happening, they need you to set up the new information you are going to discuss in a new section by helping them see how it connects back to the previous section. For example, look back at the paragraph at the start of this chapter's section on "global cohesion." The paragraph helps the readers understand how the ideas that follow fit together with the ideas they have just read. The first sentence is actually about the previous section on "coherence." It is there to start a new section with material with which they are familiar: coherence. They immediately feel comfortable because they are on the same page as you. The next sentence then makes the connection between that material and the section that follows. These connections are crucial for readers to be able to understand how everything fits together.

In a policy document, using the first paragraph of a section to build these connections is even more important because policy audiences rarely read from the beginning straight through to the end. Instead, they skim the headings as they thumb through the report, and then they may go back and read a particular section in more depth. Because they often jump in the middle of the document, it is important that the introductory paragraph in a section set the context. This may seem maddening or foolish to you, but you can't change your audience; therefore you need to create a globally cohesive document that manages their particular reading behavior.

Preview Coming New Material

The first paragraph of a section is also an important place to give a brief overview of what is coming. It signals to the audience the important themes on which they should be focusing through the remainder of the section. Sometimes this can be explicit. You can write something like, "The main three causes of flooding are subsidence, sea level rise, and more frequent storms." Making a list like this one tells your readers what to look for as the section progresses (subsidence, sea level rise, and more frequent storms) and why you are telling them about them (to understand why flooding occurs). This helpful signaling helps your readers keep track of why they are learning about the details that are coming in the rest of the section.

When your audience reads your document, they are really trying to do two things at once: learn the details and learn why they are learning the details. This is hard work, but one way you can make it easier is by using the same word for the same concept throughout your document. Imagine how hard it would be to follow in a report the effects of sinking land that alternated between subsidence, sinking, and collapse. If your reader is new to the material they will have a difficult time knowing if these are separate things or different words for the same thing. But if you always call it *subsidence* as you discuss the effects, then your audience will always connect what you are saying back to what you said at the beginning, that *subsidence* is one of three reasons why flooding is increasing.

Show Why They Learned It

The end of a section is also an important place to help the reader make connections between the sections of your document. Traditionally, you probably learned that the last paragraph in a section should say what you said again (think the fifth paragraph of the five-paragraph essay). Unfortunately, this is bad advice in a policy setting. In policy settings space and reader attention are at a premium, so you want each paragraph to add

Pro-Tip

The Importance of Endings: Opportunities for Emphasis

The topic sentence of each paragraph works to remind you and to inform your audience about why you are writing any given paragraph. But the first sentence at the beginning of a paragraph isn't the only place of special emphasis in a paragraph. The end is as well. The end of a paragraph, particularly one at the end of a section, helps to put the emphasis on an important issue. It is the last thing the reader hits and signals to them what to remember.

Consider the following two example sentences that might come at the end of a section. Both cover the same material but emphasize different things:

. . . Global warming and the associated rise in water levels could endanger marine estuaries and decimate the fishing across California, **according to the Coastal Zone Management Agency.**

. . . According to the Coastal Zone Management Agency, global warming and the associated rise in water levels could **endanger marine estuaries and decimate the fishing across California.**

The first example ends the paragraph by putting the emphasis on the agency. The second example puts the emphasis on the problem. Either choice can be appropriate as long as you make a conscious choice. The end of a paragraph or a section is a unique chance to focus the reader on an idea using memorable language. Don't squander those opportunities.

as much value as it can. So rather than using the last paragraph to repeat yourself, you should use it to sum up the main messages of the section. Don't use the last paragraph in a section to say again what was said; instead, use it to say what it means.

Bringing the audience back to the big picture helps to create cohesion between your sections. The last paragraph of a section is an opportunity to connect the content you just covered to the big picture of your document. Use the last paragraph in a section to pull your readers up from the important nuances and details you've been telling them about and remind them why they learned about those particulars. Then readers will be ready to start learning new material in the next section because they have focused again on the broad outlines of the argument and they understand why they are going to read the next section.

Conclusion

You now have the main principles you need to write policy documents. Cohesion and coherence are the most important principles you can employ to create documents that really help your audience understand what it is you are trying to communicate in each paragraph, each section, and in your document as a whole. Apply these principles and you will succeed at communicating your thinking through the documents you write.

CHECKLIST

Paragraph cohesion:

- Paragraph begins with knowledge with which the audience is familiar.
- Sentences begin with familiar information and then proceed to new or complex information.

Paragraph coherence:

- Topic sentence establishes the point of the paragraph.
- Each sentence directly relates to the point of the paragraph.
- The same idea/person/agency is referred to by the same name throughout the paragraph.

Document cohesion:

- Each section has an introductory paragraph that relates the section to the main themes of the document, previews the content of the section, and connects the content to the themes.

- Each section has a closing paragraph that reminds the reader why the section was important.

Document coherence:

- Headings correctly and clearly delineate the main sections of the document.

- Each section is on point and clearly connects to the main point of the document.

- The same idea/person/agency is referred to by the same name throughout the document.

EXERCISES

Coherence and Cohesion in Paragraphs

Applying to Your Own Writing: Select a paragraph in your current draft. Take a pen, pencil, highlighter, or paintbrush and underline the topics in the paragraph that connect together. Are the sentences in your paragraph cohesive? If not, rewrite your paragraph to make the topic at the end of each sentence connect to the one after it.

Coherence and Cohesion at the Global Level

Critique This Book: Since it's hard to provide full-length documents to critique, let's use this book as an example. Pick a section header in this chapter or one of the previous chapters. Look at the paragraphs immediately above and below the header. Do the paragraphs follow the principles laid out at the end of this chapter to encourage cohesion? If not, what could have been done differently to make the sections on either side of the header more cohesive? Alternately, look ahead to one of the sample documents in Chapters 8–13 and ask the same questions.

Applying to Your Own Writing: Now apply that same critical eye to your own writing. Pick a section header in your document. Look at the paragraphs immediately above and below the header. Do the paragraphs follow the principles laid out at the end of this chapter to encourage cohesion? If not, what could have been done differently to make the sections on either side of the header more cohesive?

BIBLIOGRAPHY

The Nature Conservancy. (2014). *Coastal resilience on Virginia's Eastern Shore.* Retrieved from https://www.conservationgateway.org/ConservationByGeography/NorthAmerica/UnitedStates/virginia/Documents/NFWF%20CR%20Fact%20Sheet%20revised%20Nov2014.pdf

5

Visually Communicating: On Creating and Writing About Tables

W hen you pick up a magazine, whether it's *National Geographic, Sports Illustrated,* or *People,* you likely flip through it, looking to see what catches your eye. You read the headlines, glance at the photographs, and finally decide if and where you are going to settle in and read. You approach reading a magazine this way for good reasons: Time is short, magazines are long, and skimming the headlines and pictures is a good way to decide what you want to read.

Policy makers approach policy documents the same way, but policy documents are slightly different than magazines (or so you may have noticed!). One conspicuous difference is that policy documents rarely include photographs as visual hooks. Instead, we use figures, tables, and infographics that we hope will pop out to policy makers and memorably tell them our story. These visual tools enable policy makers to understand and remember key themes we want to convey to them. A trend line shows that death rates for whites in America are rising at a time when all other races are falling. A convoluted organizational chart conveys why no one seems able to fix the problems of the Washington, D.C., metro system even though people are dying every year on the subway. A process map displays all the steps a company must go through to get the environmental permits needed to build a new electric vehicles plant and create hundreds of new jobs.

Visuals like these are effective because some ideas we handle in public policy are more easily conveyed visually than in text. For example, you may have read the sentence above that said, "A trend line shows that death rates for whites in America are rising at a time when all other races are falling." But you probably forgot about it quickly. Now look at Figure 5.1 below highlighting a key aspect of this terrible trend: the change in death rates of white Americans since 1990 from drugs, alcohol, and suicide, the so-called "deaths of despair."[1]

Memorable, isn't it?

And it's not simply memorable. The visual also conveys an enormous amount of complicated information in a lot less space than I could have in written form. I could have written several lengthy paragraphs discussing the

---

[1] NPR, "The Forces Driving Middle-Aged White People's 'Deaths of Despair,'" March 23, 2017, http://www.npr.org/sections/health-shots/2017/03/23/521083335/the-forces-driving-middle-aged-white-peoples-deaths-of-despair

Figure 5.1 White non-Hispanic Midlife Mortality From "Deaths of Despair" in the U.S. by Education, Ages 50–54, Deaths by Drugs, Alcohol, and Suicide

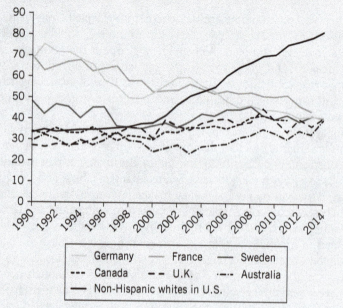

"Deaths of Despair" Rates Across Countries:
Deaths per 100,000 by Drugs, Alcohol, and Suicide Among Men and Women Ages 50–54

Legend:
— Germany — France — Sweden
--- Canada – – U.K. ·—·· Australia
— Non-Hispanic whites in U.S.

Source: "Rising Morbidity and Mortality in Midlife Among White non-Hispanic Americans in the 21st Century," by A. Case and A. Deaton, 2015, *Proceedings of the National Academy of Sciences, 112*(49), pp. 15078–15083.

changes in death rates from these causes cross-nationally by describing them over the last 25 years, then described each of the seven countries over that time and then talked about the U.S. trend in comparison . . . but that would have taken me pages and pages and you would be bored. Not because the information isn't important and shocking but because the delivery wouldn't convey the issue succinctly, dramatically, and memorably. So, instead of writing and writing, I've shown you a visual that is hard to forget.

Creating powerful and effective visuals for your audience requires the same two skills of your writing: *thinking* and *communicating*. Just like with writing, the thinking is the hardest part. It's the thinking that will help you decide what crucial point your visual needs to make, what data will back it up, or what process you need to show.

The good news is you've already done much of that thinking in your sentence outline and revisions. By the time you decide you need a figure or a table to support a point, you know what the point is, how it fits in your argument, and why the figure is so important it needs to take up a half-page of the precious, limited space in your document.

But just like with sentences and paragraphs, it's not enough simply to know what you want to create. Instead, you have to use the principles of design to make sure your visual *communicates* with your audience. Each of the three broad categories of visuals discussed in this chapter (tables, graphs, and infographics) share four audience-centered design principles to enable your visual to communicate effectively with your audience. Follow them and you'll have graphics that make your point immediately and clearly. Violate them and you'll confuse your audience and obscure more than you clarify.

Principles for Designing Visuals

1. **Make one important point per visual.** Figure 5.1 vividly shows the increase in deaths of despair for white Americans while all other peer countries are remaining low, but notice that part of what makes it memorable is that the figure only tries to make one point rather than a multitude of points. Remember, readers are often skimming through a document the first time they hit one of your visuals. *Focus them on one important point per visual.* When you do this, the visuals orient your reader to what is important in your argument, much like headers do. If you make visuals about unimportant points, your readers will focus on those to the detriment of your important points. If you make them about multiple points you'll confuse your readers because they won't know what to focus on and take away. Instead, make visuals about one important point that your readers should focus on and remember.

2. **Make visuals self-contained and self-orienting.** For a visual to communicate effectively, all the information an audience needs to understand it must be contained in it. Since readers often skim policy documents for visuals, the same way you do in a magazine, many times they won't have arrived at your visual having read the surrounding text. As such, you have to have the right information in the visual to orient them. Your visual has to provide the reader with the *who, what, when, where,*

and *how* of each visual.[2] For example, Figure 5.1 shows that non-Hispanic whites (*who*) are dying at increasingly high rates (*what is happening*) starting in about 2000 (*when*) in the United States (*where*), and we know this from a report published by the Brookings Institution (*how*).

3. **Interpret the visual in the document.** Readers will often look at your visual before they read your document, but you still need to reference and explain the meaning of your visual in the text. As you write about your visual, make sure to answer these three natural questions your readers will have:

    a. Why is the visual here? In other words, why is it important to show your audience this visual now, in this spot in the argument? What point is it there to make?

    b. What is in the visual? Describe the data and composition of the visual. The visual is a type of evidence, and you need to describe where you got the evidence. Do this by describing the information you've included in the visual (the *who, what, when, where,* and *how*) with a little bit more detail.

    c. What does the visual show? Tell your audience explicitly what the visual means. Interpret it for them. Make note of any important trends and tell them what the visual means for the problem that is important to both of you.

4. **Make it readable to people with normal vision who are in a hurry.** With the strict page limits required for many policy documents, it's often tempting to skimp on the size of a visual. Don't.

    There are two reasons why you shouldn't. First, the people who are most likely to make decisions you want to impact are often old. This is stereotypical but true. As they've aged, their eyesight has worsened. It's not because they're lame, it's because their eyes have changed as they've aged (yours will too!). Be kind to us. Work hard to make your visual readable to them in terms of colors, contrasts, and (most important) size.

    Second, when you are creating visuals you will suffer from the curse of knowledge, just like you did when you were writing. It's easy to forget that a new reader won't know all the details.

---

[2] The missing *w*, of course, is *why*. This is hard to capture in a visual unless you are reporting on a causal mechanism you identified through a well-designed research project.

Instead, you'll convince yourself that they don't really need to know some particular set of numbers and it's okay to use that eight-point font in that particular part of the visual. Don't do this! If it's important enough to include, it's important enough to make big enough for your audience to read.

In this chapter, we'll apply these principles to one of the most common visuals in public policy: tables. In the next chapter, we'll look at how to apply them to creating figures like graphs and infographics.

Problem → Solved
Which Program Should I Use to Create a Visual?

Designing and creating visuals are two different tasks. Designing a visual means envisioning which information needs to go in and around the visual. Creating a visual is the process of creating one using a particular computer program. In this chapter, we'll think a lot about design. To create the visuals, you'll need to learn a computer program or hire a graphic designer.

The good news is there are dozens of programs you can use to create the visuals: from old standbys like Word, Excel, and PowerPoint; to fancy statistical programs like SAS, R, Stata, and SPSS that you might encounter in a graduate program; to cutting-edge graphic design websites like Canva and Piktochart; to powerful graphic design tools like Adobe Creative Cloud that design professionals often use.

Each of these programs has specific user guides to help you create graphics. Whichever program you are using, consider investing in a graphics book. For example, the excellent *A Visual Guide to Stata Graphics* (Mitchell, 2012) is on the bookshelf behind me.

Alternately, it's worth considering whether or not *you* should be creating your visuals at all. If your graphic is complicated or your programing skills are limited, then it may make more sense to hire a professional graphic designer. The programs described above are complicated, they may or may not help you create what you need, and many will come and go over the years. For all of these reasons, weigh the costs of creating your graphic yourself versus paying someone else to do it. This may be a good place to learn to delegate!

Tables

Perhaps the most straightforward of the visuals in public policy documents are tables. Comprised of rows and columns that intersect to form cells, these visuals are excellent tools for communicating straightforward and precise information. In fact, in some situations, only a table will do because it can communicate exact numbers in ways a figure never could.

For example, one place where you will always see tables is budget documents. All governments and nonprofits have budgets, and the details are always conveyed in tables. These tables are the official records of how much money should be spent on a program. It's not enough to have a chart that people squint at to see how much California has allocated to spend on the National Guard this year. Having a figure that allocates somewhere between $100 and 200 million won't cut it. It's important to know that down to the cent! The same with salary tables (you want to know exactly how much you'll get paid), tax tables (how much exactly are they going to take from your paycheck?!), and tables detailing other specific numbers.

But tables can also be more than lists of specific numbers. Often tables show the summary statistics (counts, averages, medians, etc.). For example, a table could include helpful counts of the number of people served by an after-school program in different cities, the average size of farm subsidies in different rural counties, or the median household income in various voting precincts.

Elements of a Successful Table

An effective table needs to successfully fulfill the design principles laid out earlier in this chapter. It must fit into the flow of your overall document and *make one important point*. It might be there to communicate the progressive nature of the tax brackets. It might be there to show that big farms get more subsidies per acre than medium or small farms. But it should only make one point. Then the table must be *self-contained and self-orienting*. Make sure that you have the following elements included and that they are thoughtfully completed:

Title: First, give your table a number (e.g., Table 1) that you can then reference in the text so you don't have to type the whole title every time you write about it. Second, make sure the title refers explicitly to as much of the *who, what, when,* and *where* as you can.

Row and column headers: Each row and column should be labeled in a way that is easy for the reader to understand. Eliminate jargon-filled headers. You may know that your row header "*permit_any_circ*" means what percentage of people want abortions to be permitted under any circumstances, but no one else will. Similarly, make sure readers know what units you are using. Does ".29" mean that only .029% of those surveyed support abortion under any circumstances, or that 29% do? Don't leave your readers in doubt. Tell them explicitly!

Sources: Give readers confidence in your numbers by giving them some sense of how you got them. If you got the information from another source, name the organization or publication explicitly. Most tables put this information in a note at the bottom of the table labeled "Sources."

Finally, you need to make sure that the text in your table is legible to the people who are trying to read it. Font size matters, of course, but tables have other considerations as well. For example, tables that run multiple pages can be hard to read, as can tables that have too many rows or columns. These are judgment calls, so think carefully about the trade-offs of including more interesting information and the possibility of confusing your readers and them missing your main point. Use your revision principles of taking time away and asking others to read your drafts to help you decide where your table format is helping or confusing your readers.

Now let's take a look at a running example that illustrates these principles of design for better and for worse.

A Bad Example

Imagine that you've just picked up a new report on the startling increase in white death rates across the United States, and as you're flipping through it for the first time you come upon Table 5.1a. Without looking ahead, what are you able to take away from this table?

When I first read this, it took me several minutes to figure out what it was trying to convey. There were parts I was able to understand immediately, parts I was able to infer, and parts that just left me confused. You? Try saying out loud what makes it confusing or identify places that are the least

Table 5.1a Changes in Mortality Rates 2013–1999, Ages 45–54 (2013 mortality rates)				
	All-Cause Mortality	Poisonings	Intentional Self-Harm	Chronic Liver Cirrhosis
WNH	33.9 (415.4)	22.2 (30.1)	9.5 (25.5)	5.3 (21.1)
BNH	–214.8 (581.9)	3.7 (21.8)	0.9 (6.6)	–9.5 (13.5)
Hispanics	–63.6 (269.6)	4.3 (14.4)	0.2 (7.3)	–3.5 (23.1)

clear by circling them before reading the next paragraph (this will help cement the knowledge in your head).

I found Table 5.1a pretty confusing for a number of reasons. In our list of *who*, *what*, *when*, *where*, and *how*, this table only conveys one of them clearly. We know *when* (2013–1999), but even that is a really strange way to write that time period. Most people write 1999–2013. (Why stress your reader by making them read backward?) We do know a bit about *what* is happening. People are dying and we have four columns of causes, but if you're like me, you're pretty confused about what the numbers in each cell mean. Why are there two sets of numbers in each cell? What are the units?

Another problem is we're not sure exactly *who* is dying. We do know they are middle-aged, but it's not obvious what WNH and BNH mean. We're not sure *where* they are from. Nor do we know where these numbers are coming from. *How* do we know these mortality rates? I'm sure the researcher who wrote this would think we're dumb for not knowing these things, but then again, that is the very definition of the curse of knowledge: forgetting that just because you know something doesn't mean that other people don't.

Finally, notice that in this table it is even hard to know what the numbers stand for. What is in parentheses? If you work hard, you can eventually conclude that they are the overall mortality rates, but it took me several guesses to figure that out. By making you guess, these authors have distracted you from the point they are trying to make, whatever that is. That's bad writing.

A Better Example

Now take a look at Table 5.1b, which implements the principles of good visuals to make it more readable. What are you able to take away from this version? Notice that some simple fixes go a long way in making it more understandable.

The authors has defined the what a mortality rate is, written out the actual names of the WNH and BNH so we don't have to guess, added lines to help us read the table, and—importantly—separated out each of the columns into two subcolumns so we can understand what the numbers that were in parentheses in Table 5.1a mean. This table makes it a lot easier to understand what each component part means and gives us a shot at understanding why it is there.

That said, this table still has weaknesses. Think again about what confuses you here. One thing that confuses me is that it's not clear what the point of this table is! *Why* is it here? This table makes us guess at the answer. The title gives us facts, but it doesn't tell us how to think about what it means.

Best Example

Table 5.1c is a version that really focuses our attention on the point of the table. Two changes make a big difference here. First, the title is a significant

Table 5.1b Mortality Rates per 100,000 People Ages 45–54 in 2013 and the Changes in Mortality Rates From 1999 to 2013

	All-Cause Mortality		Poisonings		Intentional Self-Harm		Chronic Liver Cirrhosis	
	Mortality rate in 2013	Change 1999–2013	Mortality rate in 2013	Change 1999–2013	Mortality rate in 2013	Change 1999–2013	Mortality rate in 2013	Change 1999–2013
White non-Hispanics	415.4	33.9	30.1	22.2	25.5	9.5	21.1	5.3
Black non-Hispanics	581.9	–214.8	21.8	3.7	6.6	0.9	13.5	–9.5
Hispanics	269.6	–63.6	14.4	4.3	7.3	0.2	23.1	–3.5

Table 5.1c	Racial Differences in Mortality Rates per 100,000 People Ages 45–54 and the Changes in Their Mortality Rates From 1999 to 2013		
		White non-Hispanics	Black non-Hispanics	Hispanics
All-Cause Mortality	Death rate in 2013	415.4	581.9	269.6
	Change 1999–2013	33.9	–214.8	–63.6
Poisonings	Death rate in 2013	30.1	21.8	14.4
	Change 1999–2013	22.2	3.7	4.3
Intentional Self-Harm	Death rate in 2013	25.5	6.6	7.3
	Change 1999–2013	9.5	0.9	0.2
Chronic Liver Cirrhosis	Death rate in 2013	21.1	13.5	23.1
	Change 1999–2013	5.3	–9.5	–3.5

Source: "Rising Morbidity and Mortality in Midlife Among White non-Hispanic Americans in the 21st Century," by A. Case and A. Deaton, 2015, *Proceedings of the National Academy of Sciences, 112*(49), pp. 15078–15083.

improvement. It immediately focuses us on the key point: There are big racial differences in mortality from these causes. Second, the design of this table focuses us on these differences by showing the mortality rates of each racial group side by side, making it immediately obvious what is being compared.[3]

With these two changes, you can immediately focus on the trend that middle-aged whites have had huge increases in their death rates from each of these causes over the last 14 years. You can see that blacks in this age group have the worst overall death rate but that their health has been improving dramatically while white deaths are climbing. And you finally know from where these numbers come: a prestigious, peer-reviewed journal article.

When the table is arranged this way, when the guesswork is taken out of the column titles and units, then the readers will focus on the message that you want to convey. The readers will see patterns when before they were struggling to understand what the rows even meant! When you apply the principles of table design you can keep your readers from spending all of their energy figuring out the details as they try to construct the big-picture message. Instead, by making the table easy to read, you can have your readers focus their attention on your main takeaway.

---

[3] I did this by transposing the table—that is, by switching the columns and the rows. Now each row focuses us on the racial difference instead of the differences between the causes of death.

When you create a table, it's important to think about how exact you make the numbers in each cell. One of the curses of a calculator is that when you divide numbers or create an average, it spits out a number to the twelfth decimal place. How many digits should you use?

You should use as many decimal places as are useful to the reader and faithful to the data you have collected. For example, in the table above, the mortality data are from death records across the United States. While these data have nuances, they are pretty accurate, so the rates they calculated are faithful to the data for many more decimal places than they showed us.

The question, then, is what is useful to the reader. The authors for Table 1 decided that the death rate should be reported to the first decimal place. Why? They could have included more decimal places, but that would have made the table harder to read without adding much value to your understanding of the trends involved. If the authors had rounded to whole numbers (turning 415.4 to 415), it would have been hard to see the differences in how the suicide rate had changed. One decimal place is the sweet spot for these data. You'll need to make judgment calls for your table and get a second opinion from your friends who are helping you do revisions.

Writing About a Table

While readers will often look at your visual before they read your document, you still need to write about the table in your text. There is inevitably more that needs to be said about the message of the table than is conveyed in the table itself. Most crucially, readers will be looking for information about the three questions highlighted at the beginning of the chapter:

a. <u>Why is the table here?</u> Explicitly connect the table to the greater argument of your document, making sure you use the principles of cohesion and coherence we discussed earlier in this book. Tell your audience why it is important to show them this table at this point in your argument.

b. <u>What is in the table?</u> Describe the data and composition of the table. Your audience will want to know where your evidence is coming from and why it is trustworthy. Tell them. Make sure you give enough background to understand the specifics but that you also come to the point quickly (a tricky task!).

c. <u>What does the table show?</u> Tell your audience explicitly what the table means. Interpret it for them. Do this by describing the information you've included in the table (the *who, what, when, where,* and *how*) with a little bit more detail. Make note of the important numbers or trends and then tell them what the table means for the problem that is important to both of you.

In answering these questions, you will have to make decisions about what specific numbers or trends to discuss, how much detail to include, and more. The key question that should guide these decisions is whether or not your write-up is helping focus your audience on the key takeaways from your table. Let's look at a series of write-ups about Table 5.1c to see a gamut of table descriptions and some examples of what is helpful and unhelpful.

A Bad Example

Here is a typical example of text you might find next to Table 5.1c:

As shown in Table 5.1c, the all-cause mortality rate of WNHs ages 45–54 is currently 415.4, BNHs is 589.1, and Hispanics is 269.6. These rates have changed for WNHs by 33.9, –214.8 for BNHs, and –63.6 for Hispanics. The poisoning rate of WNHs in this age group is 30.1, BNHs is 21.8, and Hispanics is 14.4. These rates have changed for WNHs by 22.2, 3.7 for BNHs, and 4.3 for Hispanics. The intentional self-harm rate of WNHs in this age group is 25.5, BNHs is 6.6, and Hispanics is 7.3. These rates have changed for WNHs by 9.5, 0.9 for BNHs, and 0.2 for Hispanics. The chronic liver cirrhosis rate of WNHs in this age group is 25.5, BNHs is 6.6, and Hispanics is 7.3. These rates have changed for WNHs by 9.5, 0.9 for BNHs, and 0.2 for Hispanics.

This write-up fails for several reasons. The most important is that it doesn't help the reader understand the meaning of the table. Instead of focusing on the important message of Table 5.1c, this write-up simply converts the table to paragraph form without providing any context or interpretation. Also, in doing so, the author has made the write-up numbingly boring because it isn't adding value, it's only repeating information. In fact, the write-up is so boring I'll wager you didn't read it all the way through.[4]

A Better Example

Now let's look at a better version:

As shown in Table 5.1c, over the 15-year period between 1999 and 2015, midlife all-cause mortality fell by more than 200 per 100,000 for black non-Hispanics (BNHs), and by more than 60 per 100,000 for Hispanics. By contrast, white non-Hispanic (WNH) mortality rose by 34 per 100,000. Deaths from poisonings roughly tripled across the time period for WNHs while slightly increasing for other groups. Intentional self-harm mortality also increased for WNHs by 9.5 per 100,000 while BNH mortality increased by 0.9 per 100,000 and Hispanics by 0.2 per 100,000. Finally, the chronic liver cirrhosis mortality rate of WNHs increased by 5.3 per 100,000 while BNHs and Hispanics both saw important decreases in their chronic liver cirrhosis mortality rates.

This example is better. For one, it's shorter and for two, it's a lot less painful to read. The reason is that this version focuses us on the trends in Table 5.1c, rather than focusing us on the baselines. It lets Table 5.1c do the work of showing us all of the specific baseline numbers and instead makes a decision about what are the most important numbers (the changes, in this case) and focuses our attention on them.

While this version is a big improvement over the previous one (you might actually have read it all the way through!), it still isn't particularly engaging or memorable.

Best Example

Now let's look at a version that really adds value to the table:

Between 1999 and 2013, a shocking thing happened: middle-aged, white, non-Hispanic Americans (WNHs) began to die at higher rates, increasing 9% over the 15-year span (see Table 5.1c). During the same period, the mortality rate of both black, non-Hispanic Americans (BNHs) and Hispanic Americans

---

[4] If you did, then you would have noticed that the numbers in the last sentence of the write-up are wrong! But you didn't, and that's more evidence that bad write-ups are ineffective at what they claim to do: convey the basic information in the table.

dropped 27% and 19%, respectively. The increase in the death rate of WNHs is largely driven by so-called "deaths of despair" stemming from drug overdose (*poisonings*), suicide (*intentional self-harm*), and alcoholism (*chronic liver cirrhosis*). In 2015, WNHs died from drug overdoses twice as often as their Hispanic counterparts and 38% more often than BNHs. In 2013, out of every 100,000 WNHs, 25.5 committed suicide, a rate that increased 60% over the 15-year time period to the point where WHNs kill themselves 3.5 times more frequently than BNHs or Hispanics of the same age. Finally, WHNs have been drinking themselves to death at increasingly higher rates over the time frame. They now die from chronic liver cirrhosis almost as frequently as Hispanic Americans.

This write-up is significantly stronger than the previous one. It clearly and memorably tells the reader what they should pay attention to from the table. It focuses the narrative clearly on the increasing propensity of WNHs to die of external causes during this time period. Even more, it actually adds some value by comparing the changes between the three racial groups in ways that are meaningful.

Notice, though, that this version involved some editorial choices that the other, more straightforward tellings did not. I used emotional words and phrases like "shocking" and "drinking themselves to death" that were different from the more sterile language of simply describing these num-bers. I tried to have the language mirror the wrenching stories of despair that engulf many of the rural white Americans around whom I grew up in Appalachia.[5] Whether or not this kind of emotional language is appro-priate for your document depends on the audience, context, and point you are trying to make. Again, these are judgment calls, so ask those who are helping you to give you feedback about whether or not they are appropriate.

Notice also that this write-up doesn't focus at all on one of the most grievous messages of Table 5.1c: the high death rates of BNHs compared to WNHs or Hispanics. There is clearly a story to tell here, but these write-ups do not tell it. This might be justified because the report the table is illustrating focuses on the changing death rates for white, non-Hispanic Americans, or it might not be. Without knowing the context and purpose of this report, it's hard to make that judgment.

---

[5] At this time of writing, the total for drug overdose deaths in the United States was predicted to have increased from about 43,000 deaths in 2013 to about 63,000 deaths in 2016, with no end to these dramatic increases in sight. For scale, this number is about the same as the number of deaths nationwide from guns and automobile accidents combined (Katz, 2017).

Problem → Solved
Presenting Regression Tables and Results

Many public policy researchers use multiple regression as a primary tool in understanding what influences policy outcomes. These mathematical models can provide real insight into some of the policy problems you might be facing. However, the price to gain this insight is usually multiple upper-level or graduate-level classes in statistics. These courses focus primarily on understanding the math, applying the skills to a problem, and understanding the results. They typically focus very little on communicating these results to readers without statistical training. This creates two sets of challenges.

The first challenge is how to make meaning of the regression results for readers who are not trained in interpreting regression results. The best course of action in the policy documents described in this book is to banish the results tables, model descriptions, and nuances to an appendix for interested readers. It's the rare reader who wants you to tell them about the 95% confidence interval or whether or not you used robust standard errors. Instead, provide a simple interpretation of the results that laypeople can understand. Tell your reader what the point estimate of the effect is, tell them what it means, how they should think about it compared to the effect of other causes, and whether or not they should trust it.[6]

The second set of challenges is how to communicate and interpret the results to other people who know how to interpret regression findings. The good news is that new software giving us new visual tools to do this has increased dramatically in the last 15 years. Most disciplines have best practices in displaying regression results (Gelman, Pasarica, & Dodhia, 2002; Kastellec & Leoni, 2007). If you're interested, take a look at a recent article in the *Journal of the American Medical Association* to see some of the visual tools it is using (Chetty et al., 2016).[7] These visuals do a nice job because they focus on the high-level message while giving trained analysts enough in the background to have a sense for what is happening.

---

[6] If you plan to write about regression results frequently, it is worth picking up a copy of Jane Miller's excellent guide to writing about regression, *The Chicago Guide to Writing About Multivariate Analysis*.

[7] A color version of the visuals and a nice overview video about the differences in life expectancy for the poor and rich can be found at the JAMA website: http://jamanetwork.com/journals/jama/fullarticle/2513561.

Conclusion

As you've seen, when tables are done well, they can be a powerful means of communicating with your audience. Properly constructed, they can show patterns and trends in ways that are cleaner and easier than trying to describe your data simply by using prose. With your data moved to a table, you can then use your prose to help your audience understand what the data in the table mean. Then you'll have tables and table descriptions that communicate powerfully with your audience the dynamics of your problem.

As you create tables and insert them into your document, make sure you make use of the design principles laid out in the beginning of the chapter. When you apply these principles, you can create a high-quality table and accompanying write-up that dramatically increase your audience's ability to understand and resonate with your message. Now let's turn to see how figures can do the same thing.

CHECKLIST

General checklist for tables, charts, and infographics

Make sure that for all of your visuals you do the following four things:

1. *Make one important point per visual.*
2. *Make visuals self-contained and self-orienting.*
3. *Interpret the visual in the document:*
   a. Why is the visual there?
   b. What is in the visual?
   c. What does the visual show?
4. *Make it readable to people with normal vision who are in a hurry.*

TABLES CHECKLIST

1. Title: write an individualized title for each table
   a. State the purpose or topic of that table
   b. Include the context of the data
   c. Identify units, if the same for all or most variables in the table
2. Label each row and column
   a. Briefly identify its contents with a short phrase, not acronym or numeric code
   b. Specify units or categories if not summarized in table title

3. Footnotes
   a. Identify the data source (if not in table title)
   b. Define all abbreviations and symbols used within the table

4. Structure and organization
   a. Use indenting or column spanners to show how adjacent rows or columns relate
   b. Apply theoretical and empirical principles to organize rows and columns
      i. For text tables, coordinate row and column sequence with order of discussion
      ii. For appendix tables, use alphabetical order or another widely known principle for the topic so tables are self-guiding
   c. Report the fewest number of digits and decimal places needed for your topic, data, and types of statistics
   d. Use consistent formatting, alignment, and symbols in all tables in a document

5. Check that the table can be understood without reference to the text

EXERCISES

1. Mock up a table, either by hand on a piece of paper or in a spreadsheet that displays data in a way that would help your reader understand your project. Why did you choose the column and the row categories or variables that you did? Why did you give it the title that you did? Why did you include the footnote material that you did?

2. Now consider an alternate way to arrange the table. For example, you could split the table into two tables to simplify it, or include subcategories to show details of particular trends. What does it emphasize differently? What do you like better about this arrangement? What doesn't work as well?

3. Write a description of the table. What does the description do that the table doesn't do on its own? Are you satisfied with the final result? Why or why not?

BIBLIOGRAPHY

Chetty, R., Stepner, M., Abraham, S., Lin, S., Scuderi, B., Turner, N., . . . Cutler, D. (2016). The association between income and life expectancy in the United States, 2001–2014. *JAMA, 315*(16), 1750–1766.

Gelman, A., Pasarica, C., & Dodhia, R. (2002). Let's practice what we preach: Turning tables into graphs. *The American Statistician, 56*(2), 121–130.

Kastellec, J. P., & Leoni, E. L. (2007). Using graphs instead of tables in political science. *Perspectives on Politics, 5*(4), 755–771.

Katz, J. (2017, June 5). Drug deaths in America are rising faster than ever. *New York Times.*

Mitchell, M. N. (2012). *A visual guide to stata graphics* (3rd ed.). College Station, TX: Stata Press.

CHAPTER

6

Visually Communicating: On Creating and Writing About Graphs and Other Figures

W hich part of your document will be the most read? What part will your reader look at first? The answer to both questions is the same: the figures. Just like you flip to the photos first in a magazine, in policy documents the figures are the main avenue you can use to welcome and orient your audience to your document.

Audiences look at figures for good reasons. They are often eye-catching. They usually communicate a lot of information quickly. And figures are particularly good for telling stories about relationships. Human beings instinctively generate narratives out of what they see, and a figure quickly gives your audience data from which they can begin constructing a story: Are the number of Airbnb guests increasing over time? Then the problem is getting bigger. Do men or women get higher sentences for sexting? Then there might be gender discrimination in sentencing. Figures enable readers to begin to visually understand and orient themselves to the stories we are telling them quickly and powerfully.

Because readers reflexively go to the figures first, it is important to construct them using the principles the readers intuitively understand. Violate those principles and you'll discombobulate your reader instantly. Follow the principles and you'll hook your reader into the main message of your story in ways that leave them hungry to learn more.

Elements of a Successful Figure

The most significant principle for creating effective figures is that they must *make one important point.* Your point might be that white, non-Hispanic death rates have increased in the United States over the last 35 years while they have fallen in other developed countries, as shown in Figure 6.1.[1] It might show the relationship between the education level of individuals and the amount they are paid in the workplace by plotting hundreds of people's individual data on the same figure. But whatever the reason, your figure *should only make one point.*

---

[1] NPR, "The Forces Driving Middle-Aged White People's 'Deaths of Despair,'" March 23, 2017, http://www.npr.org/sections/health-shots/2017/03/23/521083335/the-forces-driving-middle-aged-white-peoples-deaths-of-despair.

Don't expect the reader to discern other, nuanced points you want them to take away from a figure. For example, even if you think the remarkably similar decline of "deaths of despair" in Germany and France over the last 35 years is the second key takeaway from Figure 6.1, someone else might think the slight increase of such deaths in Canada is. Don't leave something important to chance. If nuance is needed, either create a second figure highlighting the point or add a nuance in the surrounding text. Keep the audience focused on one takeaway per figure.

So how do you ensure that your figure is effectively making your one point to the audience?

Like tables, figures work best when they are *self-contained and self-orienting*. Make sure that you have the following elements included and thoughtfully completed. Tick these boxes first and then look to make sure that your message is clear:

Figure 6.1   White non-Hispanic Midlife Mortality From "Deaths of Despair" in the U.S. by Education, Ages 50–54, Deaths by Drugs, Alcohol, and Suicide

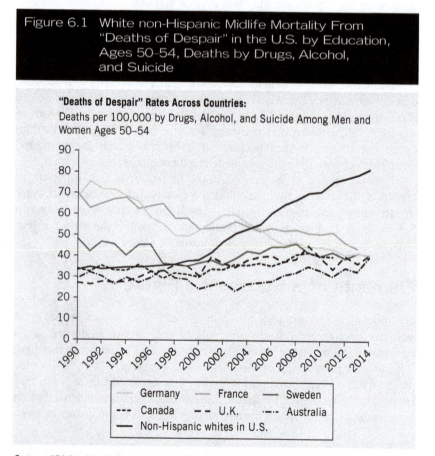

"Deaths of Despair" Rates Across Countries:
Deaths per 100,000 by Drugs, Alcohol, and Suicide Among Men and Women Ages 50–54

Legend:
— Germany — France — Sweden
--- Canada – – U.K. ·—·· Australia
— Non-Hispanic whites in U.S.

Source: "Rising Morbidity and Mortality in Midlife Among White non-Hispanic Americans in the 21st Century," by A. Case and A. Deaton, 2015, *Proceedings of the National Academy of Sciences, 112*(49), pp. 15078–15083.

Title: First, give your figure a number that you can then specify in the text so you don't have to type the whole title every time you refer to it. For most policy documents, start labeling the figures using "Figure 1," then fill in the rest of the title: "Figure 1: 'Deaths of Despair' Rates Across Countries." Second, make sure the title includes as much of the *who, what, when,* and *where* as you can reasonably fit in (try to stay under 20 words). For example, in Figure 6.1, a subtitle helps orient you to these questions.

Sources: Give readers confidence in your numbers by giving them some sense of how you got them. If you got the information from another source, name the organization or publication explicitly. Most figures put this information in a note at the bottom labeled "Sources."

Readability: Make sure that the numbers, labels, titles, and sources in your figure are legible. Font size matters, of course (remember to be kind to old people with bad eyes!), but figures have other considerations as well. The relative size of some parts of a figure can obscure other parts. For example, you might create Figure 6.2 to show that the "deaths of despair" are relatively small contributors to the overall mortality in middle age, and it would do a great job at this task. But if you wanted a figure that showed

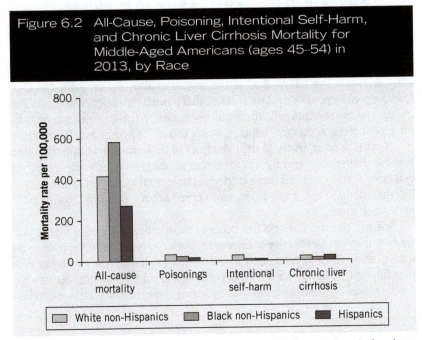

Figure 6.2 All-Cause, Poisoning, Intentional Self-Harm, and Chronic Liver Cirrhosis Mortality for Middle-Aged Americans (ages 45–54) in 2013, by Race

Source: "Rising Morbidity and Mortality in Midlife Among White non-Hispanic Americans in the 21st Century," by A. Case and A. Deaton, 2015, *Proceedings of the National Academy of Sciences, 112*(49), pp. 15078–15083.

the racial differences within each of these four categories, then Figure 6.2 would be ineffective because the scale of the first category makes the other three unreadable. Can you tell how many people a year die of poisonings, suicide, and alcoholism in each of the groups? What about comparing the causes of death between for BNHs? The numbers are probably too small to see meaningful differences, even if your eyesight is still good.

The point is that the same figure that makes one point well can fail miserably at making another one. Figure 6.2 is great at making one distinction and lousy at making the other one. The trade-offs present in Figure 6.2 are but one example of the many judgment calls you have to make when designing figures, so think carefully about how readability constrains your ability to include information in your figure.

Label your axes and convey the units:[2] While not every figure is a graph, many of them are.[3] Every graph has both an x- and a y-axis. Make sure to label both of them intelligibly and eliminate jargon. If you don't, people will spend their time trying to figure out the details rather than focusing on your one important point. You may know that your y-axis label "percent_DOA" measures the percentage of drug overdose victims who are dead on arrival (DOA) at the hospital, but no one else will. Similarly, make sure your readers know what units you are using. Does ".29" mean that only .029% of victims are DOA or that 29% are? Don't leave your readers in doubt. Tell them explicitly!

But while you must do some things correctly, you have a lot of leeway in designing your figure to communicate your point. Even more than with tables, if you are using accurate data and reporting them correctly, then the main question to ask isn't whether the figure is "right" or "wrong." Rather, ask yourself, Given that I've followed all of the principles above, *is my figure effective? Does every element work together to ensure that it meets the design principles of this chapter and communicates effectively with my audience?* These questions can help drive your revision process, which is as important for figures as it is for text.

As you've seen, many of the principles of designing tables are the same as those that enable your figures to communicate with your audience. Since you have already applied these principles in several examples in Chapter 5, I'll trust that you can apply them again here without walking through bad-better-best examples.

Instead, let's use the next few pages to show different kinds of figures and see how they can be effective at demonstrating to your audience the reality you want to show them. If you're familiar with one type, it might be worth just flipping through the figures (as a normal policy reader might), thinking about what exactly makes them effective and where you might use them in your work. When

---

[2] Picture from xkcd, https://xkcd.com/833/.

[3] For our purposes, graphs are visuals that present data along two axes. This will distinguish graphs from the various figures we'll discuss in the last section of this chapter.

Source: Randal Munroe, xkcd.com.

you get to one you haven't seen before, take a few minutes to understand what it is, how it works, and why it is a powerful tool for focusing the reader's attention.

Graphs

One traditional category of figures is graphs. Chances are you've created some of the basic versions in a spreadsheet program. However, it is still worth spending a few pages thinking about different types of graphs, some of which it's unlikely you've seen. If you have a lot of statistical training, you may sometimes neglect to use these tools when you forget to communicate the basic reality of your problem to your audience.[4] Wherever you are, it's worth remembering that a picture is worth a thousand words. What kind of graph can best make your point to your audience? It's worth taking the time to consider both the simple and the complex to find the most effective way to tell your story.

Bar Graphs

Basic Bar Graph

Perhaps the most basic graph is a *bar graph,* where the y-axis is made up of two or more categories and the y-axis is a continuous variable.[5]

---

[4] If you're a data nerd, there are great resources out there on how visually to display data. Classic books like Tufte (1983, 2006) and newer books like Yau (2011, 2013) provide wonderful overviews. For communicating regression results, I've found Gelman, Pasarica, and Dodhia (2002); Kastellec and Leoni (2007); and Miller (2013) to be particularly helpful resources.

[5] Categorical variables break up the world into different groupings, or categories. Examples include race (WNH, BNH, etc.), nationality (Chinese, Indian, Nigerian, etc.), or types of fruit (apples, oranges, pears, etc.). Continuous variables are used to measure things that can be along many different points in continuum, like height, income, or mortality rates.

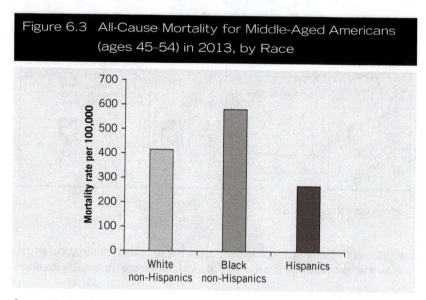

Figure 6.3 All-Cause Mortality for Middle-Aged Americans (ages 45–54) in 2013, by Race

Source: "Rising Morbidity and Mortality in Midlife Among White non-Hispanic Americans in the 21st Century," by A. Case and A. Deaton, 2015, *Proceedings of the National Academy of Sciences, 112*(49), 15078–15083.

Figure 6.3 shows the all-cause mortality rates for the different races in 2013. The x-axis has three categories: white non-Hispanics (WNHs), black non-Hispanics (BNHs), and Hispanics, into which people are divided. The y-axis is a continuous variable that shows how many people out of 100,000 die a year in each category.

Notice that this simple graph communicates a fundamentally different message than Figure 6.2. Rather than focusing you on the relatively small role deaths of despair play in overall mortality, Figure 6.2 focuses your attention on the fact that middle-aged black non-Hispanic Americans die at much higher rates than the other two ethnic groups.

Notice also that you can focus on the main message because Figure 6.2 ticks all of the boxes on our checklist from the beginning of the chapter. There is a clear title, axis labels, and source. These details make sure that the graph conveys the punch of the data: The likelihood of living or dying in middle age is significantly different for different races in America.

Clustered Bar Graph

Once you have the idea of a basic bar graph, you can then begin to see the power of its variations. One of these is a *clustered bar graph* like we saw in Figure 6.2. In clustered bar graphs, there are two categories on the x-axis, the main category of which organizes the graph into groupings of columns, and the subcategories are the columns within each grouping.

For example, in Figure 6.4 the two sets of categories are the causes of death (the main category) and the racial groups (the subcategories).[6] This modified version of Figure 6.2 is redesigned to focus the reader on how WNHs die from each cause of the deaths of despair at rates that are higher than the other groups. The racial groups are clustered by the different causes so you can clearly see how the mortality rates of each group compare within each cause of death.[7]

Clustered bar graphs are a useful tool in other policy areas as well. You could use them to effectively show how the various contributors to

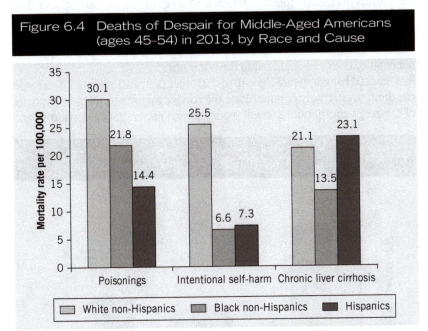

Figure 6.4 Deaths of Despair for Middle-Aged Americans (ages 45–54) in 2013, by Race and Cause

Source: "Rising Morbidity and Mortality in Midlife Among White non-Hispanic Americans in the 21st Century," by A. Case and A. Deaton, 2015, *Proceedings of the National Academy of Sciences, 112*(49), pp. 15078–15083.

[6] With a clustered bar chart, it is always possible to switch the main and subcategories. You could reorganize Figure 6.4 so that all of the WNH causes of death are together, all of the BNH causes are together, and all of the Hispanic causes are together. I usually try it both ways to see which version does a better job of telling the story I want to tell.

[7] You might also notice that I added the exact numbers into each column. It would make the same point with or without the numbers, but since this graph is fairly wide the numbers make it easier for readers to see the magnitude of the chronic liver cirrhosis deaths without tracing their fingers all the way back to the y-axis.

nitrogen loads in four different estuaries (main organizing category) were affected by farms, factories, and homeowners (the subcategories) or the three different locations of a nonprofit (the main category) served a different mix of mentally disabled patients, elderly adults, or at-risk children as clients (the three subcategories).

Stacked Bar Graphs

One other useful variation of a bar graph is a *stacked bar graph*. Stacked bar graphs allow you to show both the overall magnitude of an effect for one group of people and the distinct component parts as well. A stacked bar graph enables you to display the data from Figure 6.4 differently. Figure 6.5 stacks the "deaths of despair" together for each racial grouping. Because it does this, the reader can see that WNHs kill themselves via these three causes at roughly twice the rate of the other two groups. These numbers are the same as the previous graphs, but again, choosing a different tool enables you to tell a different story than you could using the other ones.

Stacked bar graphs are a useful tool in other policy areas as well. You could use them to effectively communicate the relative importance of different types of campaign contributions (small money donations, corporate donations, and

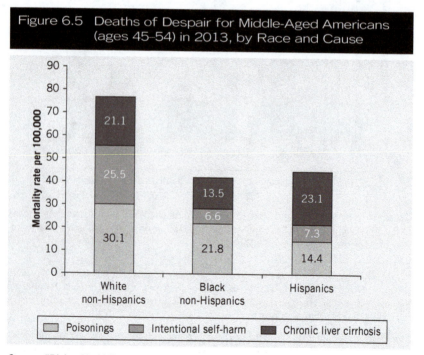

Figure 6.5   Deaths of Despair for Middle-Aged Americans (ages 45–54) in 2013, by Race and Cause

Source: "Rising Morbidity and Mortality in Midlife Among White non-Hispanic Americans in the 21st Century," by A. Case and A. Deaton, 2015, *Proceedings of the National Academy of Sciences, 112*(49), 15078–15083.

super-PACs) to different candidates, how people of different age groups spend their time each day (work, sleep, commuting, etc.), or the composition of the refugees in different refugee camps (infants, older children, adults, the elderly).

Line Graphs

Another useful graph commonly used in policy writing is the line graph. In line graphs, the x-axis usually is time (days, months, or years) and the y-axis represents the trend you are interested in showing the reader, usually continuous variables. For example, Figure 6.1 at the beginning of the chapter showed how U.S. deaths of despair have grown since 1990 while death rates in European countries have fallen from the same causes.

Figure 6.6 is another example of a line graph (Burke, 2017). Take a look and see what you're immediately able to take away.

First of all, you can see that this graphic was designed by a pro. One of the markers is how easily you are able to orient yourself. Admittedly, you've had some set-up for this, but notice how quickly you're able to grasp the point of this graph: The increase in deaths of despair for WNHs is driven by men and women with a high school degree or less. College graduates have barely seen their death rates budge.

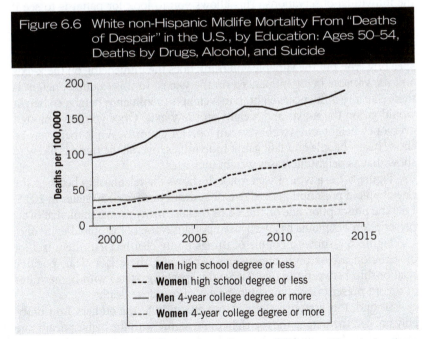

Figure 6.6 White non-Hispanic Midlife Mortality From "Deaths of Despair" in the U.S., by Education: Ages 50–54, Deaths by Drugs, Alcohol, and Suicide

Source: "Rising Morbidity and Mortality in Midlife Among White non-Hispanic Americans in the 21st Century," by A. Case and A. Deaton, 2015, *Proceedings of the National Academy of Sciences, 112*(49), 15078–15083.

I see this trend in my own life. In the college town where I live, over 50% of the residents have college degrees, and we have seen relatively few impacts from this crisis. Just 75 miles away, however, West Virginians have the lowest college completion rate in the country; they have the highest overdose rate, and the tragedy affecting their community is regularly featured in the national media (e.g., Talbot, 2017).

Line graphs are a useful tool for many different policy areas. Any time you want to show how the severity of a problem has changed over time, a line graph can help you make the point. You've probably seen line graphs charting how pollution levels, housing prices, or economic growth have changed over time. They are also particularly useful in showing how different groups perform against one another over time. They can dispel the idea that groups have the same problems or that one group is right in line with everyone else. Done well, a line graph can show key trends in ways your audience is unlikely to forget.

Scatterplots

The final commonly used graph is a *scatterplot*. In a scatterplot, individual units (people, counties, states, or countries) are displayed on a graph in a way that allows your audience to see patterns (or lack thereof) across the individual observations. This allows you to look for patterns to see if one variable influences another.

An easy and intuitive example would be to take all of the people (the unit) in a school and plot their heights and weights on a graph. Generally speaking, you put the variable you think does the influencing on the x-axis and the variable being influenced on the y-axis. In this example, height is more likely to influence weight than weight is to influence height, so height would go on the x-axis and weight on the y-axis. Once you have plotted everyone's height and weight you can look for patterns. While there may be short, heavy people and tall, gaunt individuals, overall the trend is likely to show that as height increases weight increases.

Figure 6.7 is a typical scatterplot. It shows the relationship between the rate of opioid prescriptions and overdose death rates in all 50 states in 2015. I put the prescription rate on the x-axis because many people think that over-prescription of opioids has been an important cause of the opioid epidemic.

Figure 6.7 shows a couple of things pretty clearly. First, there is a lot of variation across both dimensions. That said, there is a clear, positive relationship between the two. Generally speaking, states with higher rates of opioid prescriptions have higher rates of overdose deaths.

Second, this scatterplot also draws attention to the outliers. You probably noticed the state in the top right of the figure with the highest death rate by far. That's West Virginia. You might also have noticed that several states have prescription rates nearly as high as West Virginia but much lower death rates. The scatterplot draws attention to these states (Alabama, Arkansas,

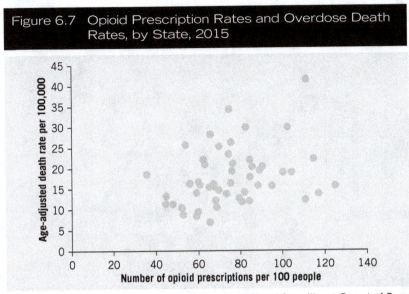

Figure 6.7 Opioid Prescription Rates and Overdose Death Rates, by State, 2015

Source: Centers for Disease Control and Prevention, *Annual Surveillance Report of Drug-Related Risks and Outcomes, United States, 2017.*

Tennessee, and Mississippi), which could lead to an interesting investigation of why so many fewer people are dying of overdoses than expected.

Scatterplots are useful tools across many different policy areas: abortion across various states (teen pregnancies and abortions), teacher performance across classrooms (children in poverty and improvement in test scores), or economic growth across countries (manufacturing jobs and unemployment). They are wonderful tools for showing overall trends to your audience. They are also wonderful tools for highlighting communities or individuals who are doing way better than they seem like they should (or way worse). In these cases, scatterplots can do more than just show raw data; they can point you to where you should learn about individual cases to understand more about your issue (McKeown, 1999; Pascale, Sternin, & Sternin, 2010).

Complex Scatterplots (or, What Hans Rosling Has Wrought)

While traditional scatterplots display data in two dimensions, new software packages have made it possible to make scatterplots more complex and interactive.[8] These packages make it possible to enhance a scatterplot from something that displays data in two dimensions to one that displays data in up to five dimensions. For example, Figure 6.8 is a more complex version of Figure 6.7.

---

[8] The late Hans Rosling was a master at using complex scatterplots to engage an audience on a policy issue. Watch his TED Talks for a taste of his entertaining style or go www.gapminder.org for a chance to explore data from around the world using his interactive software package.

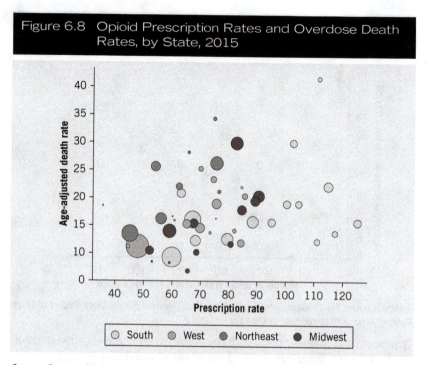

Figure 6.8 Opioid Prescription Rates and Overdose Death Rates, by State, 2015

Source: Centers for Disease Control and Prevention, *Annual Surveillance Report of Drug-Related Risks and Outcomes, United States, 2017.*

In contrast to Figure 6.7, Figure 6.8 adds two additional dimensions by varying the size and shading of the data points displayed in the scatterplot. The size shows the populations of each of the states. The shading communicates in which of the four regions of the United States each state is located.

Adding this texture to the story allows your readers to see many more patterns than they could before. Indeed, before you started reading this text, I imagine that you looked hard at the figure to try to find patterns. The good news is that you were really engaged in the data.[9]

The bad news (from my perspective) is that I don't know onto which of the patterns you latched. Was it that the most populous states have the smallest number of both prescriptions and deaths? Was it that the nine states with the highest prescription rates are all in the South? Was it that Ohio (the big dark gray dot at the top) is by far the most hard-hit of the Midwestern states? I don't know. So if I was using this in a report it would be hard to determine that you took away from it the one point I wanted to make.

---

[9] The most engaging versions of complicated scatterplots are online. These interactive scatterplots enable a fifth dimension: time. By pressing "play," you can watch the states (or countries) move over time. You can also mouse over individual scatterplots to see the state names. Head over to www.gapminder.org/tools to see the real power of these tools.

If your report is posted online, you can add a fifth dimension (time) to a complex scatterplot. By pressing "play" on the bottom left of the scatterplot you can see how the units move over time. These scatterplots can show how regional wars affect the mortality of countries as they begin and as they end. You could show how the funding (x-axis) and performance (y-axis) of universities (units) have changed over time, while layering on color coding the community colleges, four-year colleges, and research universities, as well as enrollment for the size. This complex scatterplot would allow you to understand quickly how these four variables have changed and interacted since the Great Recession. A complex scatterplot may be worth creating to explore the data yourself or to communicate your data with your audience. You should always use one if it is the best tool to make your point, but even if there isn't a crystal-clear takeaway an online version might still be worth including to engage your reader in your issue.

Figures

While the visuals above are all reasonably easy to create in Excel or another statistical package, there are other powerful visual tools that use a different framework. These data visualizations use different methods of communicating with the reader than tables or graphs using an x- and y-axis to show the pattern between two variables. They can either be static pictures or interactive, just like the examples above. I'll do my best to show you some examples below and describe what's happening, but to get the full impact of many of these tools it will be helpful to visit the URLs in the footnotes to interact with an example.

GIS Maps

One of the most interesting and useful data visualization tools is taking data from a table or a graph and mapping it using geographic information system (GIS) maps. These maps are of a specific area (counties in a state, regions in a country, etc.), and they overlay the maps with shade- or color-based data. GIS maps make clear to your reader the spatial components of trends in a way that a table cannot. For example, a table of overdose mortality rates by county in your state will tell you what the rates are, but it won't immediately make clear which parts of your state are struggling the most with the crisis; a GIS map does this instantly.

As an example, look at Figure 6.9, drawn from a report by the Centers for Disease Control and Prevention (CDC; Rudd, 2016). Here, the deaths of despair data we've been reviewing are overlaid on top of a map of the United States.[10] Because the author uses shades of gray to convey how

---

[10] For a sexier, more interactive version, check out http://arcg.is/2agsQoQ (ESRI, 2017). This report includes interactive maps of the opioid crisis at the county level for all 50 states.

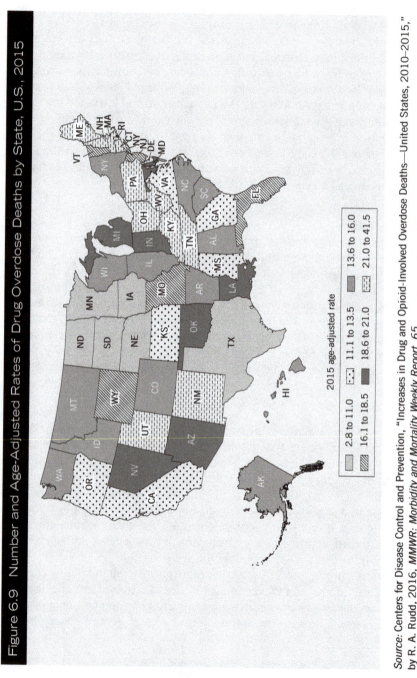

Figure 6.9   Number and Age-Adjusted Rates of Drug Overdose Deaths by State, U.S., 2015

2015 age-adjusted rate

2.8 to 11.0	13.6 to 16.0
11.1 to 13.5	21.0 to 41.5
16.1 to 18.5	
18.6 to 21.0	

Source: Centers for Disease Control and Prevention, "Increases in Drug and Opioid-Involved Overdose Deaths—United States, 2010–2015," by R. A. Rudd, 2016, *MMWR: Morbidity and Mortality Weekly Report,* 65.

severe the rate of overdose deaths is in each state, you can immediately see where drug overdose deaths are relatively high and low across the country: the states like West Virginia and others that have a significant portion of their state in Appalachia and New England. Figure 6.8 shows the audience this pattern and engages them reflexively, causing them to ask why this is the case.

When you think about your issue, you can probably quickly begin to imagine where maps could be helpful. They could illustrate student achievement across different school districts, business growth across different regions of a state, or better health outcomes across different countries of the continent on which you are working. When used well, these GIS maps can be a powerful tool for engaging and interacting with data across a variety of issues and geographies.

Resized Maps

As interesting as GIS maps are, they are often misleading because they show your reader geographic size rather than focusing on a more relevant dimension, like population or emissions. One interesting option is to resize the components of a GIS map based upon an important variable of interest, like population or emissions. These maps can be both helpful and revealing.

For example, Figure 6.10a shows a map of Virginia election results in 2017, when voters went to the polls for the first statewide election following the election of Donald Trump. Many of the areas that voted for President Trump are the closest to West Virginia and the most heavily impacted by the opioid crisis.

But as you probably noted by the vote totals on the right side of Figure 6.10a, the Democrat, Lt. Gov. Ralph Northam, roundly beat the Republican, Ed Gillespie. How is this possible, given how little of the landmass was won outright by the Democrat?

The answer, of course, is that a regular GIS map does a poor job of representing how the voters in Virginia are distributed. What Figure 6.10a doesn't show is that the three dark gray clumps are the northern Virginia area (top right near Washington, D.C.), the areas around Richmond (the middle right, the state capital), and the areas in the southeast (the Hampton Roads area). They contain over half the state's population crowded into a few, small sections of the state. Figure 6.10b shows the map of Virginia resized to reflect this reality. Suddenly, it's very clear how the Democrat won. He won most of the state's populated areas and won them handily. A resized map makes this underlying reality easy to understand.

Resized maps can be helpful in any number of situations where the geography doesn't map well to the dimension that interests you. For example, carbon emissions, where a few industrial countries produce most of the emissions and many poor countries produce relatively little, are well represented by resized maps, as are wealth concentrations, economic output, or opioid deaths. Any time the geography doesn't map reality on the ground well, a resized map can help readers understand the differences between the geography and the reality while still keeping the spatial aspects in play.

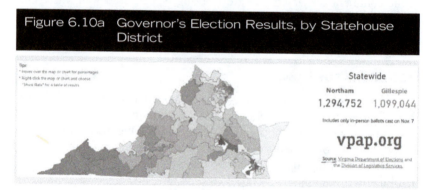

Figure 6.10a Governor's Election Results, by Statehouse District

Source: Virginia Public Access Project.

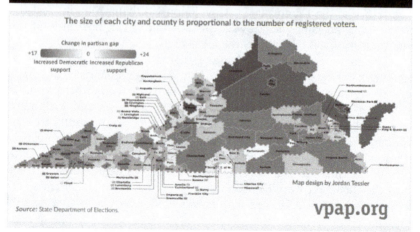

Figure 6.10b Change in Partisan Performance: Governor's Election, 2017 v. 2013

Source: Virginia Public Access Project.

Treemaps

If a resized map is one step more abstracted than a traditional GIS map, then a *treemap* is two steps more abstracted.[11] In a treemap, the visual space is divided into the different segments by the category of interest. Like a GIS map, treemaps use visual space to help readers understand an important trend. However, unlike a GIS map, treemaps don't represent a physical space.

For example, Figure 6.11 shows all of the voters in Virginia in the 2017 election, this time broken up into large counties, suburban counties and cities, and rural areas. Again, this figure shows you the relative importance of a few large cities and counties in a way a GIS map never could. Fairfax County, which is just 0.9% of the area of Virginia, has 13.6% of the population living there. This treemap conveys that reality easily.

As another example, you can also use a treemap to understand the relative impact of the opioid crisis on overall deaths for adult men in the United States. When you look at Figure 6.12, you can immediately get an intuitive sense for what men in this age group are dying from even though you might not know all of the abbreviations (in the online version you can click on each square to learn the full names and more detail). Drugs, alcohol, suicide (self-harm), car wrecks (Road Inj), IHD (heart disease), and murders dominate the landscape. With just a glance you get a sense for the scale of the problem. Notice, however, what this version of the treemap does not do well. In this format (where I have had to take a screen shot)

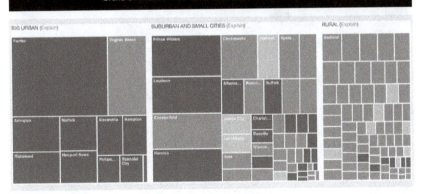

Figure 6.11 Voters by Cities and Counties in Virginia's 2017 Gubernatorial Election

Source: Virginia Public Access Project.

---

[11] All of the treemap examples here have interactive versions online. For another interesting example, find out how many jobs in your state pay $100,000 a year and which jobs earn that much. Explore these data using a treemap found here: http://flowingdata.com/2014/07/02/jobs-charted-by-state-and-salary/

it fails to implement several of the principles of good visuals: What do the shades mean? What do the abbreviations mean?

The online version is clearer and cleaner.[12] Also, the interactive nature engages you more when you play around with it. Again, just like with complex scatterplots, one trade-off of using interactive tools is that while you increase audience engagement you can lose control of the message as readers dive into the data visualization and explore themes that may be less important than the ones on which you need to focus them. I might be trying to focus you on deaths from drugs, self-harm, and poisonings, but you may have looked at this and been very interested in the cancer deaths or deaths from violence. Again, visualizations have trade-offs.

But even with those trade-offs, a treemap can be an exceptionally powerful tool for engaging your audience in understanding the right set of data. One of my favorite uses of a treemap is representing a budget. Readers can easily see where money is being spent and what an organization or government values in reality, not just in rhetoric.

Figure 6.12   Causes of Death for American Men (ages 15–49) in 2015

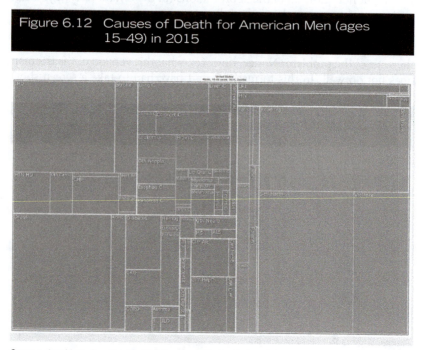

Source: Institute for Health Metrics and Evaluation, *Global Burden of Disease (GBD) 2016.* Seattle: University of Washington.

---

[12] You can recreate this treemap or explore similar treemaps for groups in the United States or for groups in other countries using the Global Burden of Disease app at http://vizhub.healthdata.org/gbd-compare (Institute for Health Metrics and Evaluation [IHME], 2016).

Process Maps

Finally, the last visualization I'll mention is the humble, but useful, *process map*. This diagram is often used to show how a process works. You may recall politicians at press conferences holding up long sheets of paper showing all the steps a company has to go through to build a new plant to decry overregulation. Or perhaps you have seen advocates for the homeless showing all the agencies a newly unhoused person must visit before they can begin to receive benefits. In both cases, the overall visual makes the point even better than the details.

Process maps can also be useful in helping audiences understand the details of particular processes. Figure 6.13 shows the process that doctors are now supposed to employ when a patient comes in asking for opioids (Hudson &

Figure 6.13 Clinic Flow Diagram

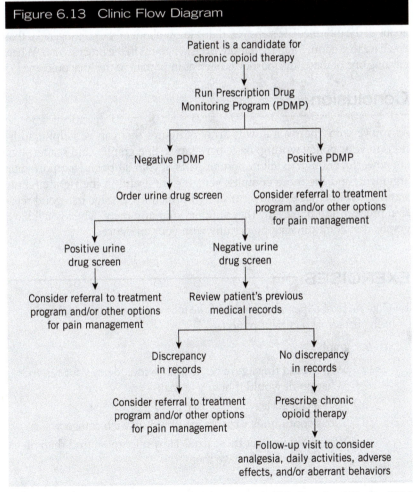

Source: Stefani A. Hudson, MD, and Leslie A. Wimsatt, PhD. Fam Pract Manag, 2014 Nov-Dec; 21(6):6–11. https://www.aafp.org/fpm/2014/1100/p6.html.

Wimsatt, 2014). From the time a patient first enters a clinic, doctors know the step-by-step process they should go through before prescribing an opioid. It documents the process from the first step of running the patient's name through the state's Prescription Drug Monitoring Program (PDMP) to see if the patient is going from doctor to doctor to get more pills (commonly known as "doctor shopping") to the event that a patient without a history of drug abuse gets an opioid prescription. This diagram is helpful, not only for teaching doctors what they should be doing, but also explaining to other audiences how this process works. You can imagine that a legislative committee might find this figure helpful in understanding how doctors have responded to their role in the opioid crisis.

When you create a process map for your document, the final product isn't the only helpful outcome. The other really helpful outcome is what you learned as you created it. As you do the research to understand the various elements in your process map and how they are connected, you will be amazed to learn about all the intermediate steps you didn't know about or the contingencies that you have to account for in the various decision points in the process map. When creating one of these, the journey is often as important as the final outcome.[13]

Conclusion

As you've seen, there are a wide array of figures that can be helpful additions in your policy writing. Basic bar graphs, line graphs, and scatterplots are powerful enough to tell important parts of your story and support your argument, and the more complex versions are useful in the right circumstances. In either case, follow the design principles, engage in a good revision process, and make sure they support your argument. Then you'll have graphs that communicate powerfully with your audience.

EXERCISES

1. On a piece of paper, sketch each of the following bar graphs by hand using data from a current project.

    a. Bar graph

        i. Why would this figure be helpful to include in your report? What point would it help you make?

        ii. X-axis categories

        iii. Y-axis continuous variable measured on each category

        iv. Where did you get these data? How might you find them if you do not already have them?

---

[13] If you want to learn more about this tool and its uses, consider taking a qualitative program evaluation course or picking up a copy of Rossi, Lipsey, and Freeman (2003).

b. Clustered bar graph

    i. Why would this figure be helpful to include in your report? What point would it help you make?

    ii. X-axis categories (clumps)

    iii. X-axis category (within clumps)

    iv. Y-axis continuous variable measured on each category

    v. Where did you get these data? How might you find them if you do not already have them?

c. Stacked bar graph

    i. Why would this figure be helpful to include in your report? What point would it help you make?

    ii. X-axis categories

    iii. X-axis categories (stacked within each category on the x-axis)

    iv. Y-axis continuous variable measured on each category

    v. Where did you get these data? How might you find them if you do not already have them?

2. On a piece of paper, sketch each of the following graphs by hand using data from a current project.

a. Line graph

    i. Why would this figure be helpful to include in your report? What point would it help you make?

    ii. X-axis continuous variable (often the independent variable)

    iii. Y-axis continuous variable (usually the dependent variable)

    iv. Where did you get these data? How might you find them if you do not already have them?

b. Scatterplot

    i. Why would this figure be helpful to include in your report? What point would it help you make?

    ii. X-axis continuous variable

    iii. Y-axis continuous variable

    iv. Where did you get these data? How might you find them if you do not already have them?

c. Complex scatterplot

    i. Why would this figure be helpful to include in your report? What point would it help you make?

    ii. X-axis continuous variable

    iii. Y-axis continuous variable

    iv. Size of bubbles

     v. Color of bubbles

    vi. Where did you get these data? How might you find them if you do not already have them?

3. On a piece of paper, sketch each of the following figures by hand using data from a current project.

  a. GIS map

     i. Why would this figure be helpful to include in your report? What point would it help you make?

    ii. What geographic boundaries would you use?

    iii. What variable would you display?

    iv. Where did you get these data? How might you find them if you do not already have them?

  b. Scaled GIS map

     i. Why would this figure be helpful to include in your report? What point would it help you make?

    ii. What geographic boundaries would you use?

    iii. What variable would you display?

    iv. Where did you get these data? How might you find them if you do not already have them?

  c. Treemap

     i. Why would this figure be helpful to include in your report? What point would it help you make?

    ii. Main variable

    iii. Subgroups

    iv. Subsubgroups (if applicable)

    v. Where did you get these data? How might you find them if you do not already have them?

  d. Flow chart

     i. Why would this figure be helpful to include in your report? What point would it help you make?

    ii. Describe what process you are sketching.

    iii. Where did you get these data? How might you find them if you do not already have them?

BIBLIOGRAPHY

Burke, A. (2017, March 23). Working class white Americans are now dying in middle age at faster rates than minority groups. Retrieved July 6, 2017, from https://www.brookings.edu/blog/brookings-now/2017/03/23/working-class-white-americans-are-now-dying-in-middle-age-at-faster-rates-than-minority-groups/

ESRI. (2017). The opioid epidemic. Retrieved July 7, 2017, from http://urbanobservatory.maps.arcgis.com/apps/Cascade/index.html?appid=f86499d99e4340b68229eaccfb02b29f

Gelman, A., Pasarica, C., & Dodhia, R. (2002). Let's practice what we preach: Turning tables into graphs. *The American Statistician, 56*(2), 121–130.

Hudson, S., & Wimsatt, L. A. (2014). How to monitor opioid use for your patients with chronic pain. *Family Practice Management, 21*(6), 6–11.

Institute for Health Metrics and Evaluation (IHME). (2016). *GBD compare data visualization*. University of Washington. Retrieved April 23, 2018, from http://vizhub.healthdata.org/gbd-compare

Kastellec, J. P., & Leoni, E. L. (2007). Using graphs instead of tables in political science. *Perspectives on Politics, 5*(04), 755–771.

McKeown, T. J. (1999). Case studies and the statistical worldview: Review of King, Keohane, and Verba's Designing Social Inquiry: Scientific Inference in Qualitative Research. *International Organization, 53*(1), 161–190.

Miller, J. E. (2013). *The Chicago guide to writing about multivariate analysis* (2nd ed.). Chicago, IL: University of Chicago Press.

Pascale, R., Sternin, J., & Sternin, M. (2010). *The power of positive deviance: How unlikely innovators solve the world's toughest problems* (1st ed.). Boston, MA: Harvard Business Review Press.

Rossi, P. H., Lipsey, M. W., & Freeman, H. E. (2003). *Evaluation: A systematic approach* (7th ed.). Thousand Oaks, CA: Sage.

Rudd, R. A. (2016). Increases in drug and opioid-involved overdose deaths—United States, 2010–2015. *Morbidity and Mortality Weekly Report, 65*. Retrieved from https://doi.org/10.15585/mmwr.mm655051e1

Talbot, M. (2017, June 5). The addicts next door. *The New Yorker, 93*(16), 74–89.

Tufte, E. R. (1983). *The visual display of quantitative information*. Cheshire, CT: Graphics Press.

Tufte, E. R. (2006). *Beautiful evidence*. Cheshire, CT: Graphics Press.

Yau, N. (2011). *Visualize this: The FlowingData guide to design, visualization, and statistics*. Hoboken, NJ: John Wiley & Sons.

Yau, N. (2013). *Data points: Visualization that means something*. Hoboken, NJ: John Wiley & Sons.

7

Pulling It All Together: Creating Professional-Quality Work

In the last four chapters, you learned the key principles for communicating with your audience. You've learned to write sentences that are actor-centered and paragraphs that are cohesive and coherent. You've seen how to create tables that are easily readable and figures that draw the attention of your audience to the themes on which you want them to focus. As you've applied these principles in your writing, you've gone through several cycles of revision and research.

Now there is just one more set of principles to pick up before you start learning the particulars of each policy-writing genre in Part 3. Let's take the time to zoom out from the content you've been focused on creating to focus on how the document looks and learn how to create a polished, professional document.

Polishing Your Document

Once you judge that your hard work in researching, analyzing, writing, and creating the content of your document is done, then it's time to do one more round of edits to get your document ready to share with your audience. In this final round, you will check all of the boxes to make sure your policy document will look as sharp as your analysis.

Focusing on how a document looks may feel like a strange exercise. Shouldn't your reader care about the content, not the appearance? Don't the facts speak for themselves? Actually, the facts don't speak for themselves. You speak for them. To do this convincingly, you need to apply standard policy formatting principles to your document. At times, these principles might feel like arbitrary conventions, but they are not. The principles you have to follow have developed informally over many years because each of them is useful for readers to navigate your document and understand what is inside of it.[1] Your audience

---

[1] In many organizations, the informal standards of what constitutes a polished document have been formalized into style guides. Style guides make sure that all of the work produced looks the same. When you enter an organization as a new employee, ask to see the style guide. You'll see quickly how it incorporates the principles below and makes decisions about the choices found in each of them. See, for example, Houston Independent School District (2016); Institute of Education Sciences, United States Department of Education (2005); Organisation for Economic Co-operation and Development (2015).

expects you to follow these conventions. When you violate them, two things happen.

First, your audience has to rapidly make a decision about why you violated standard conventions. The first and easiest answer they can arrive at is that you don't know what you're doing. That is a really unfortunate outcome for you. Your audience might not even take the time to read your document, or they might heavily discount what you have to say. If you don't know enough to format your document using the common principles of policy writing, why should they believe you know enough about your content to trust what you have to say?

Second, even if they decide that they trust you, by violating their expectations about the conventions of public policy writing you have made it harder for them to use the document. This has both cognitive and practical aspects to it. Cognitively, people only have so much bandwidth to take in information. The time they spend thinking about how to navigate your document is time they don't spend thinking about the content. That's bad for you and the message you need to convey. Practically, the conventions are there for a reason. If you don't have normal margins or spaces around headings, where will your readers take notes? If you don't include page numbers, how will they take the report to a meeting and point other policy makers to your conclusions?

Both of these outcomes are bad for you and for the people affected by the problem you are discussing. The good news is that there are some fairly straightforward principles you can use to polish your document. Employ the principles below to keep your audience engaged with your document and give them a first step in moving forward toward understanding your document.

Principle 1: Orient Your Audience From the Start

When a reader first encounters your document, they should be able to quickly orient themselves. They'll naturally ask a few initial questions before they dig in. They will want to know *why* they are holding the document, *when* it was written, and *who* wrote it.

Answering *why* for the readers is your first chance to tell them why your topic matters. Therefore, you need to think carefully about the title of your report or the subject line of your memo. Make sure it includes enough detail to accurately describe what is inside. Answering *when* is also crucial because the world may be different in a year or two than it is when you finish your report; providing a date allows readers to read your report in context. The answer to *who* isn't just about your name, but also about the organization for which you work. Providing this information gives your audience context about who you are, what slant you might have on the problem, and a starting point with how to contact you if they have questions.

You can see the difference answering these three questions (*why, when, who*) makes in the following example. A report with this title,

Retaining Teachers

by

Dan Player,

is likely to be received differently than this one:

The Problems and Promise of Matching

High-Performing Teachers and With High-Performing Students

January 2018

Professor Daniel Player

The Frank Batten School of Leadership and Public Policy

The University of Virginia.

The second one answers each of the questions more fully. By answering all of the questions an audience naturally has when they come to a document, the more complete version enables readers to quickly begin building a foundation for understanding what is to follow. For this reason, all of the genres of public policy writing have a place for this information, either in the header in a memo or op-ed, or on the cover page of a longer document, so make sure you include this information.

Principle 2: Create an Effective Executive Summary (When Needed)

Many genres (issue briefs, memos, reports, etc.) have an executive summary, which is a short paragraph or section that summarizes your report for hurried readers, as a standard component.[2] An executive summary is

---

[2] You might have noticed that the executive summary is covered in this chapter and not in Chapter 2, where you created your outlines and set about writing your paragraphs. This is because in order to write an executive summary, you need to write everything else in your document first so you will know what to summarize.

important because it allows hurried policy makers to read a brief overview of your document and understand what it will say. Past the title or subject line, this is the first substantial content they read to decide whether or not to engage with the remainder of your document. If they are in a hurry, then it may be the only part of your document they have time to read before a meeting starts. Either way, it is worth spending time polishing sentences and making every word count.

The executive summary generally ranges from three to five sentences in an issue brief or decision memo.[3] To create one, you need to boil down your paper into its major issues the policy maker should be made aware of (hint: look back at your sentence outline). Sometimes that corresponds with the major sections of your document; sometimes it is most important to focus on the takeaways rather than the background or methods sections. Ask yourself, *If my readers only read one paragraph about my document, what do they absolutely need to know?*[4]

For example, consider the following executive summary from an issue brief.[5] It is written to the school board of a large urban school district:[6]

Elementary school principals in public school systems struggle to retain high-performing teachers because they cannot pay them more than low-performing teachers due to rigid salary scales. Instead, principals reward and retain high-quality teachers by giving them students who are easier to work with: more students with higher math ability, fewer students with learning disabilities, fewer students eligible for subsidized lunch, and more female students. While this may keep high-performing teachers in the school, it also exacerbates educational inequalities by frequently matching low-performing teachers with students who need more resources to succeed.

Notice what this executive summary does well. First, it uses the best principles that we've learned in other places: The actors are clearly identified subjects of the sentences, the verbs are meaningful actions, the words are well chosen, and the executive summary functions as a paragraph that

---

[3] In longer reports (20+ pages), a full-page executive summary is appropriate. Look at comparable documents in your discipline, agency, or field to get a general sense of length in your setting.

[4] Often, you will find that when you synthesize and distill all of your paper into the executive summary you will come away with a new realization about the problem itself or the structure of your paper. When this happens, don't be afraid to engage in another round of edits.

[5] An issue brief is a 1–2 page document that briefs policy makers on an issue without making recommendations (see Chapter 8).

[6] This example is derived from research by my colleague and friend Daniel Player (2010).

is both cohesive and coherent. Second, it focuses the reader on the key aspects of the issue itself. Readers know immediately what the takeaways of the issue brief are. Even if a school board member doesn't read the rest of the issue brief and has no idea about how the researchers found evidence that principals do these activities, they can still know the main points and be ready to engage in conversation about this practice in their school system.

Principle 3: Don't Bury Important Information in the Conclusion

While the executive summary is the part of your document that is the most read, the end of a policy document is usually the least read, precisely because audiences are so busy. Unfortunately, the natural pattern of writing is to put the most important parts at the end. The natural tendency is to explain all of the research, all of the nuance, and then to come to the takeaways at the end.

That is fine for a draft, but in a polished product the important takeaways tend to be at the beginning. After all, you're not writing a novel. You won't shatter the suspense by telling your readers upfront what the punchline is. To reference a popular series of novels, your readers need to know if Harry Potter lives or dies as soon as possible in your memo because they need to begin making plans based on this information! The point is, if there's some revelation in the conclusion, then move it further up in the document and make it more prominent so it has a better chance of getting read.

Principle 4: Create a Global Map Using Headings and Subheadings[7]

Once you have your executive summary in place, then it's time to think about how your audience will navigate the rest of your document. Notice that I said *navigate*, not *read*. Policy audiences are in a hurry, so they only want to read the parts they need to read. Since policy audiences also have a wide variety of knowledge about your topic, they will use the headings to navigate to the parts of your document they find helpful.[8]

For example, someone outside of the education field might read the background of an issue brief on teacher incentives, while someone on the

---

[7] Op-eds are the one type of genre covered in this book that does not use headings.

[8] It might be helpful to think about how you design a résumé or CV. The headings and the white space you create are tools to draw the reader's eye to points and allow them to navigate your résumé quickly to decide if you would be a good fit for the position.

school board might skip straight to the findings or recommendations. In order to serve both well, it is important to create an outline that maps the various sections of your document.

How do you know where to place headings? Some genres have defined sections that always have to appear. For example, issue briefs, decision memos, and reports always have executive summaries, which always have a heading titled simply "Executive Summary." Some genres may require other sections such as a background, methods, or recommendation section.

But aside from standardized sections demanded by a genre, when should you have headings? Think back to when you began outlining your document. You broke the outline into major ideas and then broke major ideas into component ideas. At a first pass, the major ideas from your outline should be section headings and the component ideas should be subsection headings. Once they are in the document, thumb through the pages to see if they look right. How often do you hit a heading? Several on one page is probably too many; two pages between headings is probably too much.[9]

When you finalize your headings in your document, it's important to signal to the reader the difference between the main headings, subheadings, and sub-subheadings. You should do this by varying the font. In this book, the main headings are bolded, the subheadings are italicized, and the sub-subheadings are underlined, while the font size remains the same. In your setting, first look to see if there is a style guide and then look at a couple of other examples to see what the norms are.

Whatever field you are writing in, you will find it is often helpful to have descriptive headings. For example, I could have titled this subsection "*Principle 3*," but it's much more helpful to title it "*Principle 3: Create a Global Map Using Headings and Subheadings.*" That way, you could make an informed choice about whether or not to read this subsection.

Finally, headings serve another major purpose: They are the most basic form of visual design in a document. Headings should always have a line break before them and often have a line break after them. This pattern creates white space around headings that serve several important purposes. First, they draw attention to the headings themselves. Just like your eye is naturally drawn to a baseball player standing alone in the outfield in a sea of open green space, your eye is naturally drawn to the headings as they stand out on the page in open space. Second, the open space makes headers easy to read. They make their point without the clutter of lots of other words to distract from them. Third, the open white space around the headings provides the readers a chance to take notes.

---

[9] I often zoom out in my word-processing program until I can see two pages on the screen at once. With the font that small, the only thing I can read is the heading, and it gives me a good sense of how they are spaced.

Readers will often write down questions that they have in these spaces. This is great for you because the more they write down, the more they are engaging with your material.

For all of the reasons above, correctly including headings and subheadings goes a long way toward the professional look you want your document to have. At a glance, you can tell whether or not a sheet of paper is an academic paper or a policy document. You want yours to look like the latter: sharp, easy to navigate, and helpful for the reader to begin engaging with your ideas.

Principle 5: Use Bulleted Lists and Font Alterations Judiciously

Another effective way to use white space to draw attention to specific points is through bulleted lists. Bulleted lists are commonly used in policy documents because they effectively communicate with audiences by visually representing the structure of a section. Like headings, this enables readers to skim quickly and only read what they need to read. It also creates additional white space on margins where readers can take notes. In short, lists are helpful because they:

- Draw attention to specific points,
- Convey information quickly, and
- Create white space where readers can take notes.

Why It Is Important to Make Your Document Look Sharp

In the policy world, it's not just the substance that matters; it's also the appearance. As folks in the food industry often say, "People eat with their eyes first." Think about when you walk into a bakery and look inside the cases with rows and rows of colorful treats. It's the frosting on the outside of the cake or the shine on top of the tart that makes it look so tempting.

Yes, the substance inside matters. You won't buy another cake from that business unless the first one tastes good, but you're unlikely to buy the first one unless it *looks good*. It's similar for policy documents: The finishing touches make your document look sharp. They are the first signal to your audience that you know what you're doing, that you produce professional-quality work, and that they can begin to trust the substance of what you have produced.

While bulleted lists are a great tool, they should be used only under certain restrictions. First, a bulleted list is ideal for a list that fits on 1–2 pages. Past that, it is better to use regular subheadings. Second, remember that a list denotes a series of items that are like another, but the ordering doesn't matter for the cohesion of the list. For example, think about your grocery list (apples, cheese, chocolate, etc.). It doesn't matter what order you put them on the list. The bulleted list above worked because all three of the points were interchangeable.

On the other hand, a list is a poor choice for making an argument. For example, the list below is really a paragraph, making an argument about why high-performing teachers are more likely to stay in a school than low-performing ones.

High-performing teachers:

- Are less likely to transfer to a new school than low-performing teachers.

- Don't transfer as much as low-performing teachers because principals reward them with better students in their classrooms.

- Are less likely to leave teaching altogether than low-performing teachers.[10]

Here, the list doesn't work because the points are really parts of an argument that is chopped up into a list. The result is a list that's painful to read and doesn't really work. If you find yourself making connections between the points, then use a paragraph to explain your argument instead.

Like bulleted lists, there are other elements that draw your reader's eye to particular parts of your document. Headings, table or figure titles, or the title of the document can all benefit from appropriately increasing the font size, bolding, italicizing, and underlining, as we have seen above. Enlarging the font size of these elements is a helpful tool for drawing your audience's attention.

Within the main text of your document you can judiciously use bolding, italicizing, and/or underlining to draw attention to key terms, facts, or conclusions. Keep in mind that the words or phrases to which you draw attention need to make sense on their own because your reader's eye will be drawn to what you highlight and not to what is around it. These methods are particularly useful in short, half-page documents like issue briefs or decision memos that readers often read on the fly between meetings and on which they don't spend much time. In these settings, these tools are helpful in focusing the reader on a few key facts.

---

[10] From Goldhaber, Gross, and Player (2010).

But like all tools, these are dangerous if used ineptly. You must use them to serve a legitimate purpose. **Bolding (or italics) can be useful for highlighting important ideas that are self-contained**, but not for highlighting random **nouns** or *verbs*. Similarly, it can seem silly to a reader if you underline phrases that don't make sense if you read them on their own. As demonstrated in this paragraph, when you use these tools poorly, you will succeed both in drawing the reader's eye and in confusing them. Not a good combination.

Principle 6: Write in the Appropriate Tone

In all policy writing it is important to make sure that your tone is appropriate for the setting. With the exception of op-eds, which are meant to be provocative, it is important to write in a neutral, even tone. This is especially important in settings that feel informal to you (social media and email) but can be read outside of their context.

This principle is a difficult one to follow, especially when you are impassioned about an issue. One helpful principle is to remember that you'll never persuade anyone who thinks you are insulting them. It's good to be direct in your writing; it's unhelpful to be aggressive. For example, this first paragraph is less likely to get you a hearing than the second one. Both contain the same information, both are direct and to the point, but the second one is more likely to get through to people who aren't already on your side than the other.

Version 1: It is blindingly obvious that principals would be more effective in retaining excellent teachers if they could pay them more salary or award bonuses. Econ 101 students learn that people respond to financial incentives. Unions are to blame because they represent the interests of lousy teachers as well as the good ones and don't want to be held accountable through testing.

Version 2: Economic theory suggests that teachers are more likely to stay at schools if they receive higher pay or bonuses for good performance. Union-negotiated contracts often prevent principals and school systems from offering these financial incentives because they are concerned with fairness between teachers and with the accuracy of the measures.

This example may seem over the top, but remember to be on the lookout for phrases that would be quote-worthy out of context. "Don't want to be held accountable through testing" is a plum quote for the local paper, especially if you're working for the school district or for the union while you are writing this document. One way people reference this principle in policy circles is to ask if your document "passes the *Washington Post* test." What they mean when they ask this is if a reporter read your document would she be able to run a splashy headline by quoting inflammatory language in your text or would she have to focus on the facts and arguments you make? In most settings you want reporters to report the facts and make your arguments. Write appropriately so that they will.

> *Dance like no one is watching, write like it will be on the front page of the* Washington Post. (Charity Pennock, director of the Charlottesville Renewable Energy Alliance)

It is also important to write in a formal tone in a policy document. Do not use contractions. Do not use words like *ick* or *blerg* or whatever slang is cool. You wouldn't walk out of a presentation that went well and *dab* at the end of it. Don't write that way either!

Principle 7: Be Absolutely Error Free (or, Pass the Brown M&M Test)

The last principle might be the most important. This book hasn't focused on problems of grammar and spelling, not because they aren't important in the end but because you first need to focus on thinking, then communicating at the sentence and paragraph level. Now that you're at the final polishing stage, it's time to go back through and make sure that everything is right.

Being absolutely error free is crucially important because in high-stakes settings, decision makers understand that the decisions they are making might cost people their lives. If you can't catch errors in you're writing (or is it "in *your* writing . . ."), then why should they trust you to catch errors in the research or analysis you did to produce the report?

One major American institution knew this principle intuitively: the rock band Van Halen. Joe Fore (2016) tells its story well:

> As Van Halen toured the world in the 1970s and 1980s, the band brought along its contract rider, a thick document that detailed what the promoter was required to provide at the concert venue, including numerous food and drink demands. Buried among the rider's extensive food and drink requests was one very specific candy commandment: "M&M's (WARNING: ABSOLUTELY NO BROWN ONES)." The consequences for violating the clause were severe: one version of the clause warned that if brown M&Ms were found in the backstage area, "the promoter will forfeit the show at full price."

For years, the brown M&Ms ban was panned as an outrageous act of rock-star decadence—pampered musicians making a ludicrous demand just because they could. But, as lead singer David Lee Roth later explained, the chocolate clause served a purpose.

You see, at the time, Van Halen had perhaps the most complex stage show in rock history. And the band took that show into smaller venues that weren't used to hosting such a massive event. Such a complicated show had many technical needs—from having enough electrical outlets to ensuring that the building's structures were sufficiently strong to support the stage and light rigs. Those requirements were spelled out in the contract rider, but promoters often didn't read it carefully, creating disruptions, delays, and even potentially dangerous conditions.

Van Halen's front man devised the brown M&Ms clause as a test—a canary in the backstage coal mine. If the promoter had paid enough attention to remember to remove the brown M&Ms, chances are they had paid attention to the big stuff, too. And if not . . . well, Roth describes the situation: "When I would walk backstage, if I saw a brown M&M in that bowl, well, line check the entire production. Guaranteed you're going to arrive at a technical error. They didn't read the contract. Guaranteed you'd run into a problem. Sometimes it would threaten to destroy the whole show. Sometimes, literally, life threatening."

Policy audiences use grammar and spelling as their brown M&M test. It is crucial to find and fix all the errors. Everyone makes them when they write a draft. Professionals find and fix them. Each *speling* error, each *repeated repeated* word, each error in *you're* document is another death knell in your ability to be taken seriously in the policy world.

Leave time for you to revise your document. Leave time for someone else to read it over. Don't make those mistakes.

Writing Ethically: The Responsibilities of Policy Writing

The final aspect of creating professional-quality policy writing is ethics. The good news is that ethical writing isn't magic. You are capable of doing it. Sometimes it requires work. Sometimes it requires bracing honesty about the limitations of your own work or point of view. But whether or not it is time-consuming or ego-diminishing, ethical writing is foundational to professional policy writing. You need to prioritize the needs of the audience, write directly, be transparent, and be honest.

Principle 8: Be an Excellent, Audience-Centered Writer

The first way to be ethical is to do an excellent job. This might seem a strange way to start a section on ethical writing, but it serves as the foundation for all of the others. The Golden Rule says to treat others as you would have them treat you, and this applies in policy writing. When you create a document, think to yourself at every stage, *What is it that I would want from this document if I were the intended audience?*

One of the simplest and hardest aspects of meeting this high bar is creating enough time to go through a thoughtful revision process and apply the principles you have learned. Time is a key ingredient in creating high-quality work that serves the needs of your audience, both in terms of the *thinking* and the *communicating* that go into creating an audience-centered policy document.

Creating enough time to do revisions is challenging in the best of times because it is difficult to have the personal discipline to work on things that aren't urgent. But practicing that discipline in this is one of the hallmarks of a professional. How do professionals do it? Everyone has their own tips and tricks: backward timelines, a handy app that sends reminders, or software that limits your time on Facebook. One reason this book is done is that I employ all of these methods! If you struggle with discipline and time management, think about employing these or other tricks to make sure you have the time to create excellent documents for your audience.

Creating the time to be an excellent, audience-centered writer is even more challenging in a policy environment, when deadlines are of the essence. The time constraints sometimes mean you will have to push out work that isn't as polished as you would like it to be. (I was once given 2 hours to produce an issue brief for the lieutenant governor before she made a speech. Yikes!)

The good news is that writing gets easier the more you do it. You've already taken a huge first step reading and practicing the principles in this book. And the more you practice, the more second nature it becomes. In extreme circumstances, you will still have to make compromises. But with practice and good teammates you'll develop professional judgment to decide in time-constrained situations when good is good enough.

Principle 9: Don't Obfuscate (or, Write Directly)

Writing ethically in policy settings also means creating documents your audience can understand. The first aspect of this principle is to write directly about the consequences of the policy—all of them, both the good and the bad. For example, if you are writing about the new school funding formula for your city or state that decides how state tax dollars will be given to individual school districts across the state. It's tempting only to give the good news. Some of the schools will get more money to fund new programs and provide services to kids that really need them.

It's harder to talk directly about the schools that will be negatively impacted by the policy. Saying directly that wealthy districts will receive less money and will have to start taxing more won't win you any friends, but it is still important to say.

One particular temptation will be to violate the actor-centered principles from Chapter 3. Putting people at the center of problems is conflictual and challenging (Williams & Colomb, 2012, chap. 10). It's tempting to pull a punch—to obfuscate—by writing, "It was decided that the new formula would be amended to shift resources to poorer schools," instead of, "The Senate amended the bill to move money from the wealthy districts to the poorer districts."

Writing like this is harder than it seems. Real, direct writing in public policy is conflictual, and when you write honestly and directly about a policy you can receive a lot of heat because people would rather shoot the messenger than tackle this issue. For example, in 2017 the Republican-led House and Senate passed a controversial tax reform bill. The Congressional Budget Office (CBO) and the Joint Committee on Taxation (JCT), both nonpartisan policy offices created and funded by Congress, weighed in on the bill as it moved through both houses. Both the CBO and the JCT were heavily criticized by Republicans who did not like their findings. But it was their job to be direct about their professional judgments about the bills. It was the politicians' jobs to decide how to respond to them.

The second aspect of writing directly is to use language that as many people as possible can understand. Subject matter experts don't need you to write directly because they know enough about the topic to work out what you mean, even if you don't say it directly. The general public doesn't have that luxury. And because we live in a representative democracy, the public gets a say in what happens, not just through elections but also by contacting their elected officials, going to meetings, and submitting written comments on regulations. For them to do this well, you need to write clearly so they can understand the complicated reality that may feel like it is threatening their lives or livelihoods. Everyday Janes and Joes—parents with kids in the public schools or farmers facing a proposed pipeline through their field—deserve access to your findings so they can be informed and engage in the process. Ethical writing means writing, as much as you can, to make what you have to say accessible to them.

Principle 10: Give Credit Where Credit Is Due

Ethical writing is also about giving credit where credit is due. Inevitably, every policy document will build on the work of others. As such, it is important to cite the work of others when you use it in your document.

Citing your sources correctly serves two purposes. The first is to give those folks credit for the work they did in helping you—and, by extension, your readers—understand the problem. The second is to help your readers understand where you gathered evidence. Your readers can then understand the scope of what you considered and to go and read the source documents themselves if they are so inclined, either to deepen their knowledge or to double-check your work (says the cranky professor!).

Creating Bibliographies and Citations

In the past, citing references and assembling a bibliography was a fiddly nightmare. At the end of writing your document you had to go back through, find every reference you cited, create individual entries, and ensure they were formatted correctly. Every time you did a revision, you had to double-check the bibliography to make sure you hadn't added or eliminated one of them. Yuck.

Thankfully, technology has made this task a lot easier, and *citation management programs* now take care of most of this for you. My personal favorite, Zotero, allows me to insert citations as I type and automatically adds them to the bibliography.[11] When I take out a citation, Zotero removes it. Magic.

Like all of the competitors, Zotero automatically formats your citations to whichever style you are using. In policy writing, the American Psychological Association (APA) style is standard, so I use APA as the default and change it when I need to at the click of a button. I haven't looked up how to format a citation in years. I don't miss it.

---

[11] For most resources, Zotero also records citation information off of web pages with the click of a button, so I rarely type in the information to create citations. Instead, I just double-check to make sure the information has been captured correctly. Again, magic.

Principle 11: Don't Lie

The final principle of writing ethically is to be truthful. In some ways this may seem obvious, but every year there are stories in the media about people who fabricate data and every semester there are university students who are convicted of honor violations for plagiarizing. In my experience, people get into these situations for a couple of reasons.

In the university setting, the most common reason for plagiarism is poor time management. Other commitments keep students from getting an early start, then they get stuck when they start working just a day (or a few hours) before an assignment is due. Students know that plagiarism is cheating, but they rationalize it given their circumstances: "I know enough about this topic, I'm just too pressed for time to write it up properly"; or "I'll copy this text because my professor's assignment wasn't reasonable given the time he gave us."

In professional settings, people invent data when they become more invested in winning for their cause than in finding out the truth. They think something like, "I know this program is helping kids; the data just aren't fine-grained enough to show it yet"—and then they change the data to keep the program going.

It can also be the case that a boss pressures you to be dishonest (or less than honest) for similar reasons. People in these situations face extremely difficult choices about standing up to powerful people, leaving organizations that support causes about which they care deeply, or betraying those organizations by airing their dirty laundry to others without permission.[12]

In both academic and professional situations, honesty is difficult, but still crucially important. The first reason is that writing truthfully is important. It's important for the sake of the people you are serving. When you plagiarize, you haven't demonstrated that you can actually do the work, and that is bad news when it comes to actually doing it in the professional world. In the professional domain, readers deserve to know the truth about the world, even if it is unpleasant for them, or for you. To go back to the Golden Rule, you want decision makers in other policy arenas to make decisions based on accurate information. The same should apply for your domain, even if it cuts against you.

The other reason to be truthful is more self-interested. Being truthful, especially when it's hard, is the lifeblood of a professional. Once it's gone, you'll find nobody will take your calls or read your work (presuming you were able to keep your job). That's one of the reasons why, in reality, lobbyists almost never lie, despite their reputation in the popular media. They will argue one side of the story, but they do it honestly because they know

---

[12] All of these options are hard, and they involve difficult trade-offs that are worth considering at length. See Weimer and Vining (2017, chap. 3: Towards Professional Ethics) for a thoughtful debate about them.

that their effectiveness depends on decision makers seeing them as honest brokers of information. Decision makers need to be able to look at a document and trust that what is inside is truthful. Once you've planted the seed of doubt about your trustworthiness in their heads, the game is up. Be honest, be aboveboard. It's the right thing, and it's the right thing for you.

Conclusion

In sum, writing ethically and making your document shine are the last two aspects of creating policy documents that will serve your readers well. I've put a few checklists in the following pages that you are welcome to follow as you get started doing this. There is a learning curve to all of this, but it's one that many people have mastered, and you can as well. Once you've done these a few times, you'll likely find them unnecessary and you'll have yet another tool in your tool belt as a policy professional.

CHECKLIST

Making It Shine Checklist

1. Did you tell the reader who you are, when you wrote this, and what it is about in the proper place?

2. Do your headings, subheadings, and sub-subheadings make sense? Are they spaced properly?

3. Did you format them consistently (font size, bolding, italics, spacing, etc.)?

4. Is your executive summary a synopsis of the most important parts of your report, and is it the right length?

5. Did you bury anything in the conclusion that needs to be moved up?

6. Did you use bulleted lists when they might be helpful?

7. Is the tone professional?

8. Is it error free?

9. Does it look sharp?

   - Did you use standard margins?
   - Did you use a standard font and make the main text at least 12-point font?
   - Are all of the figures and tables formatted in your font?

10. Were you truthful, even when it didn't feel good?

11. Did you include a bibliography with accurate and thorough references using a standard style?

EXERCISES

Citation Management Exercise

Take the time to investigate a citation management program like Zotero or one of its 30+ competitors. Select one, read the instructions, or watch the web tutorials, and then try using it. If you need help, many universities have a paid subscription to RefWorks or EndNote, and the reference librarians can help you learn how to use it.

BIBLIOGRAPHY

Fore, J. (2016). Encourage students to eliminate the brown M&Ms from their legal writing. *Perspectives: Teaching Legal Research and Writing, 25*(1), 18–22.

Goldhaber, D., Gross, B., & Player, D. (2010). Teacher career paths, teacher quality, and persistence in the classroom: Are public schools keeping their best? *Journal of Policy Analysis and Management, 30*(1), 57–87.

Houston Independent School District. (2016). *HISD style guide.* Retrieved December 27, 2017, from http://www.houstonisd.org/site/handlers/filedownload .ashx?moduleinstanceid=91080&dataid=43950&FileName=HISD_Style_Guide-06142017.pdf

Huff, D. (2010). *How to lie with statistics.* New York: W. W. Norton & Company.

Institute of Education Sciences, United States Department of Education. (2005). *IES style guide.* Washington, DC. Retrieved December 27, 2017, from https://nces .ed.gov/statprog/styleguide/pdf/styleguide.pdf

Organisation for Economic Co-operation and Development (OECD). (2015). *OECD style guide.* (3rd ed.). Retrieved December 27, 2017, from https://www .oecd.org/about/publishing/OECD-Style-Guide-Third-Edition.pdf

Player, D. (2010). Nonmonetary compensation in the public teacher labor market. *Education Finance and Policy, 5*(1), 82–103.

Weimer, D. L., & Vining, A. R. (2017). *Policy analysis: Concepts and practice* (6th ed.). New York: Routledge.

Williams, J. M., & Colomb, G. (2012). *Style: The basics of clarity and grace.* Boston: Longman.

PART

Policy Genres and Their Purposes

The Issue Brief

Issue briefs are a common policy-writing genre, particularly in the advocacy field. For our purposes, we will define an issue brief as a 1–2 page document used to quickly inform policy makers about the basics of an issue or a program.[1] Ideally, they provide basic information on an issue in a nonpartisan fashion so that policy makers can quickly come up to speed on issues about which they know little. You may also hear the term *issue brief* applied to longer documents (4–6 pages), but anything longer probably shouldn't be described as "brief."

Issue briefs are used by advocates at every level of government who are trying to raise the profile of an issue to policy makers. In legislative bodies throughout the country, advocates for causes as diverse as children's rights, chemical manufacturing, and government agencies tour legislative offices with these two-sided, sharply designed briefs in hand. Each advocate is hoping that their brief will help educate legislators and aides about the importance of their issue.[2] After all, if legislators don't know why they should care about the issue and the basic facts about it, how can they begin to make policy about it?

Problematically for advocates, perhaps no other setting in policy making is as busy as a legislative session. To educate in this context, even some of the standard rules previously covered in this book are up for grabs: Figures and tables can be included without being described in the text, bibliographies can be consigned to a URL, photographs and quotes can be included as evidence. Scandalous? Perhaps in other genres. But in issue briefs, if it is honest and effective, then it is fair game.

---

[1] You may also hear the term *policy brief* used interchangeably with *issue brief*. There is no firm rule that distinguishes between the two. In contrast to an objectively focused issue brief, policy briefs often take a stand and advocate for it (Martin, 2014). Sometimes *policy brief* is used as an umbrella term for both advocacy and objective briefs (Food and Agriculture Organization of the United Nations, 2011). In this chapter, we will stick with *objective policy briefs*, but you can use almost all of the same rules and the formatting tools to write an advocacy brief when the need arises.

[2] As well as being hand-delivered by the advocates themselves, issue briefs are typically posted on organizations' websites, distributed to members, and mailed to relevant decision makers.

Distinctive Aspects of Issue Briefs

The audience for an issue brief is distinctive because they are insanely busy at any given moment and they are being given a document they did not request. Instead, the issue brief is a part of a sales pitch about the issue. Given these constraints, the metric by which your issue brief should be judged is whether or not a reader with no basic knowledge of the issue is able to look at the brief and understand its purpose and the basic facts of the issue in 30 seconds (Ruderman, 2012). That's the first test: to guarantee that the audience can take in the basics and then decide if they want to learn more. Let's look at some of the aspects of how issue briefs accomplish this task given their constraints.

Narrowly Focused on Communicating One Important Message

The short time your audience will spend with your issue brief means it should be fairly narrowly focused. An issue brief should focus squarely on one particular problem or program. Once you have decided what you want your reader to understand, then you can begin deciding what to include and at what level of detail.

Remember that there is a direct trade-off between focus on the particulars and establishing the context. Rather than making a sweeping overview of child poverty—its history, its causes, its variation across time and place—focus on the program the audience needs to know about in order to make a dent in the problem.

Very Brief

Issue briefs are often distributed at the start of a meeting with a legislator and entered into a large pile of papers on a decision maker's desk to be picked up later, so length matters. The shorter it is, the more likely it is to be read. Issue briefs in this context are almost always 1–2 pages long.[3]

Once you have selected an issue, then you must create a document that enables policy makers to go from knowing very little about the topic to understanding the relevant background, current trends, etc., in 1–2 pages. This is

---

[3] In some contexts, you will see the term *issue brief* used to describe a report that is 6–8 pages long. These briefs are usually produced by think tanks and written for someone who is already interested in the issue and wants more detail than a 1–2 page paper. The briefs look more like minireports than the issue briefs discussed in this chapter. They may still use some of the tools of a 1–2 page issue brief but are usually more formal. But even in this setting, an issue brief is short—no longer than 8 pages—as anything longer should really be referred to as a report, not a brief.

challenging, but it can also be a helpful exercise for you as a writer. Since you can't include everything you know about the problem, you have to be audience centered and write about what *they* need to know about the problem.

No Specific Audience

The advocates working the halls of a legislature use the same brief for Republicans and Democrats, rookie legislators and long-serving committee chairs. As such, issue briefs are rarely addressed to a particular person. Instead, they are designed to educate a general audience about the topic. To bring a wide variety of people up to speed on the issue, they need to be written using general language and broadly stated enough to educate newcomers to the topic while providing facts that will interest old hands.

Focus on Communicating the Facts

In contrast to many other policy-writing genres, in an issue brief you do not need to explain every statistic you include and how you arrived at it. Issue briefs should focus on a central message and use facts that support that message. You should understand all of the context, methods, and nuances of the data in case you are lucky enough to have your audience ask about them, but you should not put these elements in your issue brief. Write simply and directly about the facts. Those are enough here.

Heavy Use of Visual Aids

Issue briefs are the most visually engaging of all of the policy genres. Your reader will likely spend very little time with your document, so you should use all of the visual aids at your disposal to effectively grab their attention. You should think about using figures, tables, and bulleted lists, which communicate large amounts of information quickly. And, in an unusual twist, you do not need to write about the figures and tables in your main text. In an issue brief, they can stand alone, so make sure to employ the best practices from Chapters 5 and 6 to make sure they can do so successfully.

In addition to figures, you have other tools at your disposal to grab the attention of your audience. You can include callout boxes (see examples below) to highlight important points. You can include pictures or maps that help your audience connect with the issue. Whatever visual aids you use, you should always take a step back to make sure the overall visual design draws them immediately to the key points.[4]

---

[4] If you have the resources, a graphic designer can help you think about how the layout of the issue brief focuses a reader's eye and how to take advantage of the natural way we look at pieces of paper.

One simple way to enhance the design of your issue brief is to use the rule of thirds. If you have taken photography classes you know how to use the rule of thirds to compose a photograph that is visually pleasing (if not, search the web for an example or two). The same rules apply here. Envision dividing the page into nine boxes by drawing a tick-tack-toe board across your issue brief. Arrange callout boxes, tables, figures, and headers so they fit neatly within one or more of these boxes and your issue brief will look sharper.

Neutral Tone

Finally, issue briefs should be written in a neutral tone. This is because at their heart, issue briefs are about conveying a set of facts, and the facts are nonpartisan (despite recent reports to the contrary!). For example, industry groups and environmental groups should basically agree with the facts contained within each other's issue briefs. Their issue briefs may have a different focus or a different take on the issue, but even if they vehemently disagree on how the issues themselves should be addressed, the facts should be the same.

Example Issue Briefs

Generally speaking, issue briefs include an overview of the issue, identify and discuss prominent stakeholders, and discuss current policy and commonly suggested solutions to the problem. The exact format of any issue brief depends on the issue itself and what must be conveyed in order to meet the objectives.

As a result, no two issue briefs are alike, and it is difficult to know whether or not a brief will be successful without knowing the context in which it is written. This lack of a firm format can feel paralyzing or freeing, depending on your temperament. But before you make a decision about which camp you fall in, let's take a look at a couple of examples so you can get a sense of the genre.

Issue Brief Example 1: Voluntary Home Visiting in California (an Excellent Example)

The first issue brief comes from Children Now, an interest group in California that is "pro-kid" (Rothermel, n.d.). It lobbies the California legislature on a wide variety of pro-kid issues ranging from foster care to early childhood education to children's health. The following brief, "Voluntary

Home Visiting in California," was a part of its campaign in 20XX to educate legislators on the value of home visits so that legislators would consider expanding funding for the programs.

Take a minute or two to look over the example and my annotations on the side.

Now that you're back, were you able to understand the main point in less than 30 seconds? Were you able to understand the issue cleanly and clearly after a single read through?

Let's talk a bit about what this issue brief does to enable it to succeed as well as it does. The first thing you probably noticed is how sharp it looks. It's visually inviting to your eye and you intuitively are drawn to it. How did the author accomplish this?

First, notice that both pages clearly employ the rule of thirds. The header on the first page occupies the top third and the callout box fits neatly in the right-hand third. On the second page, the table takes up the top two-thirds and the recommendations take up the final third.

Second, notice how the author altered the font to draw your attention to different elements. The large numbers in the callout box draw your attention to the magnitude of the problem. The limited bolding (just two phrases) cues you into the key terms that are helpful in understanding the issue.

Finally, notice how focused the issue brief is. The text in the header and the first body paragraph work together to provide a clear and clean introduction to home visiting and why it is important. The remainder of the content fills in the details. So while this issue brief looks flashy, with lots of visual bells and whistles, the solid, focused content is also crucial to making it effective. The author did a lot of clear-headed thinking as she considered and executed the design elements.

Now think a bit about what didn't work for you. What could be done better? For starters, there is no date on this issue brief, so it's hard to know if it was written in 2008 or 2018. Second, there are a couple of small omissions that would have improved it. The table on page 2 would have benefited from a title, as well as from a URL that could have provided the sources.

In addition to the design choices, there are lots of editorial choices about the content in this issue brief. The author featured a white or Hispanic baby in the photo instead of an Asian or black baby. Most of the language is about helping families, but while moms are mentioned on several occasions, dads never are. These choices aren't wrong, per se; in fact, they probably helped make the issue brief more effective. But it is still worth noting that they are choices. Hopefully, the author actively considered them and their trade-offs while designing this issue brief.

Figure 8.1 A Strong Start for Families: Voluntary Home Visiting in California

Title immediately tells you what you are about to read about.

Picture provides visual space and the cute kid is memorable!

Clearly explains the problem.

Clearly explains how the program addresses the problem.

Bulleted list is bracketed by two bolded terms that emphasize key aspects of the program.

Call out box is eye catching and the larger font size of the number draws your eye to important facts.

Provides a URL for references instead of spending space on a bibliography.

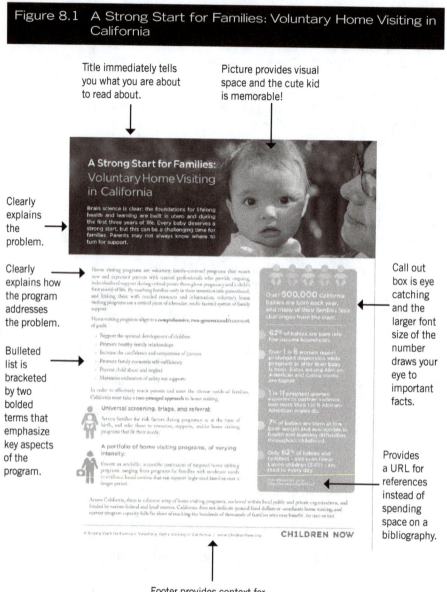

Footer provides context for the reader by identifying the organization.

Source: Children Now, https://www.childrennow.org/.

Table would benefit from a title to tell you what to expect when you read it.

Home Visiting Program	Total Counties	Families Served	Funding Sources
EARLY HEAD START — Early Head Start (EHS) provides early child development and family support services to low-income pregnant women and families with children from birth through age three.	45	8,877	Federal-to-Local Administration for Children & Families grants; First 5 Commissions; various matching funds*.
healthy families america — Healthy Families America (HFA) works to reduce child maltreatment through prenatal care, improving parent-child interactions, and promoting children's school readiness.	14	2,516	California Home Visiting Program (MIECHV); First 5 Commissions; various matching funds*.
Nurse-Family Partnership — Nurse-Family Partnership (NFP) serves first-time, low-income mothers with one-on-one home visits by a trained public health registered nurse.	21	5,206	California Home Visiting Program (MIECHV); First 5 Commissions; various matching funds*.
Parents as Teachers — Parents as Teachers (PAT) provides parents with child development knowledge and parenting support.	6	2,812	First 5 Commissions; various matching funds*.
HIPPY Program — Home Instruction for Parents of Preschool Youngsters (HIPPY) promotes preschoolers' school readiness and supports parents as their children's first teacher.	2	332	First 5 Commissions; various matching funds*.
Other evidence-based program models, meeting MIECHV evidence-based criteria but not listed above.	8	1,112	First 5 Commissions; various matching funds*.
Unique locally designed program models, specifically tailored to meet community needs.	29	20,526	First 5 Commissions; various matching funds*

From internal locally specific public and private sources.

2017 Recommendations

- **Sustain and Strengthen Funding:** Current funding is fragile and fragmented. Significant investments occur through First 5 Commissions, whose revenue is increasingly unstable due to declining tobacco sales.
  - Before September 2017, preserve federal Maternal, Infant, & Early Childhood Home Visiting (MIECHV) funding which supports 26 communities via the California Home Visiting Program.
  - Identify and facilitate opportunities to leverage additional federal dollars for home visiting programs.
- **Strategically Scale Home Visiting for Key Populations:** Home visiting gives the greatest boost to families facing the most challenges, and can drive savings across health care, child welfare, education, and social service systems.
  - Pilot projects to support specific populations within Medi-Cal and CalWORKs with home visiting.
- **Align Data & Referral Systems:** Home visiting programs have potential to be valuable data and referral hubs.
  - Enable seamless referrals between home visiting and Medicaid, WIC, CalWORKs, and other state programs.
  - Collect consistent data across home visiting programs on referrals to safety net programs, oral health, health care, and more.

For more information, contact:
Angela Rothermel
Senior Associate Early Childhood Policy
arothermel@childrennow.org

Table clearly gives an overview of relevant programs and their reach.

Unusual choice in an issue brief but it works here because the author clearly switches from providing facts above to offering opinions below.

Footer identifies who to contact if readers want to learn more.

Source: Children Now, https://www.childrennow.org/.

Issue Brief Example 2: Connecting CalWorks With Home Visiting (an Issue Brief That Could Be Improved)

Now let's look at another issue brief, again on the topic of home visiting in California (Maternal, Child and Adolescent Health Division, 2017). Take a minute or two to look it over and then flip back to this page.

Now that you're back, were you able to understand the main point in less than 30 seconds? Were you able to understand the issue cleanly and clearly after a single read through?

If you're like me, you found this issue brief much harder to understand, even though you actually knew more about home visiting when you started to read this issue brief than you did the first one. Why? This issue brief has many of the same components as the previous brief, and even some that the previous one didn't (a date, for example). The headings draw your attention well and the bolding is appropriate. What happened?

There are some easy and obvious ways to criticize this issue brief. The header is overly crowded and confusing (what is "Maternal, Child and Adolescent Health"?). There is lots of wasted space on the first page. The font choice makes it hard to read.[5] When you flip to page 2, you don't know where you should look first, and there's a spot that naturally draws your eye.

But really, all of these are minor details compared to the main problem: The *thinking* fell down here. The author lays out a clear purpose for the issue brief in the title, "Connecting CalWORKs with Home Visiting," and then fails to do just that. Instead, the issue brief provides a lot of facts, all of which are presumably correct. But the issue brief doesn't do a consistent job of making the case for how CalWORKs and home visiting are connected. It needs to provide a story that connects those facts to the overall purpose. Without the story, the brief comes across as a list of loosely connected facts. That is why this issue brief is so much harder to understand.

The lesson? Writing is both *communicating* and *thinking*, even in an issue brief. Make sure you don't forget the thinking!

Example 3: Economic Well-Being of Rhode Island Families: The Promise and Practice of Two-Generation Approaches (a Longer, Plainer Issue Brief That Is Well Written)

The previous two examples might feel overwhelming because of the extensive graphic design elements involved, but you can create an excellent

---

[5] There are two kinds of fonts: serif and sans serif. Serif fonts, like this one, have small strokes at the ends of the letters. Sans serif fonts, like the one in this sentence, do not. The small strokes in serif fonts make them easier to read, and I suggest using one in your documents.

issue brief simply by using the graphic design elements available in basic word-processing programs. To illustrate, let's look at a final example also focusing on family policy (Cooley, 2015).

This longer brief is longer than the previous two because it was written in a different context. It was distributed at a legislative advocacy event that the author's organization sponsored. Legislators, legislative aides, and agency personnel had requested a briefing on this topic. Their sustained interest allowed the author to write a longer issue brief and succeed without the flash of the other examples.

Figure 8.2 Connecting CalWORKS With Home Visiting

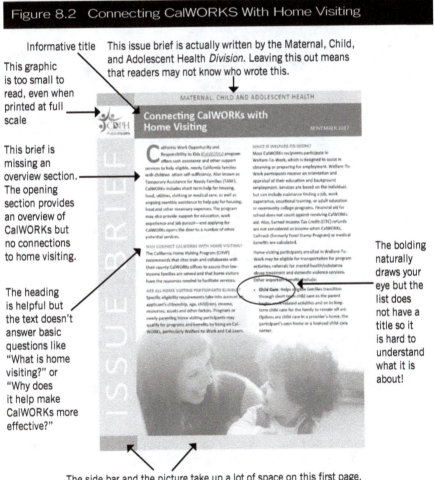

Informative title This issue brief is actually written by the Maternal, Child, and Adolescent Health *Division*. Leaving this out means that readers may not know who wrote this.

This graphic is too small to read, even when printed at full scale

This brief is missing an overview section. The opening section provides an overview of CalWORKs but no connections to home visiting.

The heading is helpful but the text doesn't answer basic questions like "What is home visiting?" or "Why does it help make CalWORKs more effective?"

The bolding naturally draws your eye but the list does not have a title so it is hard to understand what it is about!

The side bar and the picture take up a lot of space on this first page. It might have been more effective to make the rest of the page less dense, either in the header section or in the main text itself.

Source: California Department of Public Health, https://www.cdph.ca.gov/Programs/CFH/DMCAH/Pages/default.aspx.

(Continued)

Figure 8.2   (Continued)

This box works. The helpful title is bolded and in larger font to make sure you read it first. The title is informative and sets you up to learn what is inside.

A title for this box would help clarify what purpose it serves, both to the writer and to the audience. As it stands, it is confusing. Why are these four sections in one box? Two of them are about eligibility, one about guidance and one about how to follow up.

Once you have read the boxes, you naturally start reading here. Unfortunately, you have forgotten what the list is about because it spans the front and the back.

Footer identifies provides context for the organization and how to get more information about the programs. It would have been helpful to state what MCAH stands for.

Source: California Department of Public Health, https://www.cdph.ca.gov/Programs/CFH/DMCAH/Pages/default.aspx.

Now take a minute or two to look over the third example and then flip back to this page.

Now that you're back, were you able to understand the main point in less than 30 seconds? Were you able to understand the issue cleanly and clearly after a single read through?

After reading the last one, this one should feel much easier to comprehend even though it is longer. How did the author accomplish this? She doesn't do much that is fancy: just one figure and two callout boxes. The two pages employ lists and bolding effectively but nothing out of the ordinary.

So why is this brief successful? The author uses straightforward headings that allow you to easily skim the document and know what is inside it. The headings are clear and naturally follow from the previous one ("What are two-generation approaches?" → "Why use two-generation approaches?" → "Do two-generation approaches work?").

Nothing fancy, straightforward, solid *thinking*, well written, and therefore very effective.

RHODE ISLAND FAMILY IMPACT SEMINARS

April 2015   Issue Brief No. 1501

Economic Well-Being of Rhode Island Families:
The Promise and Practice of Two-Generation Approaches

Executive Summary

Children who grow up in low-income families are likely to suffer adverse long-term consequences and continue the cycle of poverty as adults. Some interventions to promote economic well-being, focused on either the child or the parent, have shown only modest effects in disrupting the pattern. Workplace development programs sometimes ignore parental constraints in participation and some early childhood education (ECE) programs do not consider the family conditions to which a child returns. Two-generation policy approaches promote family economic well-being by explicitly combining intensive, high-quality program components targeted to both adults and their children. Emerging evidence from program evaluations supports the continued consideration of two-generation policy alternatives.

Economic Well-being of Rhode Island Families

Families are responsible for several tasks essential to a well-functioning society. Families routinely provide both childcare and economic support, but sometimes they need additional assistance. Rhode Island's Temporary Caregiver Insurance program, only the third paid family leave program in the country, is a step in the right direction to support working parents and protect jobs in times of medical crisis or at childbirth. Some family economic struggles, however, represent a persistent challenge over time. According to 2013 estimates compiled by RI Kids Count, 22% of children are growing up in households with incomes at or below the federal poverty line. The unemployment rate for parents actively seeking jobs was 9% in that year. Even households with employed parents struggle for economic self-sufficiency. Among families with at least one parent working for at least a full year, 18% were still considered low-income. 34% of families with children did not have regular, full-time employment.

Child Development in Economically Disadvantaged Families

Research has repeatedly shown that children who grow up in economically disadvantaged homes are more likely to suffer adverse developmental effects than other children. Educational effects include low school readiness, low academic proficiency, and increased risk of not completing high school. Adverse health effects of child poverty include higher rates of asthma, diabetes, acute illnesses, hearing and vision issues, and speech problems. Furthermore, children growing up in poor families are much more likely to face economic disadvantages as adults, thus continuing an intergenerational cycle of poverty. The effects may be particularly acute if poverty occurs during the earliest years of childhood. Policy interventions that directly target children's developmental needs and promote parental employment simultaneously hold promise for disrupting negative consequences.

BROWN
Sponsored by the Brown University Taubman Center for Public Policy

Source: Dr. Valerie Cooley and Dr. Kenneth Wong, Co-Directors of the Rhode Island Family Impact Seminars.

(Continued)

(Continued)

The Promise of Two-Generation Anti-poverty Strategies:
Existing and Emerging Evidence
By Dr. Christopher T. King

What Are Two-Generation Approaches?

Two-generation programs seek to improve family economic well-being by explicitly combining interventions targeted at both adults and their children. In contrast, anti-poverty strategies have typically focused on adults or children. For decades, programs have helped adults through education and training or supported children through early interventions. In two-generation approaches, these essential elements of ECE for children and education and workforce development programs for adults are complemented and reinforced by additional components including support services, asset-building, health promotion, and the development of social capital networks through coaching and peer support. A particular two-generation strategy may emphasize a child or adult focus, as illustrated by the Continuum shown below, but the two-generation approach always considers the well-being of the whole family.

Why Use Two-Generation Approaches?

Poverty may affect child development through multiple mechanisms. The chronic stress associated with persistent economic disadvantage may interfere with brain development, affect cognitive functioning and emotional regulation, and increase the likelihood of physical and/or

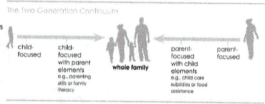

mental health issues. Limited resources and opportunities associated with low incomes, few assets, and limited parental education may also affect child outcomes. Parental employment can positively impact children through provision of role models and higher income for children, but it also decreases parenting time and increases stress, especially for parents with unstable, low-wage jobs without benefits. The variety of poverty-related factors that influence child development suggests the need for a multi-faceted, coordinated strategy focused on the whole family to disrupt pathways leading to negative outcomes.

Programs focusing primarily on either children or adults have not shown strong effects on economic well-being of families. Evaluations of ECE programs have shown mixed results, including the initial two-generation models that added low-intensity parenting components. Recent ECE evaluations highlight the challenges of replicating the positive effects found in a few early studies. Children return home from such programs to families that are likely struggling with limited income, education, and skills. Traditional workforce development programs focused on adults have produced only modest effects on parental income and employment. Intensive, sector-specific career pathway programs have yielded larger and more lasting returns on investment. Parental constraints, however, make it challenging for some low-income individuals to participate. Two-generation approaches to promote family economic well-being adopt a holistic perspective and rely on coordinated services.

Do Two-Generation Programs Work? Emerging Evidence from CareerAdvance® and Other Initiatives

Two-generation approaches have been implemented in several sites and the early results are promising. One example, CareerAdvance,® is a work-readiness and training program piloted in Tulsa, OK that helps low-income parents with young children pursue economic self-sufficiency.

Source: Dr. Valerie Cooley and Dr. Kenneth Wong, Co-Directors of the Rhode Island Family Impact Seminars.

The program equips parents through programs designed to increase employability, earning potential, and parenting skills while also promoting school readiness and socio-emotional development among children. CareerAdvance® utilizes a sector-specific career pathway of sequential trainings leading to specific "stackable" credentials needed within the healthcare sector. Key components include coaching, cohort-based training, peer support networks, and performance incentives. The program is paired with high-quality early education to specifically utilize a two generation approach. Recent results show that 95% of the initial 102 participants in the CareerAdvance® nursing pathway completed the core course, 93% passed the certification exam for nursing

> *"We constantly have the support, not only from our classmates but also from our teachers and our coach...When I was in college before it was just me against the world, basically you know. So if I dropped out, nobody cared."*
> CareerAdvance® participant

assistants, and 71% obtained employment Participants indicated that key factors in achieving success were the support of peer networks, coaching about work-family balance issues, and the acquisition of particular skills including time management and communication skills.

The Jeremiah Program and Keys to Degrees represent alternative models of two-generation programs for promoting family economic self-sufficiency. The Jeremiah Program in St. Paul and Minneapolis, MN targets single mothers and provides life skills training, individualized coaching, employment readiness and job placement services to promote economic self-sufficiency. Recognizing the challenges of single parenthood, the program also provides safe, affordable housing on a campus with other participants and on-site early childhood education. A recent study by the Wilder Foundation showed a $4 return on investment (ROI) to society for every dollar spent on a Jeremiah family.

Keys to Degrees, a program started at Endicott College in Beverly, MA, provides family-friendly housing on college campuses to single custodial parents enrolled full-time as students. Students receive group and individualized support from mentors and peers to

> *"I like how they made the program fit around the youngest child's schedule... so only during clinical times do you have to worry about before and after care. But for the most part, we cal still take the kids, kiss them good-bye, do our thing, and then be there to pick them up."*
> CareerAdvance® participant

pursue a 4-year college degree. The program also offers access to ECE and after-school programming. A recent evaluation of program sites, funded by the Kellogg Foundation and conducted by Program Evaluation and Research Group, found that Keys to Degrees participants rely less on the program over time and are making strides toward degree completion and economic self-sufficiency. Financial sustainability of the program is a concern, though, largely because campus housing is subsidized.

Key Principles in Two-Generation Policy Approaches

Two-generation approaches are also relevant to policy-level reforms and systems interventions. Developing effective and efficient policies relies on careful consideration of the particular context of economic disadvantage that families face. Two-generation approaches can assist families in fulfilling important social functions of childcare, child development, and economic support by incorporating a few key principles:

1) Effective coordination is important to address fragmentation in services for low-income families.
2) Expanding social capital networks through career coaches and cohort models is an essential component.
3) A whole family perspective can be incorporated into initial designs for new programs.

Source: Dr. Valerie Cooley and Dr. Kenneth Wong, Co-Directors of the Rhode Island Family Impact Seminars.

(Continued)

(Continued)

Policy Implications

1) Effective coordination and collaboration is important to address fragmentation in existing services for low-income families. For example, institutions of higher education and human service agencies need to work together more effectively to provide support and flexibility to low-income parents on campuses. At present, 23% of students in higher education are parents, and the figure for community and technical colleges is about twice that figure. Other opportunities exist to coordinate within and across home-visiting, Temporary Assistance to Needy Families (TANF), and healthcare expansion programs.

2) Expanding social capital networks through career coaches, cohort models, and peer supports is an essential component of effective programs. These interventions help parents address the challenge of balancing childcare and employment responsibilities. Low-income parents are resilient and have a strong motivation to improve the lives of their children, but some education and training requirements create conflicts with parenting tasks.

3) A whole family perspective can be incorporated into program designs and proposals related to opportunities for federal funding. Two-generation strategies for promoting family economic well-being can be pursued through the Workforce Innovation and Opportunity Act of 2014, ongoing Food Stamp E&T Demonstrations, and upcoming reauthorizations of TANF, Head Start, and the Elementary and Secondary Education Act. A window of opportunity exists, but the responsibility for high-quality design and implementation of programs for family economic well-being rests squarely on states and municipalities.

(This summary is adapted from several sources including Career Advance® and Capital IDEA evaluation reports prepared by Dr. King and his colleagues at the Ray Marshall Center for the Study of Human Services at the University of Texas at Austin's LBJ School of Public Affairs and Northwestern University. Dr. King was a 2012 Fellow with Ascend at the Aspen Institute. His forthcoming two-generation anthology, co-edited with Aspen Fellows, Dr. P. Lindsey Chase-Lansdale and Dr. Mario Small, is being released by the Aspen Institute on April 7, 2015.)

About the Family Impact Seminars

The Rhode Island Family Impact Seminar is affiliated with a national network of university-based sites in over 25 states called The Policy Institute for Family Impact Seminars (http://familyimpactseminars.org). In 2014, Brown University was accepted to represent Rhode Island. The Institute provides training and technical assistance to state affiliates. We receive guidance from a legislative advisory council including Senator Louis DiPalma, Senator Gayle Golden, Representative Deborah Ruggiero, Representative Marvin Abney, and Representative Antonio Giarrusso. Legislative staff including Marie Ganim, Lynne Urbani, and Kayleigh Pratt have provided insight and help. Joseph Codega coordinated the 2015 Seminar.

The Rhode Island Family Impact Seminar shares two primary goals espoused by the Policy Institute. One is to strengthen policymaking by providing timely, objective, high-quality research on current issues for state legislators and legislative staff through seminars, discussion sessions, and issue briefs. The Seminar also promotes the adoption of a family impact lens to consider the effects of policy on family functioning and the fulfillment of key social responsibilities including childcare and economic support.

 BROWN This issue brief was prepared by Dr. Valerie Cooley with Dr. Kenneth Wong, Co-Directors of the Rhode Island Family Impact Seminars. Contact valerie_cooley@brown for further information. The RI Family Impact Seminars are sponsored by the Brown University Taubman Center for Public Policy.

Source: Dr. Valerie Cooley and Dr. Kenneth Wong, Co-Directors of the Rhode Island Family Impact Seminars.

Conclusion

The three examples above will have given you a flavor of the issue brief genre. You've seen a stylish and effective issue brief, a stylish and ineffective issue brief, and a plain and effective issue brief. Each one comes from its own context and was used for a specific purpose. Now that you have seen a few examples and know the basic principles of issue briefs, it might be helpful for you to search for other example issue briefs in your area. After looking at a few of them, you'll have a sense for what works and what doesn't work in your topic area.

As you begin to write your own issue brief, make sure to keep the *thinking* front and center by employing your audience-centered writing principles. Always be thinking, *Why is it that I am writing this? What does my audience need to know? How can I best use this particular format and its particular rules to communicate with them?*

Once you have the thinking down, enjoy communicating in this unique policy genre. It's not often that public policy writers get to create something that is so visually centered. It's not quite as artistic as being a photographer, but it can be fun to design something that is both beautiful and effective.

CHECKLIST

Content and Analysis

- Demonstrates thorough understanding of the topic and its implications.
- Includes background, legislative issues, public concerns, and other aspects of the topic.
- Correctly identifies every important issue.
- Virtually all included information is relevant.
- Provides correct amount of information.

Document Formatting and Presentation

- Writes to an intelligent reader unfamiliar with specifics of topic.
- Discussion flows logically.
- Well formatted to enhance clarity by breaking content into sections with clear foci.

- Section headings preview text that follows.

- Appropriate emphasis added.

- Helpfully titled.

- Visual cues help draw the reader's eye to the relevant points quickly.

- Provides date, contact information, organization name.

Writing

- Short, precise, readable sentences that are actor centered.

- Paragraphs are cohesive, coherent, and properly emphasize important ideas.

- No grammar or spelling errors.

- No jargon.

- Passes *Washington Post* test.

EXERCISES

1. What is the purpose of your issue brief? Why are you creating it?

2. Who are the various audiences you will be targeting with your issue brief? What do they need to know about your problem?

3. Think about the content of your policy brief. What do you need to include?

4. Sketch the design elements of your policy brief on a piece of paper. What figures, tables, lists, callout boxes, etc., will you be using?

5. Create an effective 1–2 page issue brief by employing the elements of an issue brief to communicate with your audience on a core issue or program in your problem area.

BIBLIOGRAPHY

Cooley, V. (2015). *Economic well-being of Rhode Island families: The promise and practice of two-generation approaches* (issue brief no. 1501). Providence, RI: The Policy Institute for Family Impact Seminars. Retrieved from https://www.purdue.edu/hhs/hdfs/fii/publications/rhode-island-seminar-1-2/

Food and Agriculture Organization of the United Nations. (2011). *Preparing policy briefs* (Food Security Communications Toolkit). Rome, Italy. Retrieved from http://www.fao.org/docrep/014/i2195e/i2195e00.htm

Martin, S. (2014). *How to produce a policy brief* (Think Tank Initiative's Policy Engagement and Communications Program). Research to Action. Retrieved from http://www.researchtoaction.org/2014/09/produce-policy-brief/

Maternal, Child and Adolescent Health Division. (2017). *Connecting CalWORKS with home visiting* (issue brief). Sacramento, CA: California Department of Public Health. Retrieved from https://www.cdph.ca.gov/Programs/CFH/DMCAH/CDPH%20Document%20Library/Communications/Issue-Brief-CHVP-CalWORKs.pdf

Rothermel, A. (n.d.). *A strong start for families: Voluntary home visiting in California* (issue brief). Oakland, CA: Children Now. Retrieved from https://www.childrennow.org/reports-research/voluntary-home-visiting-ca/

Ruderman, M. (2012). *The art and craft of policy briefs: Translating science and engaging stakeholders*. Women and Children Health Policy Center. Bloomberg School of Public Health, Johns Hopkins University. Retrieved from https://www.jhsph.edu/research/centers-and-institutes/womens-and-childrens-health-policy-center/de/policy_brief/video

Policy History

A policy history provides an overview of important and recent policy actions taken to address a particular problem in a short memo (usually 2–3 pages). In contrast to an issue brief, which largely focuses on the particulars of the problem itself (how many homeless people? why are they homeless?), a policy history focuses on how the government has addressed the problem (what laws were passed regarding the homeless? what policies do the police use in dealing with the homeless?). *A successful policy history gives the decision maker enough context to understand what policies have been proposed and/or enacted.*

Policy histories are written for a wide variety of decision makers because new decision makers enter every policy arena each year. They arrive needing to learn what policies have been considered in the past and which ones have passed. Newly elected legislators arrive in the capitol having campaigned on the issues but needing a detailed understanding of the specific bills that have been considered before their arrival. Staffers on a governor's policy team frame the background of the new bills introduced by the hundreds of legislators in their statehouse each year. Advocacy groups engaged in new policy problems need to come up to speed quickly. All of them depend on policy histories.

Distinctive Aspects of Policy Histories

Policy histories are usually produced for a specific decision maker and focus on bills and regulations addressing a particular policy problem. With a wide range of decision makers requesting policy histories, the documents vary widely in terms of both scope and format. Any given policy history might focus entirely on one level of government, or span multiple levels. It might focus on legislative initiatives (bills and laws), agency actions (rules and regulations), or feature both. It might focus on one jurisdiction or detail how several jurisdictions have handled a particular issue differently. It all depends on the problem on which you are focusing and what your decision maker needs to know.

Despite this variety, there are some core steps at the heart of any policy history that will help you move forward as you write. The first step is deciding whether or not you need to focus on actions by the legislature, the executive, or both. Let's look at the steps necessary to produce a policy history focused on bills and laws first.

Legislative History

A legislative history focuses on explaining to your decision maker the bills considered and passed by a legislative body.[1] Legislative histories, by definition, focus on the efforts of legislators to address a particular policy challenge. During every session legislators submit bills, often having them heard in committee, and sometimes even get them passed into law. As new policy makers enter an issue area, it is crucially important to understand both what progress has been made in the legislature and what the legislature has been unwilling to do.

Finding the Bills

Compared to the other policy-writing genres in this book, the most unique aspect of a policy history is the research required to produce it. How hard could it be to research the laws that are introduced, considered, and passed around your problem? The issue is the peculiarities of the particular legislative institution you are researching. The first time you wade through its system can be excruciating.

The issue is that every legislative body is unique. The U.S. House of Representatives functions differently than the U.S. Senate. The New York State Assembly in Albany is only 150 miles from Concord, but the New Hampshire General Court couldn't be a more different legislative chamber.[2] School boards, city councils, and county governments all record their deliberations and decisions differently. Your ability to find what you need depends as much on their technological sophistication and commitment to transparency as it does on your research savvy. These systems aren't impenetrable, but it does take a lot of effort to learn them the first time.

---

[1] In the legal field, a legislative history has a different meaning than what is described in this section (Smith, 2015, chap. 5). In that field, legislative histories document and convey the intent of a specific law. They sometimes include testimony before the committee, records of discussions by committee members, and other primary documents. Because of their prominence, multiple subscriptions services provide access to legislative histories (HeinOnline, ProQuest, Westlaw). These may be available through a university library and are almost always available through a law school library.

[2] For a fascinating portrait of the 400-member-strong New Hampshire House of Representatives, take 20 minutes to listen to Part III of the *This American Life* episode, "Red State Blue State," by Glass (2012).

How should you begin researching a legislative history? I suggest a multipronged approach. The first prong is to find the relevant bill tracking system online and learn how to use it. Every state has its own bill tracking software (see Morgan [2001] for a list), as does Congress.[3] These have standard search features that allow you to enter search terms, limit dates, and search by bill sponsors.

The second prong is to talk to a librarian. Most legislative bodies have their own legislative libraries, and the librarians who work there are experts at understanding how the search systems work. They can also point you to resources that might not be immediately obvious. For example, many committees have their own websites where they post testimony, presentations, and reports that they considered when creating their bills. These resources can be enormously helpful. Additionally, many universities employ a government documents (or gov docs) librarian. This librarian (or team of librarians) specializes in navigating these complicated systems and can be a helpful resource for getting oriented in your research.

The third prong is to look for media coverage of the issue produced by traditional outlets or by advocacy groups. Use the search functions of the relevant newspaper websites to look for specific bill references. Check the Twitter feeds of reporters or advocates. Look for press releases from politicians hawking their latest bill. By checking these sources, you'll ensure your original search didn't fail because you searched for "driverless cars" instead of "autonomous vehicles." It's good to double-check!

Understanding the Bills

Once you've found the bills, then you will face the surprisingly difficult task of understanding them. Remember: Bills are meant to amend or create laws. They are written by lawyers and are almost always in legalese. Unless you have taken a course in law, the language can be difficult to understand. Thankfully, most legislatures have staff that write bill summaries to accompany the legislation. These basic overviews translate the legal wording into everyday language that an educated reader can understand.[4]

---

[3] There are also a wide variety of subscription services like FiscalNote that scrape data from the state and federal websites and compile it into more user-friendly versions. Check with your university library (or the law library, if there is a law school) to see if you have access to one of them.

[4] If you have questions about the bill that aren't addressed in the summary, consider talking to the legislative staff who helped to assemble the bill. Bill-drafting attorneys, committee staff, and research analysts can all be surprisingly accessible to the public, especially if the legislature is not in session.

Follow the Money

When creating a legislative history, it's important not just to look at the bills making something legal or illegal but also at the budget bills that fund the programs that enforce them. Increasing the fines for polluters will make little difference if the legislature cuts the staff who issue the fines. Similarly, it might be wonderful news that the legislature created a special fund to help your cause, but if it didn't put any money into that fund, that's unlikely to create change on the ground. Looking through the budget bill over the course of a couple of years can provide helpful context about how funding levels have changed for a program and how many positions have been added or cut. With any luck, you can find a report that has already pulled these figures for you. If not, you might be consigned to reading budget documents for a while!

Understand the Players

As you learn about the legislation around your issue it's worth keeping an eye on who is introducing the legislation. Think about what interests they might represent: regional, religious, racial, and others. What party are they from? Was the bill jointly sponsored with legislators from other backgrounds? As you identify patterns about which it would be helpful for your decision maker to know, make sure to include them in your legislative history. Knowing that rural Republicans and Democrats are united against a bill is a helpful context for your decision maker as they navigate the politics of the situation.

Regulatory History

While a legislative history focuses on actions taken by the legislative branch, a regulatory history focuses on actions taken by the executive branch. It looks at the rules and regulations produced by executive branch agencies to address a problem.[5] Because these rules are so specific, they can have a tremendous impact on a policy problem, and it is often worth taking the time to research and write about them for interested decision makers. Your legislative history research might tell you that Congress passed a law regulating air pollution, but only by reading the regulations produced by the Environmental Protection Agency will you learn just how much pollution a power plant is allowed to produce each year.

---

[5] For our purposes, rules and regulations can be viewed as the same thing. Both are terms used to refer to the binding directions produced and enforced by government agencies that have the force of law.

When the legislature passes a law, it often has written a law that creates policy in very broad sweeps. For example, Congress might pass a law instructing the U.S. Centers for Disease Control and Prevention (CDC) to protect the United States from highly contagious diseases that exist outside our borders. But it might give very little direction on how to do this.

By being vague, Congress enables the CDC to create rules based on its expertise and the demands of the moment. Congress may give the CDC the power to quarantine people but not specify who should be quarantined (exposed or infected people) or how long they should be quarantined. The CDC creates rules and regulations through a process known as rulemaking, and its rules reflect its expert knowledge.[6] This is one of the reasons why the CDC was so effective in keeping the 2014–2016 Ebola outbreak in West Africa from spreading inside our borders.

Finding the Regulations

When looking for recent regulatory actions on your problem, use a similar, multipronged search process like you would for a legislative history. Use regulatory websites like the *Federal Register*,[7] make use of gov docs librarians and commission staff to understand the ins and outs of the particular website you are trying to use, and employ media sources to make sure you've found all the regulations you need for your regulatory history.

Understanding the Regulations

Thankfully, regulations contain a lot less legalese than bills do. Because proposed regulations are meant to solicit public feedback, they should be written in accessible language. But even with those aspirations, they can still be difficult to understand because of the technical language. For example, a 2018 rule, "Air Quality Designations for the 2010 Sulfur Dioxide (SO_2)," has this gem in the executive summary:

---

[6] See Shambaugh and Weinstein (2016, chap. 4) for more details of regulation at the federal level.

[7] All states and many major localities have similar websites where you can see proposed and engaged regulatory actions. These may be centralized, like they are at the federal level, or they may be broken up into issue areas, with a separate process for environmental rules and regulations, workplace rules and regulations, etc.

The Clean Air Act (CAA or Act) directs areas designated Nonattainment by this rule to undertake certain planning and pollution control activities to attain the SO2NAAQS as expeditiously as practicable. (*Federal Register*, 2018)

Not exactly a paradigm of clear writing! Make sure you leave yourself enough time to understand the technical language in the rules and regulations once you find them.

Understanding the Players

Finally, regulatory policy is the result of input from many different stakeholders. It can be helpful to understand and delineate who they are as you write your regulatory history. Which agencies are involved? What is their mission, and what legislation authorizes them to take action on this policy?

It can also be helpful to think about the agendas of the individuals involved. The old saying "personnel are policy" is often true. The people in power have the ability to shape policy within the discretion of the law. Understanding their interests and communicating them to your audience will help your decision maker navigate the bureaucratic politics surrounding the problem.

How to Organize a Policy History

The structure depends on the particular needs of the decision maker for whom you are writing. You will need to make a myriad of decisions: Will you focus on bills, regulations, or both? If bills, which bills are most important? How will you make trade-offs between discussing significant legislation that occurred decades ago and how current legislation impacts your problem but just makes slight changes? How much should you focus on the individuals and organizations behind the legislation versus the content of the bills themselves?

Once you make decisions about what to cover, there are some standard ways to organize your policy history. I've listed them below and discuss some of their trade-offs:

- *Chronologically.* Some policy histories are organized as simple timelines of policy made on the issue. For straightforward issues with uncomplicated policy histories, this structure can work well. Create an overview and then walk your reader through each bill, explaining how it built on the bill before it.

- *Issue-based.* Organizing around a theme is a classic way of organizing a policy history. For complicated problems like homelessness, a policy history might helpfully be broken into sections on housing affordability, mental health, and domestic violence. Or it might be helpfully organized by subpopulation, with bills focusing on families in one section, adults in another, and veterans in a third.

- *Bill/regulation-based.* Some policy histories are focused around a single major piece of legislation or regulatory action. This might be because there is only one major piece of legislation or because a recent rule reshaped the regulatory landscape, wiping out all the rules before it. In these cases, it may be most helpful to dig into one bill over the course of the memo rather than bringing in less important pieces of legislation.

- *Organized around cross-jurisdiction comparisons.* When novel issues appear, it can often be helpful to policy makers to see what policies other jurisdictions have used to address it. For example, if you are writing why your city has never wrestled with Uber before, it can be helpful to understand how other cities have addressed the issue in the past.

Remember, the mark of a successful policy history is whether or not the decision maker gets enough context to understand what policy has been proposed and/or enacted on the problem. Do your research, use one of the structures above, and start early enough to make revisions and ask others for their feedback.

Example Policy Histories

Now let's take a look at several sample policy histories. Each is written in memo style and addressed to a particular person. The memo format means they include "To," "From," "Date," and "Subject" lines.

Just like with issue briefs, it's important to read these not just as examples of how to format a policy history but also with an eye toward *thinking* and *communicating*. Ask yourself, *Does the structure work? Do the headings allow for a quick overview? Are the sentences and paragraphs effective in helping the decision maker read and learn quickly?* These points determine the effectiveness of the policy history as much as the research and analysis of the policies themselves.

Example 1: Cyber Security Efforts by the Legislature and Commissions

The first example is a straightforward policy history that was produced for an incoming gubernatorial administration in Virginia. Cyber security is a crucial issue for state governments. They must protect the privacy of the citizens of the state and be able to provide IT services as a part of doing business. Failing to provide high-quality cyber security can be a quick pass out of office for a politician; worse, it can mean that police can't do their jobs. The new administration wanted to know what bills had been passed by the legislature and what actions had been taken by the previous administration to protect the state information technology and data from outside threats.

Take a few minutes to read over this and mark up what stands out to you. As you go through it, keep goals and norms of a policy history laid out earlier in the chapter in mind. Think about where the writer followed them and where she deviated. Consider if these choices made her more effective in educating her decision maker about the recent policies surrounding the issue in Virginia.[8]

To: The Gubernatorial Transition Team
From: Lindsay Jefferson, Gubernatorial Transition Clinic Analyst
Date: November 4, 2017
Subject: Cyber Security Bills and Executive Actions

Overview

The exponential growth of technology over the last few decades has given rise to the development of newer and more threatening cyber security attacks. The Commonwealth of Virginia has responded to these threats with continuous adaptation and support of the security of state agencies and operations. Specifically, over the last decade the Virginia General Assembly and Executive Branch have reviewed and enacted an array of legislation requiring state agencies or businesses to implement specific types of security practices, increasing penalties for computer crimes, addressing threats to critical infrastructure, adjusting funding for improved security measures, and more.

Legislative History

Much of the earlier legislation around cyber security focuses on adapting legislation, policies and definitions to accommodate for the growth of new technology and methods of cyber attacks. In 2005, the General Assembly passed H.B. 2215 and S.B. 1163. These laws modernized the Virginia Computer Crimes Act by updating definitions to comport with changing technology, such as changing the definition of "computer" and also by adding new methods of cyber attacks

---

[8] It will help to know that H.B. stands for House Bill and S.B. stands for Senate Bill. H.B. 2215 is the standard shorthand for referring to House Bill 2215.

like phishing. In addition, H.B. 2353 was passed in 2007, adding keyboard loggers, bots and zombies, and the unauthorized installation of malicious software (malware and spyware) to the list of computer trespass crimes (LIS: Virginia's Legislative Information System, "H.B.2215," 2005, "S.B. 1163," 2005, "H.B. 2353," 2007).

The General Assembly also began adapting penalties for cyber crimes in 2004 as S.B. 1147 was passed to make it a Class 6 Felony to fraudulently obtain or access from a computer identifying information (phishing) including social security numbers, driver's license numbers, bank account numbers, and more. The most recent update to cyber crime penalties came with the passage of H.B. 1815 in 2017, which increased the Class 1 misdemeanor computer trespass crimes to a Class 6 felony if the target computer is one that is exclusively for the use of, or used by, the Commonwealth, a local government within the Commonwealth, or certain public utilities (LIS: Virginia's Legislative Information System, "S.B.1147," 2004, "H.B. 1815," 2017).

In the last decade, the legislative branch has also focused on cyber security requirements for state agencies and other enterprises around the Commonwealth to ensure top rated cyber safety.

Some of the first steps toward these requirement updates began in 2004 with the passage of H.B. 1330. This law requires the director of every department in the executive branch of state government to report to the Chief Information Officer (CIO) all known incidents that threaten the security of the Commonwealth's databases and data communications resulting in exposure of data protected by federal or state laws within 24 hours of the discovery of the incident (LIS: Virginia's Legislative Information System, "H.B.1330," 2004).

More recently and most notably was the passage of H.B. 2360 in 2017. This law requires the CIO of the Virginia Information Technologies Agency (VITA) to develop policies, standards, and guidelines that require any contract for information technology with the Commonwealth's executive, legislative, and judicial branches and independent agencies to be in compliance with applicable federal laws and regulations pertaining to information security and privacy. The passage of this law made Virginia one of the first states to require federal level security standards at the state level (LIS: Virginia's Legislative Information System, "H.B. 2360," 2017). Although this law requires the development of policies, standards and guidelines by VITA, no laws have been passed that require that these standards be adhered to by every state and independent agency.

History of Executive Actions

In addition to action from the legislative branch, there has also been action from the executive branch, especially during the current McAuliffe administration. In 2015, Governor McAuliffe enacted Executive Order #39, which launched "Cyber Virginia" and established the Virginia Cyber Security Commission. Cyber Virginia details the Commonwealth's dedication to mitigate risks and safeguard the highest level of security for government infrastructure networks, foster cyber security education and awareness, incorporate innovative best practices, and also bolster business investment with public-private partnerships. Additionally, the Virginia Cyber Security Commission is responsible for:

> "identifying high risk security issues; providing advice and
> recommendations related to securing state networks, systems,
> and data, including interoperability and standardization of plans
> and procedures; providing suggestions for the addition of cyber
> security to Virginia's Emergency Management and Disaster Response
> capabilities; promoting awareness of cyber hygiene among the
> Commonwealth's citizens, businesses and government entities;
> presenting recommendations for educational and training programs
> for all ages; offering strategies to advance cyber security economic
> development; providing suggestions for coordinating the review
> and assessment of opportunities for cyber security private sector
> growth as it relates to military and defense activities in the state"
> (Commonwealth of Virginia Office of the Governor, 2015).

The Virginia Cyber Security Commission concluded its activities on March 29, 2016 and released a final report. This report highlighted the activities and actions of the Commission in the areas of Commonwealth cyber infrastructure and network protection, education and workforce development, public awareness, economic development, and development of new legislation to modernize statutes to address cyber crime. The report also provides recommendations for areas of continued emphasis (Virginia Cyber Commission, 2016).

Focus on garnering a larger amount and more specified funding for cyber security initiatives around the Commonwealth was largely started during the McAuliffe administration. Governor McAuliffe's proposed biennial budget included $22 million in planned investments in cyber security programs. The 2016–2018 budget signed into law only allotted $6.2 million specifically dedicated to these security programs outlined by the governor, leaving the funding for cyber initiatives around the state lacking (LIS: Virginia's Legislative Information System, "H.B. 1500, 2016").

Discussion of Example 1

What do you think? Classically organized, this example educates the reader about specific bills and executive actions related to cyber security in Virginia over the last 10–15 years. The author has clearly done her homework and focused the reader's attention on a few key bills and executive actions. She explains them well and connects them together. Overall, this is an effective document.

That said, it's worth noting some aspects of a policy history that the author does not include. She chooses to focus very little on the individuals involved on the legislative side. This may be because they are no longer in the legislature or because the bills were largely bipartisan. But without discussion, we're left to guess. This document also does not discuss the budgetary aspects of the problem. Yes, the legislature required VITA to develop policies, but did it provide any funding to implement those policies? That is an important question to answer.

Now think a bit about the *communicating* aspects of the memo. The writing was good enough that you likely got through it without much effort. But the author could have made a few changes to help you get through even more quickly. For example, subheadings would have helped you understand the structure more quickly.

Creating subheadings might have helped the author think about the organization of the legislative history section. It's a little disconcerting that the last paragraph starts with, "More recently and most notably." If that's really the most notable thing, then it should go first! Subheadings might have helped.

Finally, the sentences could be improved in several places. The sentence, "Focus on garnering a larger amount and more specified funding for cyber security initiatives around the Commonwealth was largely started during the McAuliffe administration," violates the actor-centered principles of good writing from Chapter 3. A little more polish here would have helped you read this policy history more quickly.

Example 2: Legislative History on American Indian Health and the ACA

Now let's take a look at a second example. Here, the author is writing to a U.S. senator who needs to learn more about how the Affordable Care Act (or Obamacare) impacted American Indian health care. Take a few minutes to read over this and mark up what stands out to you. As you go through it, keep goals and norms of a policy history laid out earlier in the chapter in mind. Think about where the writer followed them and where she deviated. Consider if these choices made her more effective in educating her decision maker about the recent policies surrounding the issue.

MEMORANDUM

TO: Sen. Udall (D-NM), Ranking Member, Senate Committee on Indian Affairs
FROM: Evelyn Immonen, Policy Analyst
DATE: October 4, 2017
RE: Legislative History on American Indian Health and the ACA

Overview

American Indians in the United States have consistently faced greater health problems than their non-Indian counterparts. The 2015 national average for American Indians in fair or poor health stands at 25%, compared to 14% for the rest of the population (Kaiser Family Foundation [KFF]). Currently, the U.S. Census estimates that 5.2 million American Indians live in the United States, of which 27% are enrolled in Medicaid, plus 50% of American Indian children (KFF). The Affordable Care Act (ACA) of 2010 brought about several important changes to the administration of health services to American Indian and Alaskan Natives by authorizing additional powers to the Indian Health Service and by expanding coverage and funding for American Indians under Medicaid.

Background

The Indian Health Service (IHS) began in 1955, after the transfer of health services from the Bureau of Indian Affairs to the Public Health Service (National Library of Medicine [NLM]). The basis of this relationship dates back to treaty provisions for health care services signed with many tribes, and the established trust responsibility between the United States and tribes. Because of this important precedent, legislation must come at the federal level out of respect to the government-to-government relationship with tribes. At first, IHS was mainly concerned with construction of clinics in remote reservation eras, but the 1970s saw an uptick in promotional material to increase awareness of the issues with American Indian health (NLM).

In 1976, the Indian Health Care Improvement Act (IHCIA) amended the Social Security Act to allow Medicaid and Medicare reimbursement for this population. This amendment created a direct relationship between IHS and Centers for Medicaid Services (CMS). The Indian Health Care Improvement Act instituted a 100% Federal Medical Assistance Percentage (FMAP) for Medicaid services for IHS or tribal facilities. Reimbursement needs to go through more accessible IHS facilities, reducing the number of patients who would have to drive hundreds of miles to access a provider off-reservation (CMS).

Section 5006 of the American Recovery and Reinvestment Act (2009) expanded some protections for Indian health. It requires states consult with tribes on a government-to-government basis on Medicaid or CHIP policies, and include their consulting process in public documents. Section 5006 also precludes states from imposing Medicaid premiums on Indian enrollees.

1955	Indian Health Service created
1976	Indian Health Care Improvement Act (IHCIA)
2000	IHCIA authorization expires
2009	American Reinvestment and Recovery Act expands protection
2010	Affordable Care Act reauthorizes and expands IHCIA

IHS Funding Problems

Indian Health Services receives annual appropriations through Congress each year, limiting the supply of services. If there is a surplus of demand, services must be prioritized or patients turned away. In 2013, IHS per capita expenditures for patient health services were just $2,849 compared to $7,717 per capita nation-wide according to the National Congress of American Indians. This affects a population whose life expectancy is 4.2 years less than the national average due to the highest rates of death by alcoholism, diabetes, unintentional injuries, and suicide compared to other racial groups (NCAI). Medicaid makes up 13% of total allocations of IHS services (HHS).

Indian Health Care Improvement Act 2010

President Obama came into office in 2008 wanting to pass major health care legislation, and he had the Democratic majority in the House to make it happen. The Senate needed the filibuster-proof 60 votes in order to pass such major legislation, and they reached that in December of 2009 by including two independents and one Republican who changed parties (Forbes). The Democratic National Committee included tribal sovereignty on their agenda in the 2008 campaign:

"In exchange for millions of acres of land, our nation pledged to provide certain services in perpetuity; we will honor our nation's treaty and trust obligations by increasing resources for economic development, *health care,* Indian education, and other important services." (DNC)

Health care services were at stake: authorization for appropriations for IHCIA had expired in 2000 (IHS). Obama acted on his campaign promise and held a White House Tribal Nations Conference in 2009, providing an opportunity for public comment from tribal leaders on the Affordable Care Act. On March 23, 2010, President Obama signed IHCIA reauthorization into law permanently as part of the Patient Protection and Affordable Care Act. Unlike in previous years, there was no expiration date on IHCIA authorization, ensuring it would continue into subsequent administrations (IHS).

New Provisions in the Affordable Care Act

The Indian Health Care Improvement Act signed in 2010 included many changes from the original 1976 legislation to facilitate the delivery of health services (IHS).

- Increases authority for IHS Director, including to enhance tribal consultation within HHS

- Provides authorization for long-term, hospice, or community-based care

- Extends the ability to recover costs from third parties to tribally-owned facilities

- Updates laws on reimbursement of Medicaid, Medicare, and CHIP by IHS facilities

- Allows tribes to purchase health benefits for IHS beneficiaries

- Authorizes collaboration between IHS and VA or Defense to share facilities and services

- Extends health benefits to program employees in Indian education or urban Indian health

- Authorizes Community Health Representative program in urban Indian areas

- Directs IHS to develop a comprehensive behavioral health program

Impacts of the Affordable Care Act on Coverage for American Indians

The ACA offered an optional expansion for states to cover low-income adults up to 138% of the federal poverty line. Some states with a relatively high population of American Indians chose to expand (California, Arizona, New Mexico), while others have not as of 2017 (Oklahoma, Texas, South Dakota). The passage of the ACA has positively impacted insurance coverage for American Indians. The Kaiser Family Foundation found that from 2013 to 2015 the uninsured rate fell from 24% to 17% among American Indians. This impact was slightly higher than on the non-Indian population, who saw the uninsured rate fall 6% in the same time period (KFF).

Finally, the ACA also impacted revenues for IHS and tribally-operated facilities. Nationwide, IHS program funding from Medicaid revenue increased from $720 million in 2013 to $810 million in 2017 (IHS). Transferring funds from the annually-appropriated IHS budget to the nondiscretionary Medicaid budget increases the proportion of guaranteed funds for IHS clinics, more proportional to expenses of the population they serve.

Discussion of Example 2

What do you think? This policy history does a nice job on several counts. First, it provides enough context for the reader to understand how the ACA fits into the broader history of Native American health care policy. This sweeping history cites legislation passed in the 1950s and alludes to a long history of Native American and U.S. government relationships before that. It sets up the new issues. Second, the frequent and informative headings help the reader move quickly across the memo to get a sense of the sweep, and they are detailed enough to get an idea of what is in each section.

From a structural perspective, I can't help wondering what would have happened if the author had flipped the memo, placing the last paragraph just under the overview section and rewriting the memo from there. In this structure, there would have been a clear focus on the ACA and she could have filled in details about the IHCIA as needed. If the point of the history was to focus on how the ACA affected Indian health, then that change would have been worth considering.

Whether or not she had flipped it, this policy history would have benefited from several additional revisions focused on the communication aspects of it. For example, the sentence, "The basis of this relationship dates back to treaty provisions for health care services signed with many tribes, and the established trust responsibility between the United States and tribes," is difficult to follow because it violates several of the principles from Chapter 3.

Example 3: Regulatory Actions by the United States' Office of Foreign Assets Control (OFAC)

For our final example, let's take a look at a policy history focused on regulatory actions. This memo is drawn from the international arena, but the frameworks remain the same. Take a few minutes to read over this and mark up what stands out to you. As you go through it, keep goals and norms of a policy history laid out earlier in the chapter in mind. Think about where the writer followed them and where she deviated. Consider if these choices made her more effective in educating her decision maker about the recent policies surrounding the issue.

To: Stephen O'Brien, Under-Secretary General and Emergency Relief Coordinator, United Nations Office for the Coordination of Humanitarian Affairs (UN-OCHA)

From: Anna Troutman, Policy Analyst

Date: November 4, 2017

Subject: Regulatory Actions by the United States' Office of Foreign Assets Control (OFAC)

Executive Summary

The Office of Foreign Assets Control (OFAC) is the Department of the Treasury division responsible for crafting and implementing U.S. sanctions policy. Headed by a political appointee, the Department's policy is entirely aligned with and driven by the Executive's foreign policy and national security agendas. Recent exceptions allowing U.S.-based activities in Hamas-controlled Gaza Strip/Occupied Palestinian Territory (OPT) created unprecedented license for humanitarian response. While future regulation allowing humanitarian response in terror-related crises is dependent on Executive policy, these updates have increased the possibility of similar sanctions exceptions across the board.

Agency Profile

The Office of Foreign Assets Control (OFAC) is the division in the Department of the Treasury responsible for determining, governing, and applying economic and trade sanctions based on U.S. foreign policy and national security goals. Operating under presidential national emergency authority and the International Emergency Economic Powers Act (IEEPA), OFAC executes executive mandates freezing foreign assets through regulations on financial institutions and their holdings. Though OFAC receives general regional and conflict-based targets from Presidential executive orders, its Office of Global Targeting (OGT) is responsible for generating and designating final individual targets for sanction. OFAC has the power to levy significant financial penalties against U.S. individuals or groups violating regulations, including imposing fines, freezing assets, and even barring violators from operating in the U.S. (Department of the Treasury, 2017). The department generates the regulations blocking humanitarian aid in designated conflict zones, and regularly penalizes U.S.-based organizations who choose to operate in contested areas.

OFAC has existed in some form since the War of 1812, when the U.S. levied its first sanctions as a nation against Great Britain. The most modern agency, the Division of Foreign Assets Control, was established in 1950 following the People's Republic of China's entry into the Korean War. The Division grew into OFAC in 1962 by Treasury Department order. Located in the Treasury Department headquarters in Washington, D.C., OFAC currently employs 200 lawyers and intelligence analysts with an annual operating budget of 30.9 million dollars (Department of the Treasury, 2017). John E. Smith serves as the Director of OFAC, a politically appointed position that does not require congressional approval. The directorate is the only politically appointed position within OFAC (House of Representatives, 2017).

Though it is a Treasury Department division, OFAC's foreign policy orientation requires regular collaboration with the Department of State, the National Security Council, and other foreign affairs agencies. The Executive's foreign policy strategy drives the designation of organizations and individuals subject to sanctions. As such, regulations put forth by OFAC directly reflect developments in international affairs and U.S. foreign policy. OFAC maintains and enforces its regulations through two vehicles: national sanctions programs, and a list of specially designated nationals and groups. While national sanctions programs block transactions with entire states, the specially designated nationals list prohibits U.S. citizens from transacting with specific foreign nationals and organizations. Both vehicles further Executive counterterrorism policy, with three sanctions programs specifically addressing terrorists and terrorist organizations: the Terrorism Sanctions Regulations (31 CFR Part 595), Global Terrorism Sanctions Regulations (31 CFR Part 594), and Foreign Terrorist Organization Sanctions

Regulations (FTOSR) (31 CFR Part 597) (Department of the Treasury, 2017). Establishing and updating these regulations is an entirely federal operation. OFAC waives the usual public consultation portion of regulatory procedure due to the foreign affairs function of these rules.

Though it is not possible for the public to weigh in on OFAC regulations, U.S. citizens and organizations can obtain exceptions to sanctions through OFAC's tightly regulated "licensing" process. OFAC has the power to grant exceptions to large sections of its sanctions regimes through "general licenses," allowing all U.S. citizens and organizations to continue work in sanctioned nations. Additionally, OFAC may grant "specific licenses" allowing certain U.S. citizens and organizations to continue work with OFAC-designated entities (Department of the Treasury, 2017).

Recent Key Regulations

Recent OFAC-generated updates to the Code of Federal Regulations (CFR) have primarily established new sanctions regimes and incorporated new licenses to existing sanctions. The CFR was updated in 2017 to block transactions with all ISIL affiliates, and updates have reaffirmed blocks to aid-giving in the ongoing humanitarian crises in Somalia and South Sudan. However, revisions to the FTOSR (31 CFR Part 597) have had the most impact on blocking or enabling humanitarian aid in terror-related crises (Government Publishing Office, 2017; Government Publishing Office, 2010; Government Publishing Office, 2006).

One update and two general licenses have been added to the FTOSR in the past decade with significant impacts to humanitarian intervention, particularly in the Gaza Strip/OPT. In 2006, the OFAC-designated terrorist organization Hamas gained a majority in the Palestinian Legislative Council and took control of the Prime Ministry. In response to this international affairs development, OFAC determined that Hamas now held significant sway over the Palestinian Authority (PA) government of Gaza/OPT. In light of existing sanctions prohibiting U.S. citizens from dealing with Hamas, OFAC updated the FTOSR and specially designated nationals list accordingly. The PA, previously a partner for many U.S. organizations and operations, was designated a "blocked" organization and all transactions with the PA (including providing aid through local government channels) were made illegal (Government Publishing Office, 2006).

Due to the entrenched nature of many U.S. organizations' work in Gaza/OPT, however, OFAC granted a general license softening the sanctions regime against the PA. Recognizing the split nature of foreign policy at the time, OFAC authorized U.S. persons to engage in transactions in Gaza/OPT in which the PA had an interest. These transactions included all licensed United Nations (UN) business and government transactions, provided they did not debit blocked accounts affiliated with the PA. The language of 31 CFR Part 597 was written liberally to include the International Monetary Fund, the World Bank, the World Food Programme, and the World Health Organization under the UN umbrella of exempted humanitarian organizations operating in the region. Additionally, OFAC granted license for in-kind donations of medical aid to areas under PA jurisdiction, widening the historically allowed fields for humanitarian engagement (Government Publishing Office, 2006).

The second general license and most recent update to the FTOSR granted permission in 2010 for use of funds in blocked accounts to pay for legal representation and related expenses. This created a significant exception to not only FTOSR sanctions, but also to the IEEPA and U.S. criminal statutes prohibiting U.S. citizens from contributing services to designated terrorists and terrorist organizations. Under this general license, U.S. actors may provide legal assistance to holders of blocked accounts seeking to contest their designation (Government Publishing Office, 2010). This upends previous interpretations of codes governing counterterrorism, which viewed services as a form of material support to terrorist organizations.

Anticipated Future Regulation and Recommended Action

Future regulatory action taken by OFAC will likely be in response to developing international affairs, and will be determined by the Executive's response agenda. Barring a massive international incident, OFAC regulatory policy developments affecting humanitarian response will be limited to new sanctions on international crises and the addition or removal of individuals and groups on the specially designated actors list. Counterterrorism-related updates will likely focus on the evolving situation in Syria, ISIL operations, radicalization in Bangladeshi Rohingya camps, and ongoing terror-related crises.

Previous updates to the CFR have set a new precedent for humanitarian operations in terror-related crises, and serve as the groundwork for a more nuanced policy on aid. However, any further policy updates will likely come as the result of a top-down Executive policy shift, similar to the shift excepting transactions with the Hamas-majority PA in 2006. As current Executive foreign and national security policy is highly focused on domestic security and does not prioritize foreign aid of any kind, it is unlikely that this shift will occur within the Trump presidency.

Advocates will best achieve initial reforms to regulations on humanitarian aid by applying for general licenses allowing operations in terror-related crises. The absence of a public review period on any OFAC updates to the CFR limits direct external stakeholder involvement to this channel. Additionally, U.S.-based aid organizations should continue to lobby Congress to shape foreign and national security policy such that it prioritizes access for humanitarian organizations in terror-related crises. Ideal OFAC regulatory policy would include a standard general license for designated humanitarian actors to continue monitored operations under all future counterterrorist sanctions regimes. Given the proper Executive policy conditions, this step from the current PA-specific license under FTOSR to standardized OFAC regulatory practice would be eminently achievable.

Discussion of Example 3

What do you think? While this example focuses almost exclusively on executive branch actions, it still reads similarly to the other two. It is most impressive for educating the reader about a complex and important issue—in this case, how the government regulates business dealings of U.S. citizens with actors in areas with terrorist bases. One reason why you can take in such complicated information is that the author *communicates* well. The sentences and paragraphs are well constructed, allowing you to get through the information quickly.

The *thinking* is also done well. The author has a clear purpose. The information she chooses to include and the way she has assembled it work, which means that even in a content-heavy document, you can get through it in a straightforward manner, without a lot of head scratching. Of course, the document isn't perfect. Subheadings would have helped, and another round of edits would have shortened it a bit; but overall, it educates the decision maker effectively in terms of content and style, and that is what makes it effective.

Conclusion

The three examples above have given you a flavor of the policy history genre. You've seen a policy history focused on legislative actions, one focused on executive actions, and one splitting the difference. Each one comes from its own context and was created for a specific decision maker. Now that you have seen a few examples and know the basic principles of policy histories, you are ready to research and communicate the policy history surrounding your issue.

As you begin to write your own policy history, make sure to keep the *thinking* front and center by employing your audience-centered writing principles. Always be thinking, *Why is it that I am writing this? What does my decision maker need to know? How can I best use this particular format and its particular rules to communicate with them?*

Once you have the *thinking* down, then enjoy *communicating* in this unique policy genre. Writing a policy history will not just provide value for your decision maker, it can also give you a new perspective on your problem. You'll have a better sense of the government actors who are engaged in addressing it. You'll know more about what they have and haven't tried. This knowledge will aid you as you move forward in helping people address your problem.

CHECKLIST

Content and Analysis

- Demonstrates thorough understanding of the topic and its implications.

- Includes background, legislative issues, public concerns, and other aspects of the topic.

- Correctly identifies every important issue.

- Virtually all included information is relevant.

- Provides correct amount of information.

Writing

- Is directed to an intelligent reader unfamiliar with specifics of topic.

- Short, precise, readable sentences that are actor centered.

- Paragraphs are cohesive, coherent, and properly emphasize important ideas.

- Discussion flows logically.

- No grammar or spelling errors.

- No jargon.

- Passes *Washington Post* test.

Document Formatting and Presentation

- Header provides date, contact information, and organization name.

- Helpfully titled.

- Well formatted to enhance clarity by breaking content into sections with clear foci.

- Section headings preview text that follows.

- Appropriate emphasis added.

- Visual cues help draw the reader's eye to the relevant points quickly.

EXERCISES

1. What is the purpose of your policy history? Why are you creating it?

2. Who is your audience for the policy history? What do they need to know about your problem?

3. Think about the content of your policy history. Should you focus on legislative actions, executive branch actions, or both?

4. Write a sentence outline of your policy history. Why did you organize it the way that you did?

5. Create an effective, 1–2 page policy history targeted to a specific decision maker that gives them enough details about the relevant policies that have been proposed and/or enacted and provides the context to understand them.

BIBLIOGRAPHY

Federal Register. (2018). *Air quality designations for the 2010 sulfur dioxide (SO_2)* (rule no. 2017–28423). Washington, DC.

Glass, I. (2012, November 2). Red state blue state. *This American life.* NPR. Retrieved January 1, 2018, from https://www.thisamericanlife.org/radio-archives/episode/478/red-state-blue-state

Morgan, J. (2001). *State legislative history research guides inventory.* Retrieved January 8, 2018, from http://law.indiana.libguides.com/c.php?g=19813&p=112411

Shambaugh, G. E., & Weinstein, P. J. (2016). *The art of policymaking: Tools, techniques, and processes in the modern executive branch* (2nd ed.). Washington, DC: CQ Press.

Smith, C. F. (2015). *Writing public policy: A practical guide to communicating in the policy-making process* (4th ed.). New York: Oxford University Press.

CHAPTER 10

The Decision Memo

D ecision-forcing memos, commonly called *decision memos*, are documents that focus decision makers on a pressing problem on which they need to take action and persuade them to take a particular action using evidence and logic.[1] Emergencies, actions by opponents, or new information about how a situation is changing may call for new action by decision makers.

If decision makers recognize these decision points in advance, they may request a decision memo to trigger the careful consideration of the problem by subordinates. Other times, subordinates may see the problem first and write these 1–2 page memos to force decision makers to make a decision. Because decision memos are focused around action, they have a highly standardized format. Decision memos frame the problem, discuss options for action, and make a recommendation about what to do.[2]

Like any policy genre, *thinking* is key to success. To succeed, you must decide what the core problem is, create multiple options that address the problem, determine the criteria you will use to decide between them, discuss the trade-offs, and make a recommendation, all in 1–2 pages. The format forces concision, and concision forces clear thinking. These page constraints demand your best *thinking* and *communicating*.

Distinctive Aspects of Decision Memos

The audience for a decision memo has a pressing need to make a good decision about the issue you are presenting to them. That's good news because they are more likely to give your memo sustained attention than many of the other policy-writing genres. The bad news is they are still in a hurry and, with enormous pressures of the decision weighing on them, they are just as demanding readers as in any of the other genres.

---

[1] Depending on the setting, decision memos may be referred to by different names. For example, the White House refers to them as decision-forcing memos (Shambaugh & Weinstein, 2016, chap. 6), while the Veterans Administration refers to them as executive decision memos (EDMs).

[2] Garfinkle (2012, chap. 6) provides strategic advice about when and how to use decision memos to shape policy.

Memo Format

Decision memos are, first and foremost, memos. As such, you must begin your memo in a standard format with "To," "From," "Date," and "Subject" lines. These are important, so don't overlook them. Remember that your decision memo, even if requested by the decision maker, is one of dozens of documents they might see on a given day. Orient them by assuring them the document is addressed to them, who wrote it and what your title is, what the date is, and what the memo is about. The date is particularly important because in fast-moving situations, they need to make sure your memo is still relevant.

The subject line serves as the functional title of your memo. Make sure your memo is descriptive. Don't just say the noun involved (i.e., DACA). Instead, provide a title that is both descriptive and orienting (Options for Passing DACA Given the Current Political Landscape in the House).

Finally, make sure to use the various formatting practices described in Chapter 7. As you will see in the examples, decision memos use headings, subheadings, bullets, and spacing liberally, as well as italicized and bolded text when appropriate. All of these are useful and appropriate tools in decision memos.

The information in the header is also important because it's likely that your memo will end up in the hands of others. For example, you may be writing to the chief of staff, but if it's good he may pass it up the chain of command to the senator. Or if the governor requested the decision memo, she might have it distributed to the cabinet before the meeting. In either case, make sure the heading is complete and correct so everyone can be on the same page.[3]

Abbreviated Policy Analysis

At its heart, a decision memo is a policy analysis compacted to fit a 1–2 page memo. While you can intuit how to organize a policy analysis by using the headings below, your *thinking* will be sharper and your analysis better if you've already had some training and practice in policy analysis.

Policy analysis is a difficult skill to master (Cooley & Pennock, 2015). Deciding on the right problem definition is notoriously difficult. It's a challenge to discern crisp and distinct alternatives. Deciding which criteria are appropriate is surprisingly problematic. And that's just the *thinking* bit; once those are in place, then you have to do the long, hard work of gathering data, considering trade-offs, and making the decision (Bardach &

---

[3] It is, of course, possible that people outside your office may read it too. It might be distributed by staff, it might be leaked, or it might be read by outsiders using the Freedom of Information Act to request a release.

Patashnik, 2015). If you haven't learned about policy analysis, or it has been a while since you've studied it, it's worth reading or reviewing a guide on the topic.[4]

Example Outline for a Decision Memo

To: President Trump

From: Joe Smith, National Security Analyst

Date: January 10, 2018

Subject: Foreign Intelligence Surveillance Act (FISA) Renewal

Executive Summary: The Foreign Intelligence Surveillance Act (FISA) . . .
. . . I recommend that you support passage of the law.

Background: The original legislation was . . .
. . . *the issue on the table now is whether or not to renew FISA in its current form.*

Options: In response to the actions by Congress, you should choose one of the following options based on . . .

Option 1: Support FISA Renewal

Paragraph 1: Detail option.

Paragraph 2: Detail impacts and discuss pros and cons.

Option 2: Oppose FISA Renewal

Paragraph 1: Detail option.

Paragraph 2: Detail impacts and discuss pros and cons.

Option 3: Push for FISA Changes in Exchange for Support of Renewal

Paragraph 1: Detail option.

Paragraph 2: Detail impacts and discuss pros and cons.

Recommendation: I recommend that you support the law. It is the best option because . . .

---

[4] See Kraft and Furlong (2013, pt. II), Bardach and Patashnik (2015), or Weimer and Vining (2017) for training or a refresher on the context behind this.

While decision memos are usually focused around policy, they are also appropriate for overtly political situations. A political decision is still a decision. An issue is on the table, options need to be considered, and a recommendation needs to be made. The same set of principles apply to political decisions (or any decision, really), and the same format can help move toward a good outcome.

Highly Standardized Structure and Headings

Decision memos are organized around a standard structure. They contain an executive summary that allows decision makers to overview the memo quickly, a background section to bring the reader up to speed, two to four options (or alternatives) for action, and a recommendation. Each section has a descriptive header that helps quickly orient the reader.

Deciding About a Criteria Section

The one nonstandard aspect of decision memos is where to put the criteria section. You have three choices. The first is to have a standalone criteria section between the background and the options. This mirrors the standard format of a full-length policy analysis where there would be some discussion of why you chose the criteria and how they are operationalized. But in decision memos you have other choices. The second choice is to insert a brief paragraph at the beginning of the options section that details what they are. The third is to include the criteria as you discuss the options.

Which should you choose? If you can, do what is standard in your arena. Look at samples or ask people what is normally done. If you're writing without explicit guidance or samples to review, then consider the following advice: Have the criteria stand alone if the criteria are controversial. This allows you to defend why you chose them. If they are important but not controversial, then consider including a brief paragraph about them at the start of the options section, before you begin detailing the options. If they are obvious and noncontroversial, then I suggest working them into the discussion of each option in the details.

Assuring Alignment

Finally, as you write, make sure to keep alignment in mind. The parallel structure of a decision memo focuses readers on your argument. If you don't align your argument throughout your memo, people will notice. For example, writers of decision memos often struggle with evaluating each alternative using the same criteria. If one of the benefits of Option 1 is that it saves lives and reduces costs, then you need to talk about whether or not Option 2 saves lives and reduces costs as well.

Similarly, it can be difficult to maintain alignment of the terms throughout the paper. Make sure to use the same language throughout. Don't refer to the same set of people as constituents in the background section, voters in the options section, and citizens in the recommendation section. Align the language throughout and your reader will be able to follow along more quickly.

Example Decision Memos

The rigid analytical and visual structure of the decision memo means there isn't the same amount of variation as in most policy genres. However, there are some differences in style. The memos below have been selected to show you how these differences function. They are by three different authors, and each slightly varies the format without breaking the rules. Let's take a look at each of them to learn from what they do well and where they could improve.

Example 1: Responding to Lead Poisoning in New York City[5]

In the 1960s and early 1970s, New York City (NYC) began to grapple with the lead poisoning epidemic facing the city's children.[6] The effects of lead as a neurotoxin were just beginning to be fully faced at the time and lead would quickly be removed from new paints and from gasoline. However, lead remained in paint in and around buildings around the United States, and this posed a particular danger for children. They were especially in danger because they were more likely to be exposed to lead by crawling and putting things into their mouths, and they were more likely to be harmed by the neurotoxin because their brains were still forming.

In NYC, political activism surrounding a number of high-profile lead poisoning cases pushed the mayor to consider making lead poisoning a policy priority. In response, the new health services administrator, Gordon Chase, had to decide how to respond to the mayor's interest. The following memo addresses that question directly.

---

[5] This memo is a sample decision memo written using information from the time period (Rosenthal, 1992). *It does not reflect current understanding of lead poisoning, lead in NYC, or lead effects in children.* If you are interested in this topic, many current resources and research are available online, especially given the lead issues in Flint, Michigan.

[6] See Rosenthal (1992) for details.

To: Mr. Gordon Chase, New York City Health Services Administrator

From: Aiden Brown, Policy Analyst

Re: Responding to Lead Poisoning in New York City

Date: January 3, 1970

Executive Summary

Lead poisoning is a preventable disease with 120,000 children at risk in New York City. Though the City has historically lacked a large-scale plan or a reasonable budget to fight this health problem, public support for a government response has grown in recent years, and now Mayor Lindsay is prioritizing reducing the prevalence of the disease. Consider these two options to address the issue: allow Commissioner McLaughlin to implement her strategy as planned, or create a task force to rewrite the department's lead poisoning policy to actively fight the disease. Continuing with Dr. McLaughlin's plan is the most effective, feasible, and beneficial to the department's relationships.

Background and Problem Definition

Lead poisoning is a serious medical condition that, if left untreated, can cause mental retardation, epilepsy, kidney and nervous system problems, coma, and death. The disease threatens children in low-income homes who may ingest lead paint chips from tenement walls. Caring for afflicted children poses a significant financial burden to society, but patients face little long-term risk if treated quickly.

The current process for dealing with lead poisoning involves many different city departments, doctors, and tests. There is no active search to find and treat cases in at-risk populations. Instead, most diagnoses come from children showing signs of symptoms in standard physical examinations. In October, Commissioner McLaughlin secured $150,000 funding to begin to improve the Health Department's policy related to lead poisoning. Her efforts further increased the pressure from prominent politicians and interest groups to take a more decisive action. Neglecting lead poisoning will leave many children with lasting health problems and reflect poorly on the Mayor's ability to accomplish his priorities.

Alternatives

I will evaluate these two alternatives based on three criteria. First, the effectiveness of the policy in identifying and treating possible cases of lead poisoning.

Second, the feasibility of implementing the policy given constraints of Health Department resources. Finally, how the policy will affect the Department's relationships in-house and with outside parties.

Alternative 1: Allow Continued Implementation of the Commissioner's Strategy

This option follows the plan set out by Dr. McLaughlin when she secured $150,000 from the Budget Bureau to fight lead related ailments. She aims to revise the health code to make landlords cover lead-painted walls, develop a small staff to handle lead issues, study the ALA test (a urine test for lead-poisoning that has not proven to be effective), and purchase equipment to measure lead levels in walls and potential victims.

This plan appears an effective use of funds. It will increase identifications by 2,500 cases at a cost of $60 per case. The estimated lifetime costs of a brain-damaged child to society include $17,000 for special education and $220,000 for institutional care. This plan saves many children from short and long-term damage and saves society the money needed to care for them. The Department can feasibly proceed to implement it. The current funds appear sufficient, but the Health Department and the Budget Bureau agree additional future funding is needed to significantly fight the epidemic. Allowing Dr. McLaughlin's plan to proceed will also ease the transition between administrators. However, by taking a more passive approach to the problem, politicians and interest groups will continue to express discontent, but this could benefit the department by drawing more attention to the issue in order to secure more funding.

Alternative 2: Actively Fight the Epidemic Through Redesign of Department Procedures

This option proactively overhauls the Health Department's policy on lead poisoning. The first step is to create a task force to deal specifically with lead poisoning issues. This group will simplify the treatment process by having all cases referred to the Social Hygiene Clinic; requiring public health stations in sixteen poverty districts to routinely test for abnormal lead levels in children ages one to six; and sending out simple informational flyers in English and Spanish with welfare checks.

This option addresses lead poisoning more aggressively than the first alternative, so we can assume it would identify at least as many cases (>2,500 case increase annually). It is important to note that the costs of this program will be relatively more expensive, but the Budget Bureau has recognized the need to increase funding for lead poisoning. They will decide to increase the budget based on the results of a case study in December. This risk makes the project less feasible, as the funding is not there right now to implement it. Announcing a program before it receives adequate funding could reflect poorly on the Health Department and the Mayor. It is important to account for the effect this action would have on the relationships within the department and with politicians. Taking such a bold plan as a newcomer to the department could serve to alienate established and more experienced members. However, it could appease public and political outcry for a response. There is an upside to retaining public displeasure, as the more attention activists and politicians draw to the issue, the more funding the department will receive to fight it. This alternative would have a mixed effect on relationship dynamics.

Recommendation

I recommend allowing Commissioner McLaughlin to proceed with her plan. This decision is more effective, feasible, and department-friendly than an aggressive approach. The cost effectiveness is clear. There is an estimated 2,500 case increase at a cost of only $60 per case. The low financial costs also make the plan more feasible. Deferring to the health care expertise of the Commissioner will help build relationships in the department as the newcomer. The more passive response will also allow time to study the disease and to formulate the best robust response for when funding increases. Finally, this action will increase public and political outcry, raising awareness about the issue and helping to secure more funding. If the Health Department and Mayor's office clearly communicate their desire to do more if given the funding, this could prove to be a successful first step in solving a major health problem.

Discussion of Example 1

What do you think? The effectiveness of a memo like this can be hard to judge without knowing the technical or political details of the situation. Without that context, let's take the memo at face value and see if it does its job well. Does it clearly lay out the decision to the decision maker? Are the trade-offs evident? Is Mr. Chase ready to make this decision?

Let's start by discussing what the author does well. First, perhaps my favorite part is how he ends the background section. This is a key spot in the memo because the ending of any section provides a chance to focus the reader. He ends this first section with the sentence, "Neglecting lead poisoning will leave many children with lasting health problems and reflect poorly on the Mayor's ability to accomplish his priorities." With that he clearly and succinctly encapsulates the whole of the problem, both in terms of the children and the effect of that problem on Chase's boss (the mayor) and his agenda. That's memorable.

Second, he does a nice job of only including details in the background section that are relevant for the decision itself. He could have included stories about the particular children who have been in the media, or the names of the activists who have been driving the issue forward. Instead, he neatly packages them and moves them aside to focus on what should be done now.

Third, notice how he chooses to discuss the criteria included at the beginning of the options section. This choice works in this memo because it provides a frame for you to begin to read the options themselves and know what he will be discussing in them.

So these elements work well. What could he have improved? I found the second paragraph in each alternative section hard to follow. Was the discussion aligned with the criteria he laid out? Hard to tell; the writing wasn't cohesive enough to really follow. He would have been well served to focus on making those paragraphs work or breaking them up to make sure we could follow them.

Example 2: H1N1 and School Closures in Texas[7]

Now let's shift gears and years and look at another example. This example is a memo written to Dr. Valadez, the Assistant Commissioner for Prevention and Preparedness Services at the Texas Department of State Health Services. In 2009, Texas became the first state to be hit by the H1N1 influenza virus, popularly known as swine flu. At the time, the death rate from the virus was unknown and many feared that it would be as deadly as SARS, which killed one in 10 victims in 2003 before it was contained.

The first cases in Texas appeared in a high school in Guadalupe County, near San Antonio. Quickly, the local school district had to consult with the Texas Department of Health and the CDC to decide whether or not to close the school. They did close the school, and as the flu spread across Texas more schools closed, with nearly 500,000 students missing school that spring (Giles, 2011). In the after-action report the following summer, both the State Department of Health and the schools faced a choice about how they would respond to flu outbreaks in the winter. This decision memo puts that choice squarely before the policy makers. Take a look.

---

[7] This memo is a sample decision memo based on the information in the case (Giles, 2011). *It does not reflect current understanding of pandemic response or school closures.* The U.S. Centers for Disease Control and Prevention (CDC) has excellent resources on current state-of-the-art responses to flu epidemics.

Date: August 12th, 2009

To: Dr. Valadez, Asst. Commissioner for Prevention & Preparedness Services, DSHS

From: Charlotte deButts, Policy Analyst

Subject: H1N1 Caused Texas School Closures

Executive Summary

With the outbreak of H1N1 in Texas, state officials must find a way to keep its citizens safe. This past spring, Texas closed schools with confirmed cases of H1N1, but this is not the only policy option. For a second option, Texas can take a more drastic approach and shut down all schools and public facilities in districts with cases of H1N1. It is also possible to keep schools open, while only sending home infected children. This third option allows most children to stay in school and stay safe.

Background & Problem Statement

In March of 2009, a new strand of influenza called H1N1 started spreading throughout Mexico. People panicked, flocking to hospitals, and Mexico responded by closing all schools and public facilities. Naturally, we began to prepare for the virus to spread across the border. The first case came in late April 2009 at Steele High School. This marked the beginning of the first flu pandemic in 40 years. Little was known about H1N1 at first, but it spread quickly and was also relatively mild.

In 2005, the Bush Administration put together guidelines for pandemic cases like H1N1. It laid out how federal, state, and local governments should handle these emergencies. The Texas Department of State Health Services (DSHS) decided within the first few days after the first H1N1 case was confirmed that the pandemic was a Category 5, the most severe rating. Based on this assumption, and with the recommendation of the Centers for Disease Control and Prevention (CDC), many counties throughout Texas closed their schools and cancelled inter-district activities. 500,000 students had their school year disrupted and there were 5,200 cases of H1N1. As we are about to start the new school year, we must balance the safety and wellbeing of Texas students and with the value of an undisrupted education.

Criteria

Safety: One of the most important roles of government is to ensure the safety of its citizens and their wellbeing is a top priority.

Feasibility: In emergency situations with little time to plan and react, the feasibility of policy is very important. It is not enough for the policy to sound like it would work, it must actually work effectively and efficiently.

Personal Freedom: People should have as much choice as they can without harming society. This includes going where they choose, working when they want, and seeing who they wish.

Alternatives

Alternative 1: Selective School Closures

This is the policy that Texas state officials used this past spring. Many districts shut down schools for two weeks, disrupting 500,000 students' school years. This also means that many parents had to miss work to take care of their children. This policy was meant to keep children from spreading H1N1 to each other at school, but many children simply shifted their interactions to other public spaces like the mall or to each other's houses.

Alternative 2: Widespread Closure of Schools and Public Facilities

In this policy option, every possible closure is utilized. If a total quarantine is desired, then every affected county should shut down all schools, public facilities, and any activities that involve cross district mixing. This option prioritizes the safety of Texan citizens above all else. Though it may seem extreme, if the goal is to keep citizens from each other and especially the infected, this is the most effective way to keep contamination at a minimum.

Alternative 3: School Closures When 10% or More of Students Are Ill

In this policy option, schools would only be closed when 10% or more of the students are ill. This middle ground allows schools to stay open even if children are sick while allowing for school closures in extreme cases. This would allow most students to continue uninterrupted and most parents to continue working.

Recommendation

I recommend that you choose Alternative 3 and only close schools in extreme cases. This option allows families to keep their personal freedom to attend school and extracurricular activities. It is also very feasible because it requires little work on the part of state or local government. Keeping schools open does put more citizens at risk of illness, but with a disease that spreads so quickly, but is relatively mild, an extreme quarantine is not necessary.

Alternative 2, which requires shutting down most of the state, would keep people the safest, but the effects on personal freedom are extreme. It is also not very feasible. Economic activity in Texas would be reduced for a substantial amount of time and it still won't keep people from interacting privately. Alternative 1, which requires that any affected school close, worked in that it kept rates of infection down, but it kept an immense number of students from school. It limited people's personal freedom and was only feasible on a small scale.

Alternative 3 is feasible, allows citizens freedom of choice, and still protects their safety. Going forward, it is the best policy option when responding to H1N1.

Discussion of Example 2

What do you think? Again, the effectiveness of a memo like this can be hard to judge without knowing the technical or political details of the situation. Without that context, let's take the memo at face value and see if it does its job well. Does it clearly lay out the decision to the decision maker? Are the trade-offs evident? Are government officials in Texas ready to make this decision?

Let's start by discussing what the author does well. First, she uses the headings to create a clear road map of the memo. Each one of them has a descriptive title, including the criteria that are pulled out from the alternatives (options) section and discussed separately. Second, her short paragraphs in both sections allow the reader to move through her analysis quickly. Finally, she also keeps her alternatives section clean by moving the discussion of the trade-offs to the recommendation section.

So these elements work well. What could she have improved? Alignment is one area. Alternative 1 discusses the drawbacks to parents of children missing school, but that theme isn't touched on in the others, even though there would be a clear impact on parents in each course of action. Another area is the content of the background: Why does the reader need to know about H1N1 coming from Mexico? That background doesn't set up the rest of the case and could be cut.

Example 3: Raising Virginia's Felony Larceny Threshold

For our final example, let's take a look at a criminal justice issue: felony larceny thresholds. Simply put, each state chooses a cash value that divides petty larceny (or small theft) from felony larceny. This distinction matters because a felony conviction carries much higher consequences for the convicted including higher fines, more jail time, and in some states loss of voting rights. This threshold varies from state to state and is therefore often under debate. This memo steps into that debate. Take a look.

To: Del. William Howell, Speaker of the Virginia House of Delegates

From: David Smith, Legislative Aide

Date: October 9, 2016

Re: Raising Virginia's Felony Larceny Threshold

Executive Summary: Virginia's $200 felony larceny threshold is the lowest in the nation. As a result, criminals in Virginia often receive felony charges for crimes that other states would consider misdemeanors. The General Assembly last updated Virginia's felony larceny threshold in 1980 and bills have been introduced to raise the threshold many times since. These attempts have all been successfully blocked in large part by retailers' groups, who fear that raising the threshold will increase shoplifting. *Virginia should raise the felony larceny threshold to $585, index the threshold for inflation, and include a specialized statute to increase the petit larceny punishment for stealing from a retailer.*

Background: Felony Larceny in Virginia: Virginia's felony larceny threshold is $200, the lowest in the country and well below the national average of $1,005. The General Assembly last updated Virginia's threshold in 1980 when they raised it from $100.6 to $200 in 1980, which is equivalent to approximately $585 today.

In Virginia, felony larceny charges contribute significantly to the felon population. From 2008 to 2015, the average number of felony sentencing events in which larceny was the most serious offense was about 5,500. In all other states except New Jersey, many of those convictions would have been considered misdemeanors. Many studies show that having a felony greatly limits the opportunities of people returning to their communities after incarceration as felons often face barriers to housing, employment, and education once they return from prison or jail.

For the past decade, lawmakers have worked to raise Virginia's felony larceny threshold. In the 2015 General Assembly session alone, both the Virginia House and Senate introduced bills (HB 1369 and SB 1234) that would have raised the felony larceny threshold to $500.80. The Virginia Retail Federation and the Virginia Retail Merchants Association successfully blocked each bill. As this issue will likely come up again in the next legislative session, this memo explores Virginia's options for changing its felony threshold.

Option 1: Keep Virginia's felony larceny threshold at $200.

This option maintains the status quo, keeping Virginia's felony larceny threshold at its current $200.

Pros:

- *Supported by powerful advocacy groups:* The Virginia Retail Merchants Association and the Virginia Retail Federation support this option.

- *Falling burden of felony convictions:* Policies across the state have lessened the consequences of a felony larceny conviction. This year, Gov. McAuliffe has worked to restore voting rights to all felons. Further, several cities have removed questions about prior convictions on city job applications. Both lower the impact of a felony conviction.

Cons:

- *Current policy doesn't reflect original intent:* Virginia's felony larceny threshold is much more severe than lawmakers intended when they raised it from $100 to $200 in 1980. $100 in 1980 is worth $292.30 today.

- *High costs:* In 2008, the Virginia Department of Corrections estimated that increasing the felony larceny threshold to $500 would save $3.5 million in prison bed costs in 2013 alone.

Option 2: Raise the felony larceny threshold & index to inflation with retail carve out.

This option would raise the larceny threshold to $585, the equivalent of $200 in 1980. Further, it would include a provision to index the threshold for inflation. To make this change less objectionable to opponents, a special provision is included to punish stealing from a store.

Pros:

- *Reduced costs:* According to the Justice Policy Institute, raising the felony larceny threshold from $200 to $600 could save Virginia approximately $22 million over six years.

- *Reduced burden of felony conviction:* Raising the threshold to $585 would reduce the number of low-level larceny offenders up for felony conviction.

- *Inflation indexing keeps limit in line with original intent:* An indexing measure will maintain the current intent of the law over time.

- *Retail carve out reduces political opposition:* The Virginia Retail Merchants Association and the Virginia Retail Federation are staunch opponents of efforts to raise the threshold but a carve out may reduce opposition.

Cons:

- *Burden shift to local jails:* Local jails see more misdemeanor offenders because they are no longer felons.

- *Carve out privileges businesses over individuals:* Current law treats stealing from individuals the same as from businesses. Punishing theft from businesses more severely implies that individuals' property is less valuable than business property.

- *May increase theft:* Lower punishments may result in higher crime rates. However, the DCJS finds no conclusive evidence that neighboring states saw crime increases when they raised their larceny thresholds.

Recommendation:

I recommend Option 2, raise the felony larceny threshold to $585 and index the threshold for inflation. Option 2 reduces policy drift and saves the state money by reducing the number of felons. At the same time, you should work to educate the Virginia Retail Federation and Virginia Retail Merchants Association, about evidence that raising the limit does not increase theft.

Discussion of Example 3

What do you think? Let's start by discussing what the author does well. This memo is straightforward in its language and argumentation. Readers can get through it quickly. Part of this is because the issue is relatively straightforward, but notice how the writing helps. First, the executive summary is helpfully written. If you've read the executive summary, you really have the bones of the argument. The remainder fills in the details, but it ends with a clear takeaway, helpfully italicized in case you were tempted to skip over it!

Second, she takes the memo format and breaks it up even more than the previous example. Here, the pros and cons of each option are clearly listed separately. The bullets and italicizing mean the reader can get through the argument even more quickly.

So these elements work well. What could she have improved? The end of the background section is a lost opportunity. It ends with, "As this issue will likely come up again in the next legislative session, this memo explores Virginia's options for changing its felony threshold." The end of a section, especially a background section, is a chance to memorably frame the problem. Instead, the author provides a bland overview of the memo halfway through it. She could have used this spot as a chance to highlight the need to win over these interest groups. Or she could have used it as a chance to focus attention on the gap between the intent of the law 40 years ago and how it functions today. Either way, this was a missed opportunity.

Conclusion

The three examples above will have given you a flavor of decision memos. You've seen how they vary within the strict framework by which they are bound. Each example is drawn from a different context and was used for a specific purpose. Now that you have seen a few examples and know the basic principles, it might be helpful for you to search for other examples in your area. After looking at a few of them, you'll have a sense for what works and what doesn't.

As you begin to write your own decision memos, make sure to keep the *thinking* front and center. Once you know the format, following it is easy. Deciding what problem you should focus the reader on, what alternatives you should propose, and how to decide between them—that's hard. As with all genres, the more time you give yourself to think and to get feedback, the better-quality product you'll produce.

Finally, enjoy writing these! Decision memos, by definition, are produced when there is an opportunity to shape policy. Issue briefs and legislative histories lay the groundwork for change, but decision memos are written for the moment of change itself. When you're in the middle of writing one, frustrated by how hard it is, it can be helpful to remember that this is the reason why most people go into public policy; to help make the change on difficult issues to help people. That's work worth doing.

CHECKLIST

Content and Analysis

- Executive summary contains all vital information.
- Background section provides relevant information without unneeded detail.

Background

- Demonstrates thorough and coherent understanding of the problem and its implications.
- Correctly identifies every important issue and provides the precise amount of information for the reader.

Analysis and Recommendations

- Presents clear, distinct, and specific options appropriate to the problem.
- Appropriately analyzes alternatives and counterarguments.
- Final recommendation clearly and logically supported by analysis.
- Analysis aligns across the memo as a whole.

Writing

- Is directed to an intelligent reader unfamiliar with specifics of topic.
- Short, precise, readable sentences that are actor centered.
- Paragraphs are cohesive, coherent, and properly emphasize important ideas.
- Discussion flows logically.
- No grammar or spelling errors.
- No jargon.
- Passes *Washington Post* test.

Document Formatting and Presentation

- Header provides date, contact information, and organization name.
- Helpfully titled.

- Well formatted to enhance clarity by breaking content into sections with clear foci.

- Section headings preview text that follows.

- Appropriate emphasis added.

- Visual cues help draw the reader's eye to the relevant points quickly.

EXERCISES

1. What is the purpose of your decision memo? Why are you writing it now? What has changed in the world that makes this the right time for action?

2. Who is your audience for the decision memo, both in terms of to whom it is addressed and who else might see it? What background will you need to know about your problem?

3. How will you organize your decision memo? How will you incorporate the criteria into it?

4. Create an effective 1–2 page decision memo targeted to a specific decision maker that makes a clear recommendation between different alternative courses of action.

BIBLIOGRAPHY

Bardach, E., & Patashnik, E. M. (2015). *A practical guide for policy analysis: The eight-fold path to more effective problem solving* (5th rev. ed.). Washington, DC: CQ Press.

Cooley, V., & Pennock, A. (2015). Teaching policy analysis through animated films: A Mickey Mouse assignment? *PS: Political Science & Politics, 48*(04), 601–606.

Garfinkle, A. (2012). *Political writing: A guide to the essentials* (1st ed.). New York: Routledge.

Giles, D. W. (2011). *On the frontlines of a pandemic: Texas responds to 2009 novel H1N1 influenza* (case program no. 1940.0). Cambridge, MA: Harvard Kennedy School of Government.

Kraft, M. E., & Furlong, S. R. (2013). *Public policy: Politics, analysis, and alternatives* (4th ed.). Washington, DC: CQ Press.

Rosenthal, B. (1992). *Lead poisoning (A)* (case program no. C14–75–123.0). Cambridge, MA: Harvard Kennedy School of Government.

Shambaugh, G. E., & Weinstein, P. J. (2016). *The art of policymaking: Tools, techniques, and processes in the modern executive branch* (2nd ed.). Washington, DC: CQ Press.

Weimer, D. L., & Vining, A. R. (2017). *Policy analysis: Concepts and practice* (6th ed.). New York: Routledge.

CHAPTER 11

Op-Eds

When you open a newspaper, or read one online, you will see two kinds of content: news articles and opinion pieces. The news of the day comprises the vast majority of content: reporting on what is currently happening with current political drama in Washington, D.C., economic trends in the heartland, or turmoil abroad.

While there is no place for opinions in the news section, there are two places in the paper where opinions are published (Shipley, 2004). In the editorial section, the editorial board of the paper shares its opinions on the major topics of the day. It endorses candidates and derides specific pieces of legislation. In contrast to the news, editorial boards often have a distinctive liberal or conservative slant. They publish their editorials on the editorial page, which you can usually find on the third to last page in the main section.

Opposite the editorial page in a printed paper, on the second to last page of the main section, you will find the opinions of individuals who are not on the editorial board of the paper. These articles are called *op-eds* because they are opposite the editorial page in a printed paper. Op-eds are published with the aim of presenting challenging ideas to the public, ideas that challenge both the public's opinions and the opinions of the editorial board of the newspaper in which they appear. For example, the *New York Times* says the objective of the op-ed section is to:

> afford greater opportunity for exploration of issues and presentation of new insights and new ideas by writers and thinkers who have no institutional connection with The Times and whose views will very frequently be completely divergent from our own. (Tumin, 2017)

With this in mind, major papers employ columnists who represent a diversity of viewpoints (Republicans and Democrats, religious and nonreligious, different racial backgrounds) to produce about half of the op-eds they publish.

The other half of the op-eds newspapers publish come from writers outside the paper who submit op-ed pieces with their perspectives on important issues of the day. Sometimes the paper solicits writers, but most times the op-ed editorial board looks through many articles submitted by the public on topics of the day.

This opening provides public policy advocates a chance to talk to the readers of the paper (possibly hundreds of thousands of them) about their issue directly. Moreover, op-eds don't just educate readers about the facts surrounding an issue; they also ask readers to care about the moral aspects of an issue. They ask readers to decide that the solutions they recommend in the op-ed aren't just technically feasible but also are the right things to do.

The ability to make a moral case for your topic while simultaneously educating the public about the facts of your issue make op-eds a policy genre worth mastering. It's the rare chance you have to shape public debate and discussion on an issue. Let's learn more.

Distinctive Aspects of Op-Eds

Successful op-eds don't simply have a topic (climate change); they have an issue (the adoption of a renewable energy standard) that advocates a clear action people should be for or against (May, 2012). You're not just providing facts about the issue to the reader; you're bringing a slant, a take, and a recommendation.

To do this effectively, you need to know and practice the aspects of op-eds. Like almost all forms of policy writing, op-eds come in many different forms. We'll look at the norms of the format below. But the truth is that while 90% of the op-eds you'll see look like this, a fair number of them don't. The best way to understand what the abnormal ones look like is to start reading op-eds, preferably in several different papers. As you start reading them and then turn to writing your own, I encourage you to keep the guidelines below in mind and then branch out in your own writing once you have a sense of the wide variety of op-ed styles that exist.

Your Values Matter Here

The first distinctive aspect of op-eds is that you're not just allowed— but are encouraged—to bring your values into the writing. There aren't many types of public policy writing where it is appropriate to give your opinion. Most of the time, your job is to provide the facts and, if asked, lay out a reasoned case for any recommendations you might make. These recommendations are carefully made on the basis of objective facts: increasing the mental health budget will enable the Department of Health and Human Services to serve 10,000 more veterans, the new antidiscrimination law will mean 500 more people with disabilities will be hired across the state, or some other factually based argument.

But an op-ed is different. Here you can, and often should, use moral claims in your arguments. It's not just that the new mental health program will serve more veterans; it's that those veterans *deserve* mental health care. They went into harm's way to protect us and now we should protect them. It's *wrong* to discriminate against people with disabilities, so we *should* make laws to protect them. Morality matters in public policy, and op-eds are one of the few places that admit a frank discussion of it.

You Can Be Literary

Another major difference between op-eds and the other genres of policy writing is that they are designed to be written by real people with a

---

Using Social Psychology to Engage the Other Side on Moral Issues

The social psychologist Jonathan Haidt argues that there are five fundamental values present in all human societies: fairness, harm, loyalty, authority, and sanctity (Haidt, 2013). Almost everyone agrees that it is important for public policies to be fair and not to harm others.[1] But there is disagreement between the right and the left on the importance of the other three values. Conservatives resonate much more strongly with appeals to loyalty, authority, and sanctity than do liberals. There is a reason why American flags are so much more common at a NASCAR race than at an academic conference (loyalty), environmental groups have so much trouble working together (authority isn't a value), and conservatives work to keep illegal drugs illegal (they care a lot about the sanctity of the human body).

Understanding these differences can be helpful when trying to frame an issue that cuts across a partisan divide in an op-ed. For example, instead of pitching gun control as an issue that will protect everyone, liberals could try talking more about how gun control could help protect police officers (authority figures). Conservatives could try to interest liberals more in pro-life perspectives by shifting their sanctity-centered rhetoric, with which liberals don't resonate, to discussions of how abortions disproportionately affect minority communities (fairness).[2]

---

[1] Admittedly, "fair" is a complicated concept. See Stone (2011, chap. 2: Equity) for a thoughtful discussion of our various notions of fairness.

[2] For a slightly longer but still quick introduction to the topic, see Haidt's TED Talk (Haidt, n.d.).

point of view on a subject. This means that you can write more conversationally than you might in other contexts. For example, you can write in the first person. And you can use memorable anecdotes from your own personal experience.

Additionally, your writing doesn't have to be in the neutral tone that is required in other policy writing. You can have opinions and express them. You can use judgmental words like *inappropriate, suitable,* or *luxurious.* Your op-ed should take a clear, provocative stand about how policy surrounding your issue should be different. Op-eds are not about being balanced and nuanced. Rather, they are about advocating for a particular policy position. To do this, you should briefly acknowledge the viewpoints of the other side before rebutting them, but you shouldn't give them more than one or two brief paragraphs. The op-ed is about asserting your opinions, not theirs.

Finally, if you are feeling particularly literary, you can use irony, wit, paradox, or metaphor—just be careful not to be mean spirited or ugly in your writing (Garfinkle, 2012). You're unlikely to change minds by demeaning people or being ugly toward things that are important to them.

While Your Opinion Matters, the Facts Still Count

While op-eds should be peppy and opinionated, it is also crucially important that they be factually correct. Newspapers have a responsibility to publish credible points of view. A good op-ed contains lots of solid facts, even if they are not cited in the final version of the paper. For example, the *New York Times* often requires 25 citations for an op-ed. Yours need not be that well researched, but your submitted op-ed should cite a variety of solid sources, even though they won't appear in the final, printed product.

Balance the Prescriptive and the Descriptive

The rough rule of thumb for op-eds is two-thirds descriptive material (history, facts, anecdotes, etc.) and one-third prescriptive material. Use the descriptive material to explain the issue to the audience. For example, if you start with an anecdote about discrimination against a particular disabled person, then explain to the reader how the anecdote is part of a broader trend. Use the prescriptive material to explain why it matters and what should be done about it. You can put the prescriptive material at the front of the op-ed, at the back, or sandwiched in the middle, depending on which works best.

Create a Lede (Narrative Hook)
That Grabs Your Audience

Like all public policy writing, you don't have the luxury of a captive audience. Newspaper readers are thumbing through the paper over breakfast or skimming the website during a break at work. To get them interested in your topic it's important to have a *lede* (newspaper speak for a narrative hook) that is reflected in the title as well as in the first paragraph. Think, *What's the newsworthy element of this topic that most people haven't seen? How am I going to interest them in it?*

There are lots of effective techniques for doing this. One of the easiest is to *look for a timely tie-in to your issue.* What is hot in the current news cycle? A recent chemical spill in the news is a chance to revisit the consequences of a recent regulatory action. What will be discussed soon? If you're writing about discrimination, readers might be particularly interested around August 6, the anniversary of the Civil Rights Act of 1965. If you're writing about homelessness, look to tie into a study that was just released with shocking or encouraging results. Finally, you could use a current pop culture reference to draw people in (Op-Ed Project, n.d.). *House of Cards* might be a nice lede for an op-ed on political corruption. Or Apu, the convenience store owner in *The Simpsons,* might connect with readers when discussing how South Asians are stereotyped.

Another effective way to draw readers into an op-ed is to write from a deeply personal experience, so *look for a way to use personal experience and personal voice.* What got you interested in the issue? What did you experience as you researched it? How could these personal experiences tie into broader issues for society? For example, moving to a new state might give you fresh perspective on how inefficient government might be. An encounter with a bully or bigot might serve as an entrée into an op-ed on racial tensions. If you had a harrowing health experience, you might be well positioned to write about the need for health education. Consider using your personal experiences to capture the audience's attention.

Limitations of the Genre

While op-eds allow freedoms that other genres do not, there are some tight stylistic restrictions by which you have to abide. First and most important, there are strict word limits. Major papers never accept op-eds over 850 words, and many papers have a 700-word limit. Make sure your op-ed fits in the framework of the paper to which you are submitting.

Second, long paragraphs are particularly bad form because the columns of a newspaper make them look unending. Instead, limit all of your paragraphs to just a few sentences and strive to create really short paragraphs; even the occasional one-sentence paragraph will do (Garfinkle,

2012). For similar formatting reasons, figures, tables, headers, and other formatting tools are out as well. Finally, op-eds are the wrong place for a lot of quotes. Use one short quote per op-ed at most, two if you absolutely must have them (Garfinkle, 2012). People are reading the piece for what you have to say, not somebody else.

Example Op-Eds

While all op-eds need to abide by the principles listed above, there is still a lot of leeway in how they are written. As a result, no two op-eds are the same, and wildly different ones can be successful. Like issue briefs, this lack of a firm format can feel either paralyzing or freeing, depending on your temperament. But before you make a decision about which camp you fall in, let's take a look at a couple of examples so you can get a sense of the genre.

Example 1: "Don't Get Sick Past July"

The first example appears below. Take a few minutes to read over it and mark up what stands out to you. As you go through it, keep the norms of an op-ed listed earlier in the chapter in mind. Think about where the writer followed them and where she deviated. Consider if these choices made her more effective in educating you about the topic and agreeing with her about her conclusions.

"Don't Get Sick Past July"

Continued lack of funding stains a failing health system for America's first people

Evelyn Immonen, Policy Analyst
November 13, 2017

Growing up on a reservation, there are a few rules you learn to live by. If you've got any elderly relatives, make sure they live with an able-bodied adult and a car with a tank full of gas, because the ambulance isn't going to make it. If you want an appointment, call at 7am the day of. Days when the Indian Health Service is doing free dental sealants for kids, make sure you're in line with any nieces or nephews you've got. But most important of all, don't get sick past July.

That's because the Indian Health Service (IHS) receives a set amount of money each year to take care of 2.2 million people—no matter the need. American Indians have the lowest health outcomes of any population in the country. Yet compared to other populations, funding is nowhere close to where it needs to be in order to address the needs of those who were here first.

American Indians today have a life expectancy of 4.4 years less than the population at large. They die from alcoholism at five times the rate of the average American, nearly twice the rate from diabetes, and are 138% more likely to die of unintentional injuries.

If that's not enough to argue for a better funded health system, then perhaps fatal disease rates are: mortality rates from cervical cancer are 1.2 times the average, from pneumonia are 1.4 times the average, and maternal deaths are 1.4 times the average. Many of these diseases would be preventable with early, regular care—the care that's being put on hold when resources are scarce.

A GAO report in 2016 on patient care at the IHS was prompted by congressional reports that IHS patients were made to wait for months on end for primary care and days even in emergencies. The GAO exposed that the agency doesn't have metrics in place to assess wait times, let alone improve them. As a result, IHS has implemented a minimum wait time of 28 days for primary care and 48 hours for emergency care. While measurements won't come in for another several years, the agency's ability to single-handedly deliver quality care with a cost ceiling is unknown.

When the government doesn't have enough funding to support the next patient, the IHS implements a waitlist, reprioritizes care, or goes into debt. That debt keeps growing, not only in the direct costs of providing health care, but also from the wear and tear of facilities. Deficiencies in resources to address ongoing operations, such as equipment, facilities, and maintenance, get added to backlog expenditures. The backlog is currently $515 billion.

The Indian Health Service, like other partner agencies including the Bureau of Indian Affairs, emerged from a trust relationship with the federal government, where American Indian tribes are both self-sovereign governments and wards of the state. The visual image often called to mind is indifferent Indian agents distributing rations as tribal members wait in line, hungry and cold. Since before the 1800s where at least one set of rations included smallpox-infected blankets, American Indians have remained behind in health. Smallpox and tuberculosis evolved into alcoholism, diabetes, and cancer, but the modern health care system ultimately retains the same character as those original rations.

The government continues to fall short of its responsibilities. At the current rate of IHS funding, the government spends $2,849 per patient, compared to health care spending equivalent to $7,717 for the general population. Yes, even prisoners receive more funding than Natives.

This remains true despite evidence that poor health outcomes increase costs in issue areas like job employment, education, and housing. Poor housing conditions are associated with a range of negative health outcomes, including mental health, injuries, respiratory illnesses, and lead poisoning. For American Indians, 30% of housing is overcrowded, with as many as 20 family members packed into a single home. While overcrowded conditions might exacerbate health conditions, they also may be due to them as relatives are afraid of leaving family members uncared for.

Now, with an ongoing debate in Congress over health care and budgeting and the Thanksgiving holidays around the corner, it's more important than ever to discuss that what the average American has to be thankful for remains a pipedream for American Indians relying on the Indian Health Service. A system that was already underfunded is being severely damaged by ongoing sequestration and budget caps. Left as is, the Indian Health Service will continue to fall victim to the fiscal constraints of the federal budget, unable to provide the benefits promised to its beneficiaries.

Discussion of Example 1

Whew. What do you think? First of all, it's worth acknowledging that the op-ed deals with a particularly heavy topic, especially if you are a Native American or have friends or family that are part of a tribe. Part of what makes it feel heavy is the writing helps you feel the moral weight of the topic. The author points out that the Indian Health Service (IHS) violates some of our key values. It doesn't seem fair that the government spends $2,849 per patient, compared to health care spending equivalent to $7,717 for the general population. It doesn't seem fair that Native Americans die at such higher rates than others. It also seems harmful to cut off health care in July. As you can see, the author does a nice job of making moral points about the dysfunction of the IHS and buttresses this moral issue with lots of facts and figures.

The second thing worth noticing is how effective the lede is. The author immediately grabs your interest with a series of anecdotes that you likely haven't thought of, even though they make sense, and then surprises you with a final one that doesn't seem to make sense. This disconnect then motivates you to read the rest of the article to understand it, which is also why it makes for such an effective title. She also uses the lede to imply that she knows a lot about growing up on a reservation. The lede is personal, but the op-ed quickly turns to the larger problem. It's an effective strategy here.

What could the author have done better? My main critique is that the author pulls her punch at the end. She's convinced me that this situation is morally appalling and should change, but she hasn't recommended how. She should have seized her chance to ask for something more than a discussion. She should have asked for change. The writing could also improve in a couple of spots (as you may have noticed). Perhaps I should send her a copy of this book. . . .

Example 2: "Amazon's HQ3 Won't Be in the U.S. Unless Something Changes"

For the second example, let's turn to a different issue in health care: economic development. At the time I was writing this chapter, Amazon was deciding where in the United States to locate its second headquarters (HQ2). Cities around the country put in bids, hoping they could lure Amazon to locate in their region. With the newspapers swirling with gossip about the decision, the politically focused *The Hill* published the following op-ed (Gray-Little & Nelms, 2018). Take a few minutes to read it through. As you do so, keep the norms of an op-ed discussed earlier in the chapter in mind. Think about where the writers followed them and where they deviated. Consider if these choices made them more effective in educating you about their topic and agreeing with them about their conclusions.

Amazon's HQ3 Won't Be in the US Unless Something Changes

March 21, 2018

By Bernadette Gray-Little and David W. Nelms.

Amazon is nearing a decision on where it will locate its second headquarters— HQ2. The company is planning to spend more than $5 billion and eventually create up to 50,000 high-paying jobs.

The announcement will bring an end to a closely watched competition that sparked important debates about what it would take to win. But it's not too early to start thinking about HQ3.

Amazon listed specific criteria for selecting the winner, such as: the site and buildings, including specific tax incentives to build them; transportation networks; culture and quality of life; and a labor force with a strong pipeline of talent.

The company gave particular emphasis to sites with a strong university system, asking cities to identify universities and community colleges with relevant degrees and quantify the number of graduates who have attained those degrees over the last three years.

After Cincinnati's regional development spokesperson, Ed Loyd, received a briefing on why Cincinnati did not make it into the final 20, he stated, "Talent was the most important factor out of everything they looked at."

Amazon's 20 finalist cities have a robust high-tech talent pool. Between 2013 and 2015 many of these regions created 10,000 to even 31,000 new high-tech jobs, with many witnessing double-digit growth over this two-year period.

Given Amazon's hiring record, it's not surprising that the quality of the labor force that will surround HQ2 is the top priority.

Many of Amazon's top decision makers—and, indeed, the workforce that has made the company so successful—graduated from colleges and universities five, 10 or 15 years ago when the United States still ranked high internationally in college-degree attainment.

America's international ranking has been deteriorating rapidly, not so much because the United States has dropped substantially, but because other countries have made enormous investments in higher education and are graduating new entrants into the labor force at much higher rates.

In 1995, the United States was first among OECD member countries in the number of college graduates. By 2012, the U.S. dropped to No. 19 out of the 28 OECD countries.

In five years, it is likely that Amazon will be looking for a third headquarters, or HQ3. Will the company be able to restrict its next competition to North America? It is doubtful, unless the United States gets serious about higher education.

New data from the Lumina Foundation show there were small gains in degree attainment in 2016, but persistent gaps remain by race and ethnicity, with the fastest growing populations lagging the most. Our nation's diversity is our greatest competitive advantage, but only if we provide opportunities to grow talent and career mobility.

If we are serious about ensuring that Amazon's HQ2 and HQ3 remain in North America, it is time to invest in higher education.

Only 10 of the leading high-tech cities of the world are in North America, and three of those are in Canada. Unlike the U.S., our northern neighbor continues to be a world leader in higher-education graduation rates.

Amazon will have a hard time denying the other top 25 high-tech cities in the world—such as Berlin, Shenzhen, Bangalore, Stockholm, Seoul and Hong Kong—from competing for the HQ3 site. Doing so would significantly lower the bar for the quality and quantity of high-tech talent.

A group of industry, higher education and government leaders on the National Commission on Financing 21st Century Higher Education published recommendations for how the U.S. can attain an internationally competitive 60 percent postsecondary graduation rate.

Supported by the Lumina Foundation, the commission identified specific policy recommendations designed to increase degree attainment, including the following:

- Realign incentives and retarget existing funds to make the entire system more affordable.

- Create innovative models in the delivery of postsecondary education that can make the entire system more productive.

- Identify options from all levels of government and the private sector to increase funding for higher education.

Now is the perfect time to embrace this international challenge and make higher education a national priority before Amazon's HQ3 goes to Europe or Asia—and is followed by Google, Apple and other firms that require a highly educated, high-tech labor pool.

Bernadette Gray-Little is chancellor of the University of Kansas. David W. Nelms is chairman and CEO of Discover Financial. Gray-Little and Nelms serve on the nonpartisan National Commission on Financing 21st Century Higher Education, formed by the University of Virginia's Miller Center of Public Affairs (@Miller_Center).

Discussion of Example 2

What do you think? The first thing you might notice is the pivot. The authors begin with a topic that everyone was talking about at the time (HQ2) and use it to discuss what they want to discuss. HQ2 was such a big deal that cities and states made promotional videos and launched marketing campaigns aimed at securing the 50,000 new jobs and $5,000,000,000 in investment. The authors use the enthusiasm for HQ2 to focus readers on one particular criterion in Amazon's decision process: higher education. It's a great hook.

Second, you might notice that this piece is chock-full of effectively cited facts and figures. International education statistics, a quote from a stakeholder, and a major new public policy report all feature prominently. The authors use these sources to buttress the logical argument that flows from the beginning to the end of their op-ed.

Third, notice how the authors aren't personal in this piece at all. They don't even hint at a personal connection, despite their being a university president and a CEO. Instead, their comments about the current state of affairs are aimed squarely at the facts on the ground. They put the question, "What should America do about our higher-ed system?" front and center, and then they provide solutions.

Finally, notice that the pairing of the authors might have turned your head when you got to the end and understood who they were. A university president and the CEO of a major corporation don't always agree on the same things, so people pay attention when they do. This unusual combination helps strengthen their case. Overall, it's well done.

Example 3: "The Dignity of Choice in Terminal Illness"

For the third example, let's look at an op-ed on one last issue in health care: physician-assisted suicide, alternately known as death with dignity. Again, a heavy issue.

Take a few minutes to read it through. As you go through it, keep the norms of an op-ed listed earlier in the chapter in mind. Think about where the writer followed them and where she deviated. Consider if these choices made her more effective in educating you about the topic and agreeing with her about her conclusions.

"The Dignity of Choice in Terminal Illness"

By: Mary Greeson

I'll never forget that Thursday morning phone call. "I'm in the ambulance with your father. He can't breathe—you should come up."

That weekend ended my father's five-year struggle with stage-IV colon cancer. Doctors ran out of treatment options after four long years, and the final year of my father's life was one of seemingly endless pain. A Virginia resident, opioid-based pain management was his only option, one he refused.

Physician-assisted suicide could have been another option for my father. Also known as physician aid in dying or death with dignity, physician-assisted suicide provides terminally ill patients access to the knowledge and means to end their lives. Patients must be terminally ill with a prognosis of six months or less to live to qualify for physician-assisted suicide.

My father was diagnosed with stage-IV colon cancer on his 50th birthday. He started chemotherapy treatments one week later, and over the next four years, he endured seven rounds of chemo and five surgeries. He fought hard to beat this disease, but to no avail.

When doctors gently suggested that additional treatments were unlikely to work, my father sought second and third opinions. Stage-IV colon cancer has an average five-year survival rate of 12%, and we were sure he was one of the lucky ones.

It took my father weeks to accept the prognosis. Then his doctor offered him a morphine prescription for regular daily use. "This will ease your discomfort," his doctor said. My father refused.

He could accept the limits of modern medicine, but he was not ready to give up control of his body and his life.

Morphine causes drowsiness and brain fog, so he would not have been able to continue doing the things he loved while taking it. Without his work, his hobbies, his quality of life would have diminished. To maintain some degree of normalcy, he chose to suffer.

There is little dignity to a slow and painful death. My father could work without morphine, until the pain prevented him from driving, and then even riding in a car. My father could work on his programming hobby until the pain made him too dizzy to sit for more than 20 minutes. My father could read his favorite books, until the pain blurred the words on the page.

Through all of this, you must be wondering why he didn't fill the morphine prescription. I know I asked myself this question every time I saw him struggle to move. And one day I asked him. "After every surgery, I was given morphine during recovery. It made me feel like I was losing myself, and I don't ever want to feel that way again."

Feeling in control was important to my father, as it is for many other patients with terminal illness. Indeed, records in Oregon and Washington show that patients seeking physician-assisted suicide are primarily motivated by autonomy and dignity rather than pain. In a study of Oregonians requesting physician-assisted suicide, 19.6% reported filing the request to "feel in control."

To this day, almost three years later, I wonder what choice my father would have made if physician-assisted suicide was available as an option. Today, Virginia is one of 45 states in the U.S. which does not authorize physician-assisted suicide. Five states, beginning with Oregon in 1997, have authorized physician-assisted suicide in response to public demand. A 2016 Gallup poll reported that 69% of Americans support physician-assisted suicide.

Some critics of physician-assisted suicide accuse patients of taking the easy way out, or worry that vulnerable populations will be euthanized instead of empowered. However, existing statutes have explicit requirements about a patient's mental and emotional fitness, and often require multiple requests to be submitted before a patient is considered for physician-assisted suicide. Furthermore, 42% of patients in California who obtained prescriptions to end their lives chose not to use them. Merely having the option empowered them to make the right choice for their end-of-life care.

We live in a country where citizens are empowered to make their dreams a reality, through hard work and perseverance. Why then, when a patient has fought hard and lost, are brain fog or excruciating pain the only options?

Discussion of Example 3

Again, whew. What a heavy topic. Every one of us has relatives and friends who have taken this journey, and many of us have walked in the same shoes as this author with our own relatives.[3] That's part of what makes the author's lede so effective. It is deeply personal, and the op-ed as a whole is much more personal than the other two examples. Here, her personal anecdote is woven together with the policy issue itself. Her experience with her father's death is deeply personal, and she uses it to connect the readers to the issue in a deeply personal way. Whether or not you agree with her, it's hard not to consider her point of view, as personal as it is.

This op-ed is also effective because the author plays by the rules of the genre. She addresses an issue and takes a stand. The argument, as personal as it is, uses facts and figures to connect it to the broader experience of the country. She acknowledges one of the main objections of some opponents and provides evidence to challenge it. She has a clear prescription.

---

[3] I highly recommend surgeon Atul Gawande's thoughtful and helpful book, *Being Mortal: Illness, Medicine and What Matters in the End*, as we walk with others or take that final journey ourselves (Gawande, 2015).

Where could the author have been more effective? My main complaint is that the writing needs some polishing—in this case, the structure of her argument. This is best seen at the end of the last paragraph, which lands awkwardly, just as we saw in the first example. Rather than ending with an appeal for "hard work and perseverance"—themes she hasn't developed in the op-ed—she could have wrapped back around to her father's death and her walking with him in his pain. That would have carried the deeply personal theme of the op-ed back full circle.

Conclusion: Writing (and Publishing!) Your Own Op-Ed

As you've seen from the three examples, while op-eds can differ greatly in terms of style and topic, following some core rules is key to successfully engaging the readers of a newspaper with your ideas. The good news is that you can write one as well.[4]

Once you've written one, you'll have to follow a few more steps to get it published. The first step is to select a paper to which to submit. Most important is to figure out who you want to sway about your issue. If you're interested in affecting policy in your city, don't submit first to national newspapers, even though they might have bigger names; instead, write for your city's major paper. Not only will it be more likely to be read by the people who matter, you're also much more likely to be selected for publication, as national newspapers receive hundreds of submissions a week—much more than the average city paper.

Most papers have directions about how to submit op-eds on their websites. Follow their directions for submission, taking care to be professional about your submission (i.e., follow their rules and be polite). One professional best practice is to submit your op-ed to only one paper at a time. If you haven't heard back within a week, then you should assume it won't be used and you are free to submit it to other places.[5]

Don't be discouraged if your op-ed doesn't get picked up by the first paper to which you submit it. If the *Los Angeles Times* isn't interested (circulation ~800,000), the *Sacramento Bee* (circulation ~300,000) might be. If it is picked up, you'll work with the op-ed editor and their staff on your writing so that your points will shine through on the printed page.

---

[4] Every year I ask my students to write them for class and every year a student has decided to submit their op-ed and had it published in one of the major newspapers in the state.

[5] Hall (2013) has a nice piece about how the inside of the submissions process works at the *New York Times*.

Finally, don't be discouraged, if even when published you don't feel like your op-ed changed the trajectory of your issue. Even professional op-ed columnists have trouble getting their audience to engage in important stories (Kristof, 2017). Remember, you're educating and persuading with an op-ed. Raising the profile of your issue is a long process, and an op-ed is one step in laying the groundwork for effective change. Use your op-ed to keep creating change on your problem, one step at a time.

CHECKLIST

Content

- Have a clear vision of what unique and provocative perspective you're bringing to your issue.
- Create an attention-grabbing title.
- Have a narrative hook to capture the audience's attention.
- Stay within the word limit for the paper to which you are submitting (usually between 700–850 words).
- Include sources to support your claims.

Writing

- Directed to an intelligent reader unfamiliar with specifics of topic.
- Short, precise, readable sentences that are actor centered.
- Paragraphs are cohesive, coherent, and properly emphasize important ideas.
- Discussion flows logically.
- No grammar or spelling errors.
- No jargon.
- Passes *Washington Post* test.

EXERCISES

1. Identify a newspaper where it would be helpful for you to publish an op-ed on your topic. Why is this the right paper for an op-ed written by you on your topic?

2. Read three to five op-eds published recently in that newspaper (preferably on your topic, if you can). What do you notice about them? Who wrote them? What makes them effective or ineffective? Do they represent the point of view that you bring to the issue?

3. Write an op-ed on your issue employing the principles from this chapter. Decide what kind of lede you want to use and which facts will be most helpful in providing evidence for your claims. Decide if you want to use one of the moral foundations discussed earlier in the chapter as a framework for your argument.

4. Submit your op-ed to a newspaper.

5. Write an op-ed that argues against yours. What moral claims would you make? What evidence would you marshal?

BIBLIOGRAPHY

Garfinkle, A. (2012). *Political writing: A guide to the essentials* (1st ed.). New York: Routledge.

Gawande, A. (2015). *Being mortal: Illness, medicine and what matters in the end* (int. ed.). New York: Picador.

Gray-Little, B., & Nelms, D. W. (2018, March 21). Amazon's HQ3 won't be in the US unless something changes. *The Hill*. Retrieved May 4, 2018, from http://thehill.com/opinion/education/379532-amazons-hq3-wont-be-in-the-us-unless-something-changes

Haidt, J. (2013). *The righteous mind: Why good people are divided by politics and religion* (reprint ed.). New York: Vintage.

Haidt, J. (n.d.). *The moral roots of liberals and conservatives*. Retrieved May 4, 2018, from https://www.ted.com/talks/jonathan_haidt_on_the_moral_mind

Hall, T. (2013, October 13). Op-ed and you. *New York Times*. Retrieved May 4, 2018, from https://www.nytimes.com/2013/10/14/opinion/op-ed-and-you.html

Kristof, N. (2017, December 21). My worst columns. *New York Times*. Retrieved May 4, 2018, from https://www.nytimes.com/2017/12/21/opinion/nicholas-kristof-worst-columns.html

May, T. (2012). *Op-eds: Writing for social change* (Electronic Hallway). Seattle, WA: Evans School of Public Affairs, University of Washington.

Op-Ed Project. *Op-ed writing: Tips and tricks*. (n.d.). Retrieved January 3, 2018, from https://www.theopedproject.org/oped-basics/

Shipley, D. (2004, February 1). And now a word from op-ed. *New York Times*. Retrieved May 4, 2018, from https://www.nytimes.com/2004/02/01/opinion/01SHIP.html

Stone, D. (2011). *Policy paradox: The art of political decision making* (3rd ed.). New York: W. W. Norton & Company.

Tumin, R. (2017, December 3). The op-ed pages, explained. *New York Times*. Retrieved May 4, 2018, from https://www.nytimes.com/2017/12/03/insider/opinion-op-ed-explainer.html

Legislative Testimony and Public Comment: Writing to Persuade the Government

Every day, policy makers face decisions about new policies, even the simplest of which have far-reaching repercussions. They learn about these repercussions through feedback from individual citizens and organized interest groups. A good policy-making process invites the perspectives of all of the stakeholders affected by an issue, and does so in a formal way in which stakeholders can anticipate and participate.

These stakeholders then help decision makers understand the consequences of their policies, both legislative and regulatory, by testifying and providing public comments. In legislative bodies, committee hearings provide a formal space where elected officials hear testimony from various stakeholders about what a policy will mean for them and why they support or oppose it. In regulatory processes, decision makers hear from stakeholders through hearings and by soliciting written public comments.

For example, imagine a city council member hears from a constituent who couldn't find parking on his street after work and had to walk several blocks home with his groceries and children in the driving snow. Appalled, the council member drafts an ordinance mandating that parking permits be distributed to residents of the neighborhood and nonresidents be banned from parking on the streets. Like almost all legislation put forward, it's a well-intentioned attempt to solve a real problem.

The rub is any given solution needs a lot of consideration. It might just affect the one problem or it might have many secondary effects. Take the parking permit system as an example. As soon as the ordinance is introduced, the council member will find a surprising number of people with opinions. Local businesses will worry about how customers from other neighborhoods will find parking to visit their stores. Other local residents will wonder where their out-of-town guests will park when they come to visit. Police might balk at handing out parking tickets as yet another distraction from their mission to keep people safe. City hall officials might wonder how they will check to make sure people who get the passes actually live in the neighborhood. Other council members will wonder what other program will lose money to fund this one. Will taxes be raised?!

This might seem like a lot of conflict over a small issue, but at its best, this is how government works: All of the impacted parties help the decision makers understand the consequences of a policy before they make a decision.

Because new issues and ideas like this come up every day, policy makers need dependable systems to educate themselves. Testimony and written comments are two of the most common ways stakeholders communicate with decision makers in a system.

Distinctive Aspects of Testimony and Comment

The goals of submitting either testimony or public comment are to educate and persuade policy makers.[1] Your first goal is to educate them by providing information they might not yet have considered. Often, policy makers simply need to hear the perspectives of people the policy impacts. They need to know how this policy will affect you. For example, they might not understand how creating a permitted parking system would affect students attending a local college in the neighborhood. Providing testimony at a hearing is a chance to educate them.

You can also help educate decision makers by offering expert perspective on the topic. If you work for the local Chamber of Commerce, then you can help decision makers understand the impact of the parking permit system on small businesses. If you know the science, you might be able to point out that fewer cars in a neighborhood might result in less air pollution and fewer children with asthma. Decision makers might not even know about these impacts, but you can tell them.

When you educate and inform policy makers in these settings, keep in mind the distinctive aspects of testimony and comment that will help make you effective.

You're an Advocate, Not a Neutral Policy Analyst

While you are aiming to educate decision makers, your second goal is to persuade them to adopt or reject a particular policy to help the group of people you are representing. Sometimes your recommendation will help everyone, but more likely you will be arguing that they should help your group while hurting others. A parking permit system might help alleviate parking problems for local residents, but it will cause harm for people who drive into the neighborhood to work.

---

[1] Depending on the setting, you may have the opportunity to read your testimony out loud or you may simply be able to submit a written copy. Even if you know you will be able to read out loud, it's a good idea to have a polished, written version to submit for the record.

When you advocate for something publicly, you should be prepared for other people to disagree with you, sometimes strenuously.[2] It is, of course, helpful if you can propose a compromise solution that solves everyone's problems. Depending on the issue, it might be the case that no one has ever thought to propose the solution that you see. Talk about it!

As an advocate, it's important to argue with all of the tools at your disposal. Provide data to underscore your arguments. Talk about what happened when this policy was tried in a different community. Show them what scientists say about the impact of the policy. Like any good argument, it's helpful to acknowledge the perspective of the other side. Acknowledging where the evidence the other side brings to the table is accurate before discussing why it isn't applicable in your situation is much more persuasive than simply bringing your own set of facts to the conversation (Regulations.gov, n.d.).

Finally, whatever ends you advocate for, remember that advocates need to be scrupulously honest. Decision makers have to be able to trust your figures, arguments, data, and assertions. You don't have to make the argument for the other side, but everything you say has to be 100% true, both in fact and in spirit.

Understand the Context

Like any writing you do in public policy, it is crucial to understand the context in which your document will be read. For example, it is important to understand the other stakeholders who will be giving input. If you are one of five witnesses at a hearing, you should understand what material they will be covering so you can decide what niche your testimony should fill. Likewise, if you are educating regulatory policy makers who have been working on a topic for years and are steeped in the science, then your testimony can be more technical than if you are writing for legislators who haven't encountered the topic before the hearing.

Memo Style

Both testimony and written comments are best written in a memo style.[3] Like all memos, it's important to have the correct headers with the requisite "To," "From," "Date," and "Subject" lines. Particularly when

---

[2] Creating change is hard. It is hard to accomplish, and it is hard to experience other people's anger in the process. I highly recommend *Leadership on the Line* (Heifetz & Linsky, 2017) as an introduction to how to create change and endure the inevitable pushback that follows.

[3] Some testimony and some written comments are submitted in a letter format. The header is slightly different than that of a memo, but the rest of the format is largely the same. Look at testimony and comments in your issue area for examples.

giving feedback on bills that change as they move through committees, it's important to note that your testimony is targeted at the bill in a specific setting on a specific date. The reason is that your testimony might actually change the bill! If you don't include a date and a hearing, then someone might find your testimony later and think you oppose a bill that you currently support.

Make Sure to Introduce Your Organization

Finally, make sure in your testimony or written comment that you are clear about who you are and what you represent. Policy makers want to have some context about who you are. As you'll see in the examples below, it's customary to include a brief paragraph about your organization: How big is it? What is its mission? Why do its members care about this topic? If you're a student, you might reflect on your university training and why you care about the bill. If you're a community member, you might give them some context about how long you've lived in the district and what connections you have to the topic.

Don't Bury the Lede

Attention in these settings is always limited, so use the time you have with policy makers to focus them on your main point. State clearly and directly whether you oppose or support the policy and clearly and briefly state your reasons. As you'll see in the examples, testimony is often just a page or two long. Use your time to focus on your main point(s)!

Thank You's Matter

Finally, it's traditional to thank the committee hearing or agency reading your testimony. You can thank them at the beginning, the end, or even both if your document is on the longer side. It may be their job to read your written comments, but saying thank you is still the right thing to do. Bureaucrats and elected officials are people, too, and a thank you can go a long way, if not on this issue, then by being welcomed back to the table for the next one.

Legislative Testimony

Simply talking about "legislative testimony" can be a bit of a misnomer. Sometimes what you say will be the same as what you write, but other times you will be asked to write two different pieces: the testimony you'll read and the testimony you'll submit. The way to find out ahead of time is to ask the legislative staff what the norms of their committee are. They can tell you all of the details that inevitably vary across the country: Can you speak, or will you only submit a written memo? If you speak, will you be asked questions? How long can you speak? Will you stand or sit?

Once you have the answers, then it's time to think a bit about shaping your message, given the particulars of the committee and the setting. Start by thinking about the context. Is this a topic the committee has been discussing for years or for the first time? Touch base with staff ahead of time and get a feel from them about what will come. Staff often write the questions for the committee members and will share them with you. For the most part, lawmaking at this level is about everybody clearly understanding the policies, not about asking "gotcha" questions. Staff want the information you have and will generally ask you clear questions about your topic.

If you're invited to give your testimony orally, be prepared for a couple of unusual features of testifying. First, lawmakers are the ones who set the rules. Therefore, they can be the ones who break them. Don't be surprised if they interrupt you and ask questions mid-sentence. You'll have to think on your feet as you respond, and be careful never to provide an answer you're unsure of. It's always better to say, "I don't know, but I will find the answer for you," than to assert something and be wrong. Often, lawmakers know the answer to the question they are asking. They ask you so that other committee members hear that information from you instead of from them. Since they sometimes know the answer to the questions they are asking, you're playing a dangerous game if you speak confidently about something that you don't already know.

Second, hearings can be a circus. If you've never been to one, try to go to one before you testify. Depending on the situation, the sheer number of people or the emptiness of the room can be disorienting. While witnesses are testifying, committee members sometimes step out, have side conversations, or appear disinterested. Keep your poise and keep talking. You'd be surprised at how good they are at keeping an ear out for what you have to say.

Finally, if you appear on TV, think through the special demands that brings. Dress appropriately for the occasion. If you normally wear makeup, make sure to do so this time, as lights and cameras aren't kind. Make sure you go to the restroom before testifying. Being seated in front of a committee for 2.5 hours of questioning can be uncomfortable, but doing so after consuming three cups of coffee is worse. You can't excuse yourself mid-hearing on live TV, so make sure you've taken care of business so you can take care of business when they ask you a question.

Example 1: Evidence Shows That
"Ban the Box" Doesn't Work (and Might Hurt)

The example testimony below was given by my friend and colleague Jennifer Doleac (2017). Professor Doleac is an expert on criminal justice policy, and she was invited by staff of the U.S. Congress to testify before the Full House Committee on Oversight and Government Reform about the effectiveness of so-called "ban the box" policies.

"Ban the box" policies refer to a box on a job application that asks if applicants have ever been convicted of a felony. Businesses love them because they can quickly identify ex-felons and not hire them. Other advocacy groups argue that they disproportionately affect black men caught up in the mass incarceration movement. These advocacy groups have lobbied governments to pass laws that prohibit employers from asking if applicants have been convicted of a felony in their job applications.

Professor Doleac was invited to speak because she has empirical answers about the effect of "ban the box" policies (Doleac & Hansen, 2016). Lawmakers and their staff invited her to testify alongside five other people—three government officials and two advocates—all of whom were working in the area. Here is the testimony she read.

Chairman Gowdy, Ranking Member Cummings, and other members of the Committee:

Thank you for inviting me to testify in this hearing about prisoner reentry. I am an Assistant Professor of Public Policy and Economics at the University of Virginia. I am also the Director of the Justice Tech Lab, which works to find effective, scalable solutions to criminal justice problems.

In addition to my roles at UVA, I am a Senior Social Scientist at the Lab @ DC, a research group in the Mayor's Office here in the District, and a Non-resident Fellow in Economics Studies at the Brookings Institution. I am also a member of the Poverty, Employment, and Self-Sufficiency Network organized by the Institute for Research on Poverty at the University of Wisconsin.

To each of these roles I bring my expertise in the economics of crime and discrimination. In recent years, I have been particularly focused on the issue of prisoner reentry. In addition to a number of ongoing studies testing the impacts of new interventions on reentry outcomes, I have studied the effects of Ban the Box policies (also called Fair Chance policies). This is the topic I will focus on today. Though I will note that the views I express here are my own and do not represent those of any of the organizations I am affiliated with.

Two-thirds of people who are released from prison will be arrested again within three years. This high recidivism rate signals our collective failure to help this group successfully reintegrate to civilian life. The question facing policy-makers is what we can do to facilitate more successful reintegration and break this cycle of incarceration.

Those who go through the criminal justice system face a wide array of challenges that make this task difficult. These challenges include low education, limited and interrupted work histories, lack of stable housing, and high rates of substance abuse, mental illness, and emotional trauma. All of these factors help explain why this population has trouble finding stable employment upon release from prison.

Ban the Box aims to increase access to jobs by prohibiting employers from asking job applicants about their criminal histories until late in the hiring process. The hope is that if some people with records can get their foot in the door, those who are a good fit for the job will be able to communicate their work-readiness during an interview, before the employer runs a background check.

But work-readiness—the ability to show up on time every day and do a good job—is difficult to discern from a job application, and even from an interview. Employers clearly believe that a criminal record is a negative signal about work-readiness, and are also worried about negligent hiring lawsuits or bad press that might result from hiring someone with a record. Unfortunately, BTB does not do anything to address the reasons employers might be reluctant to hire someone with a criminal record. It just tells them they can't ask.

Since many employers still don't want to hire people with criminal records—especially those with recent convictions—they may try to guess who has a record when they aren't allowed to ask up front. In the United States, young black men who don't have a college degree are much more likely than others to have a recent conviction that might worry an employer, and so employers who want to avoid interviewing people with recent convictions may avoid interviewing applicants from this group. As a result, we might see BTB hurt this group more than it helps them. Indeed, this is what has happened.

In the written testimony I submitted to this Committee, I summarized the empirical evidence from the best studies on this topic, as well as the broader literature on how information affects discrimination in the labor market. This evidence can be summarized as follows:

- First: Delaying information about job applicants' criminal histories leads employers to discriminate against groups that are more likely to have a recent conviction. This hurts young, low-skilled, black men who don't have criminal records.

- Second: The best evidence suggests that Ban the Box does not increase employment for people with criminal records, and might even reduce it.

- Third: These findings are consistent with empirical evidence from other contexts, such as drug testing and credit check bans. Studies consistently show that removing information about characteristics that disadvantage protected groups actually hurts those groups more than it helps them. In the absence of information, employers do not simply assume the best about people. They try to guess who has the characteristics they are trying to avoid. Rather than reducing discrimination, this approach effectively broadens it to the entire group.

- Finally: Effective approaches to this policy problem are likely to be policies that directly address employers' concerns, such as investing in rehabilitation, providing more information about applicants' work-readiness, and clarifying employers' legal responsibilities in the hiring process.

Overall, the academic literature provides strong evidence that—despite the best intentions—BTB has not helped people with criminal records, and has harmed young, low-skilled black men without records, who already struggle in the labor market for a variety of reasons. Based on this evidence, I urge this Committee to reject the Fair Chance Act and focus on other policy options that are likely to be more successful.

Thank you.

Discussion of Example 1

What do you think? Professor Doleac does a nice job here of employing standard best practices for testimony. First, she says thank you (always important!). Second, she identifies herself and the organizations with which she is affiliated. Fully one-third of her testimony is setting the context for her remarks so the representatives have a clear sense of where she is coming from. Third, she uses straightforward language that the committee can understand. That's not easy for anyone discussing a technical issue, but it is especially hard for an economist! Finally, it's hard to see simply by reading her testimony, but she chooses what to focus on in light of the other people testifying. She's able to focus narrowly on the effectiveness of "ban the box" policies because others are talking about other aspects of prisoner reentry.

It's also worth noticing how she advocates for a particular position about "ban the box" policies. She is clearly against the policy but doesn't come off as a jerk. The tone of her testimony might strike you as pretty different than the testimony you might see on the nightly news or West Wing, but this is the way that most testimony works. There is no grandstanding. She doesn't degrade the other side. She gives a clear, straightforward argument supported by lots of evidence. She makes a clear recommendation at the end. Textbook.

You might also have noticed that she references her submitted written testimony. Her oral testimony was aimed at the lawmakers in the room. She was also asked to submit a longer, written testimony that was more likely to be read by staff who are experts in this issue area than the lawmakers themselves. Her 26 pages, complete with dozens of academic references, are the right level for the staff and the wrong level for the legislators. By asking good questions of the staff ahead of time, she was able to know how to be effective in both settings.

Example 2: Renewable Energy in Rhode Island

Now let's look at testimony in a different setting. The following example comes from a renewable energy industry advocate in Rhode Island. Her organization, the New England Clean Energy Council (NECEC), represented renewable energy businesses that want the government to create policies that allow renewable energy to compete fairly with other energy sources.

In this case, a bill before the Rhode Island Senate proposed that the power company would be required to continue paying consumers to make their homes more energy efficient. This policy is known as "Least-Cost Procurement." The reason is because reducing electric consumption is the least costly way to have more electricity available on the grid, since making homes more efficient is less costly than building new power plants.

The testimony was given during a public hearing in the Rhode Island statehouse. The committee sat behind old oak tables, and members allowed anyone who wanted to speak about the bill time to testify on a first-come, first-served basis. Citizens, lobbyists, and businesses all lined up (literally) to speak on the bill. Here's the testimony the lobbyist prepared.

Senate Bill 733:

System Reliability and Least-Cost Procurement

Submitted by

Charity Pennock

Rhode Island State Coordinator

March 26, 2015

Chairman Picard and Members of the Senate Commerce Committee:

The New England Clean Energy Council (NECEC) greatly appreciates the opportunity to comment on the Senate Bill 733 related to System Reliability & Least-Cost Procurement (LCP).

NECEC is the lead voice for hundreds of clean energy companies across New England, influencing the energy policy agenda and growing the clean energy economy. NECEC's mission is to accelerate New England's clean energy economy to global leadership by building an active community of stakeholders and a world-class cluster of clean energy companies. NECEC is the only organization in New England that covers all of the clean energy market segments, representing the business perspectives of investors and clean energy companies across every stage of development. NECEC members span the broad spectrum of the clean energy industry, including energy efficiency, demand response, renewable energy, combined heat and power, energy storage, fuel cells and advanced and "smart" technologies. Many of our members are operating and investing in Rhode Island, and more are interested in doing so.

Senate Bill 733's long-term commitment to the first source of energy cost savings—energy efficiency—is critical to the growth of clean energy jobs and businesses in Rhode Island. By extending the program now, clean energy businesses have a clear market signal that there will be sustained demand for their products into the future. Having a stable market encourages companies to invest in both people and new products creating jobs and wealth across the Ocean State.

The impacts of Rhode Island's LCP are proven. According to Acadia Center, for every $1 spent on energy efficiency, Rhode Island consumers have realized $3.50 in economic benefit totaling nearly $2 billion since 2008. In addition, by reducing energy consumption of residential, commercial, and industrial energy users, more money remains in the pocketbooks of homeowners, small businesses, and manufacturers to spend on other critical services such as housing and health care and to support job growth and business expansion.

For these reasons, NECEC supports Senate Bill 733. In addition, NECEC recommends extending the LCP extension to 2038 as recommended by Article 24 of the Governor's 2016 budget.

Thank you again for the opportunity to offer these comments. Please consider NECEC a resource for information on clean energy and energy policy as you continue your deliberations.

Sincerely,

Charity Pennock

Rhode Island State Coordinator

Discussion of Example 2

What do you think? Again, it meets the standard best practices of legislative testimony: thank you's, context about the organization and those it represents (businesses), supporting facts, and a clear declaration of support for the policy. That said, this testimony does differ from the first example. It's considerably shorter, because the lobbyist knew from attending previous committee meetings that she had to be brief. It's also interesting in that the testimony ends with an invitation to dialogue. It's clear that she and her organization want to establish themselves as experts to whom legislators can turn as they have questions after the hearing.

One interesting twist is that what you read above wasn't what she said.[4] The hearing was running late into the night, and the lobbyist was going to be one of the last ones speaking. As she watched the senators' growing weariness with the long-winded folks testifying in front of her, she decided it was better to paraphrase. She introduced her organization in a sentence or two, stated its support, and offered to talk more when the senators wanted her to. That made more of an impact than saying every word she had written, some of which overlapped with what they had heard before. To be effective, she read her audience and adjusted. Context matters. Noticing the situation and adjusting made the policy makers more interested in listening to her the next time around.

---

[4] Copies were given to staff for the record and posted on the organization's website so interested parties could see their position.

Public Comment for Regulations[5]

Regulatory decision makers often solicit public feedback on a policy by asking for regulatory comment. When regulators propose to change a regulation, they do so by publicly announcing the changes they are considering and asking for feedback through public comment letters.[6] At the federal level, this allows stakeholders from around the country to give feedback on the proposed policy without traveling to Washington, D.C.

In some ways, writing public comment is easier than writing for a public hearing. First of all, your audience is the specific government agency proposing the rule. That agency is usually staffed by people who have worked on the topic for years. This means that your comments can include fairly technical information if need be (while still being written clearly, of course!). Second, rules rarely change more than once as they move through the policy process, so there are fewer versions to keep track of than the average bill.

Example 3: Public Health Association for Trans-Fats Regulation

For our regulatory comment examples, I've pulled two of the 201 comments submitted to the U.S. Food and Drug Administration (FDA) about its proposed rule to ban trans-fats from foods in the United States.[7] Those 201 comments constitute part of a heated debate about what companies are allowed to put in the food you eat, how affordable it will be, how good it will taste, and how quickly it will kill you.

At the heart of the debate is the question about whether or not companies can use trans-fats to make their products. For a little background, many of the foods we eat have some sort of fat added to them, from butter in a cake to the cream in our coffee. Normal plant-based oils (sunflower, corn, or canola oil) are useful in a lot of settings, but they aren't great for foods that have to keep for a long time on a shelf. However, these oils can be transformed by adding a hydrogen atom to create a trans-fat (sometimes called partially hydrogenated oil, or PHO). On the good side, trans-fats are

---

[5] Regulators also hold public hearings. For advice on writing for those settings refer to the section above on legislative testimony.

[6] At the federal level, the *Federal Register* is the website where new rules are announced, comments are received, and then—several months later—final policies are announced. All 50 states have similar processes and venues for commenting on their regulatory changes.

[7] Of the 201 comments, several were form letters that were submitted several hundred times. They were identical and therefore are listed once on the *Federal Register* website, with a note saying how many copies were submitted.

great for creating baked goods, as they prolong the shelf life of the foods in which they are used. The bad news is that they are bad for you. Really bad. As you'll see below, when Denmark reduced trans-fat consumption by 85%, the heart disease rate fell by 50%![8]

In the early 2000s, the FDA was concerned enough about trans-fats that it mandated that food labels include information about how much trans-fat was in them. By 2013 the FDA had become convinced by the science that trans-fats were so dangerous they should be banned from food starting in June 2018. The FDA proposed the rule banning them in the *Federal Register* (2015), instigating a firestorm of comments from public health officials across the country like the Association of State Public Health Nutritionists, business groups representing food producers like the National Frozen Pizza Institute (yes, that's a real interest group), patient advocacy groups like the American Heart Association, and many individual citizens.

The first example is a comment letter from the American Public Health Association weighing in on the rule. Take a look and see what you think.

March 7, 2014[9]

Division of Dockets Management (HFA-305) SUBMITTED VIA: Regulations.gov

U.S. Food and Drug Administration

5630 Fishers Lane, Room 1061

Rockville, MD 20852

Re: Docket No. FDA-2013-N-1317

On behalf of the American Public Health Association, a diverse community of public health professionals who champion the health of all people and communities, I write to express our strong support for the Food and Drug Administration's quick action on a final determination[10] to remove partially hydrogenated oil from the food supply. Thank you for this opportunity to provide comments on the tentative determination regarding partially hydrogenated oils as APHA

---

[8] If you're interested in the story about why companies began using trans-fats in the early 1900s, take a few minutes to listen to Gladwell's (n.d.) podcast episode, *McDonald's Broke My Heart.*

[9] This document has been edited for length. The original can be found on the *Federal Register's* website; https://www.federalregister.gov/documents/2015/06/17/2015-14883/final-determination-regarding-partially-hydrogenated-oils.

[10] A *determination* is regulation lingo for a ruling.

recognizes that a healthier food supply is absolutely critical in supporting good health and reducing chronic disease related to poor nutrition, overweight, obesity and food insecurity.

APHA has long supported an FDA determination that partially hydrogenated oils, which are the primary dietary source of industrially-produced trans fatty acids, or trans fat, are not generally recognized as safe for any use in food, based on current scientific evidence that establishes the health risks associated with the consumption of trans fat. New scientific evidence and the findings of expert scientific panels have revealed the very serious impact of PHOs in the food supply.[11]

By FDA's estimation, PHO is causing 3,000 to 7,000 deaths per year and should be phased out of the food supply as rapidly as possible. The Danish government's efforts to decrease the intake of trans fat from 6 grams per day to 1 gram per day over a 20-year period is thought to be related to a 50 percent decrease in ischemic heart disease. Furthermore, FDA has concluded that the economic benefits of eliminating the use of partially hydrogenated oil greatly outweigh the costs of switching to healthier oils. Over 20 years, it is estimated that the benefits would total between $117 billion and $242 billion while the costs would total between $12 billion and $14 billion.

Given the impact trans fat intake has on health, APHA makes the following comments on removing trans fat from the food supply:

There is no safe level of trans fat: PHO is both harmful and unnecessary and should therefore be eliminated from the food supply. Recently an Institute of Medicine panel concluded: "It is recommended that trans fatty acid consumption be as low as possible while consuming a nutritionally adequate diet." In a subsequent press release, IOM stated, "Because they are not essential and provide no known health benefit, there is no safe level of trans fatty acids and people should eat as little of them as possible while consuming a nutritionally adequate diet." Currently, many labels indicate 0 grams of trans fat per serving, but contain up to 0.49 grams of trans. Even this seemingly small amount promotes heart disease, especially in segments of the population that consume large and multiple servings of such foods over the course of a day. To protect the public's health, FDA should bar the use of PHO in all amounts and all foods.

---

[11] A *PHO* is a partially hydrogenated oil. It would have been helpful if the APHA had been clear about that.

Reasonable time frames for industry action: In the early 2000s, FDA finalized its trans-fat labeling regulation. The action spurred forward-thinking companies to switch from PHO to more healthful oils. Between 2006 and 2010, restaurants and bakeries responded successfully to local regulations limiting trans fat, even though they had little experience reformulating foods and fewer alternative oils were available than are today.

FDA should set one standard for all oils, regardless of their end use. By focusing on the manufactured oils, instead of oil-containing foods, FDA's enforcement task would be greatly simplified. If this approach is adopted, FDA should set a compliance deadline of 18 months from the date of the final decision.

While some companies might argue that 18 months is not enough time, any longer would continue the uneven playing field that disadvantages those companies that have replaced hydrogenated oils in their products. Companies should not be put at a competitive disadvantage for being forward thinking and attentive to this important public health concern.

Experience demonstrates small business can act quickly: Small bakeries and restaurants in New York City and elsewhere have shown that it is possible for these sectors to comply with replacing PHO in an 18-month period. An 18-month deadline from the date of a final FDA decision should be sufficient for all manufacturers, bakeries and restaurants, big or small, and producers of both fried foods and other foods.

Among restaurants, all of the largest companies and many smaller ones now fry in trans-free oils, while some have continued to use PHO. Likewise, many food manufacturers have largely or totally switched from PHO to more healthful oils, though some companies continue to use recipes with PHO.

If small companies need technical expertise to reformulate their foods, FDA could encourage major trade associations to set up a national help center, much like New York City. An appropriately staffed telephone line, along with an informative website, could help many small companies and their oil suppliers.

Alternatives available to industry: In the United States, substitutes for PHO are readily available for virtually all types of food, and the food industry, oil processors, seed companies and farmers deserve great credit for the progress that has been made over the past decade in reducing trans fat levels in processed and prepared foods by about 75 percent. This effort has likely saved several hundred thousand lives over the years.

In summary, APHA strongly endorses the need to remove partially hydrogenated oil from the food supply and urges FDA to make the necessary changes. By doing so, FDA will help ensure that Americans have a healthier food supply contributing to better health and well-being. Thank you for this opportunity to share the public health community's support for eliminating PHOs from the food supply.

Sincerely,

Georges Benjamin, MD

Executive Director

Discussion of Example 3

What do you think? Notice all of the things this comment letter does well. First, it's easy to read. Even with a complicated topic, in a comment written by one expert to an agency full of other experts, you were likely able to pick up most of what Dr. Benjamin wrote. This is in part because of the clear sentences and paragraphs and in part because he used the formatting templates we've discussed in the book—the bullets and bolding are effective. Second, he follows the same rules as the testimony we saw above. At the beginning of this comment, he explains who he is, what his organization does, what issue he's addressing, and his position. He's direct without being a jerk. Third, he employs a lot of facts to support his point of view. The evidence is clearly on his side, and he uses it. He directly addresses the objections of his opponents, directly addressing claims that businesses aren't able to change course or that some trans-fats are still safe. In sum, it's a professional letter, and there isn't much to criticize.

Example 4: Corporate Comment on Trans-Fats Regulation

While the public health community was strongly for the rule, the business groups were against it. Dozens of industry groups opposed the ban, including the Popcorn Institute, the Grocery Manufacturers Association, the Snack Food Association, and Long John Silver's. Nestlé, the international food conglomerate, also had some concerns about the rule. Take a look at its comment letter.

March 8, 2014[12]

Division of Dockets Management (HFA-305)

Food and Drug Administration

5630 Fishers Lane, Rm. 1061

Rockville, MD 20852

Re: Tentative Determination Regarding Partially Hydrogenated Oils; Request for Comments and for Scientific Data and Information (Docket No. FDA-2013-N-1317); Food and Drug Administration

To Whom It May Concern:

Nestlé in the US ("Nestlé") is proud to be part of the leading food, nutrition, health and wellness company in the world. We sell a wide range of products, managed by our businesses, including Nestlé USA and Nestlé Nutrition. Individually, each business focuses on its expertise to provide nutritious and preferred choices in its category. Together, as one company, we share a commitment to safety, health and quality. Our mission is to deliver Good Food, Good Life through foods and beverages, nutrition knowledge and services that can improve the lives of our consumers.

Nestlé in the US, with 2013 sales of $25 billion, is part of Nestlé S.A. in Vevey, Switzerland with 2013 sales of $99 billion. In the US, we have over 50,000 employees and 140 locations based in 47 states.

We manufacture a large variety of FDA-regulated food products including some of our billion-dollar brands such as Stouffer's®;, DiGiorno®; and Coffee-mate®;. We manufacture many of America's most trusted brands including Gerber®; and Nestlé Toll House®. Our portfolio includes a wide range of products including frozen meals, ice cream, chilled pastas and sauces, confectionery products, dehydrated and liquid beverages, infant, toddler, health care and performance nutrition products.

In all that we do, we have a commitment to nutrition, health and wellness that is reflected throughout our worldwide organization. . . .

---

[12] This document has been edited for length. The original can be found on the *Federal Register's* website; https://www.regulations.gov/document?D=FDA-2013-N-1317-0182.

. . . It is in this light that we offer the following comments to the Food and Drug Administration (FDA) on its tentative determination that partially hydrogenated oils (PHOs) are no longer generally recognized as safe (GRAS).

Nestlé's Experience With Reducing PHOs

Globally, Nestlé is committed to removing trans fat originating from PHOs from all of our food and beverage products. To this end, we have been actively working to remove from our products PHOs that are added as functional ingredients. As a result, PHOs are not added as functional ingredients in the vast majority of our products. Furthermore, our global commitment is to remove trans fat originating from PHOs from all our food and beverage products sold for human consumption by the end of 2016.

Consistent with our global ambition, Nestlé in the US is on target for removing all PHOs as functional ingredients by the end of 2016—and it is likely we will meet this goal in 2015. These efforts include removal of PHOs as functional ingredients from our coffee creamers and frozen pizzas portfolios, two categories of foods specifically noted by FDA in its tentative determination and supporting documents as containing PHOs. As indicated above, we have been actively working on removal of PHOs from these products for some time, and we are nearing the successful conclusion of this process with little to no increase in saturated fat levels. For example, in 2010, 38% of the products in our Nestlé Pizza Division had labeled trans fat greater than 0 g. This percentage was reduced to 20% in 2011, 14% in 2012, and 2% (mostly from cheese and meat ingredients) in 2013. And we anticipate removing all PHOs used as functional ingredients in our pizzas by the end of 2014.

Additional Comments

Nestlé has participated with the Grocery Manufacturers Association (GMA), American Frozen Food Institute (AFFI) and other food trade associations in developing comments on FDA's tentative determination on PHOs, and we generally support the extensive comments submitted by these food trade associations. We would like to take this opportunity to highlight and reinforce a number of issues of particular importance to Nestlé, which focus on several specific concerns about the following approaches taken by FDA in its tentative determination.

- FDA has not specifically defined "partially hydrogenated oil" and, thus, it is unclear what range of trans fatty acid content in these oils would be covered under any final agency decision. We recommend FDA provide a definition of "partially hydrogenated oil" and a subsequent opportunity for public comment on this definition before finalizing any further regulation of PHOs.

- Nestlé recognizes that FDA is focusing its tentative determination on PHOs because they are the primary dietary source of industrially-produced trans fat. While we support this focus, we would not support any extension of the assessment to trans fat occurring naturally in meat or milk, which are foods that have a long history of safe consumption as part of a balanced diet.

Nestlé greatly appreciates the opportunity to submit these comments and share our experience with reducing PHOs in the foods we manufacture. Please do not hesitate to call on us if we may be of assistance as FDA continues its efforts to evaluate the regulatory status of PHOs.

Respectfully submitted,

Timothy A. Morck, PhD, Vice President, Scientific & Regulatory Affairs, Nestlé Corporate Affairs, Washington, DC

Mark Nelson, Director, Regulatory & Scientific Affairs, Nestlé USA, Glendale, CA

Cheryl A. Callen, Director, Regulatory Affairs Nestlé Infant Nutrition, Florham Park, NJ

Discussion of Example 4

What do you think? Even though this example is written by a professional team of corporate lobbyists from one of the world's biggest corporations, it still follows the same outlines as the other examples we've reviewed: Same introduction to who they are. Same clear writing. Same memo skills. A thank you at the end.

One interesting thing to note here is that the letter doesn't take a clear stand on the rule itself. In contrast to a normal comment, it doesn't speak for or against the rule. The authors don't comment on the science or attack the FDA findings like some of the other comment letters from other industry groups. Instead, they ask for the FDA to define what a "partially hydrogenated oil" is and to seek comments about it. Without knowing the particulars of the situation, it's hard to know if this is an industry leader pointing out a fixable problem with the rule or if it's a delay tactic. It would be interesting to know why the authors asked for a delay in finalizing the recommendation.

Conclusion

As you've seen above, writing legislative testimony and regulatory comments is a straightforward process. The examples I've used above are largely from business groups. There's a reason for that. Business groups do almost all of the lobbying on the vast majority of issues before legislatures and regulatory agencies (Baumgartner & Leech, 2001). Environmental or health-related lobby groups sometimes lobby on their issues, but they are usually outmanned and outgunned by the business groups.

There is a logic to this system. A few companies can reap huge benefits from changing policy while the vast majority of individuals have little to gain from most policies we've considered. Energy companies have a big interest in power pricing. Citizens, just a little. Trans fats were a hot topic to food companies and health professionals, but not to the average citizen—even one who eats a lot of frozen pizza.

But that doesn't mean that citizens shouldn't be a part of the policy conversation on these issues. In fact, this book is in large part an effort to equip you to do just that. Controversial projects like oil and natural gas pipelines go through regulatory processes every year. Even if you don't work for an advocacy group you can use the principles shown here to speak up as a citizen. Lawmakers designed the system so that you can have a voice in the laws and rules they make. Use the lessons in this chapter to use your voice to help them make good decisions.

CHECKLIST

Content and Analysis

- Provides context for who you are, what organization you represent, and why you are engaged in this issue.

- Demonstrates thorough understanding of the topic and its implications.

- Provides correct amount of information.

- Clearly states support for or opposition to the proposed change.

Document Formatting and Presentation

- Writes to an intelligent reader unfamiliar with specifics of topic.
- Discussion flows logically.
- Well formatted to enhance clarity by breaking content into sections with clear foci.
- Section headings preview text that follows.
- Appropriate emphasis added.
- Visual cues help draw the reader's eye to the relevant points quickly.
- Header provides date, contact information, and organization name.

Writing

- Short, precise, and readable sentences that are actor centered.
- Paragraphs are cohesive, coherent, and properly emphasize important ideas.
- No grammar or spelling errors.
- No jargon.
- Passes *Washington Post* test.

EXERCISES

1. Identify a legislative committee to which you would ideally give testimony. What would be the purpose of your testimony? Why would you be giving it?

2. Who comprises the audience for the testimony? From whom else would they be hearing?

3. Write a sentence outline of your testimony. Why did you organize it the way that you did?

4. Write an effective 1–2 page testimony targeted to a committee that gives members enough details about you, the organization for which you are writing, and your reasons for opposing or supporting the proposed legislation for them to understand how to consider your testimony.

5. Identify a regulatory matter to which you would ideally submit a comment letter. What would be the purpose of your letter? Why would you be submitting it?

6. Write a sentence outline of your comment letter. Why did you organize it the way you did?

7. Write an effective 1–2 page comment letter that gives enough details about you, the organization for which you are writing, and your reasons for opposing or supporting the proposed regulation for your audience to understand how to consider your perspective.

BIBLIOGRAPHY

Baumgartner, F. R., & Leech, B. L. (2001). Interest niches and policy bandwagons: Patterns of interest group involvement in national politics. *The Journal of Politics*, 63(04), 1191–1213.

Doleac, J. (2017). Oversight of the Bureau of Prisons and Inmate Reentry, § Full House Committee on Oversight and Government Reform. Washington, DC. Retrieved from https://oversight.house.gov/hearing/oversight-bureau-prisons-inmate-reentry/

Doleac, J., & Hansen, B. (2016). *Does "ban the box" help or hurt low-skilled workers? Statistical discrimination and employment outcomes when criminal histories are hidden* (working paper no. 22469). National Bureau of Economic Research.

Federal Register. (2015). *Final determination regarding partially hydrogenated oils* (docket no. FDA-2013-N-1317). Washington, DC. Retrieved April 19, 2018, from https://www.federalregister.gov/documents/2015/06/17/2015-14883/final-determination-regarding-partially-hydrogenated-oils

Gladwell, M. (n.d.). *McDonald's broke my heart*. Retrieved January 22, 2018, from http://revisionisthistory.com/episodes/19-mcdonalds-broke-my-heart

Heifetz, R. A., & Linsky, M. (2017). *Leadership on the line: Staying alive through the dangers of change* (rev. ed.). Boston, MA: Harvard Business Review Press.

Regulations.gov. (n.d.). *Tips for submitting effective comments*. Washington, DC. Retrieved April 19, 2018, from https://www.regulations.gov/docs/Tips_For_Submitting_Effective_Comments.pdf

CHAPTER 13

Writing for Nontraditional Formats: Email and Social Media

Email

While other policy-writing genres may seem more impactful, by far the most common type of writing you will do in public policy is email. Both a blessing and a bane, email takes up 28% of the average worker's daily effort (Chui, Manyika, Bughin, Dobbs, Roxburgh, Sarrazin, Sands, & Westergren, 2012). The sheer frequency of email you send as a policy writer makes an investment in emailing better worth your time. Every time you email well you make other people's lives better. Every time you email poorly, you make other people's lives worse, and sometimes you have the potential to make your own life *a lot* worse. Almost nothing else you write professionally will establish your reputation like your email.

As you know from your daily life, email is a crucial tool for getting work done. Most helpfully, it allows people to communicate with you without interrupting what you're doing. I would never have finished this book if every time someone sent me an email they had knocked on my door. Rather than interrupting my work flow to ask a question about a problem that could wait, they sent an email and I got back to them when it was convenient. But, as convenient as it is, email also creates problems, some of which apply to everyone who emails, and some of which are unique to emailing in a public policy setting.

You're Always on the Record

When you email in a public policy setting you should always assume you're on the record. There is a good chance that your emails will be seen beyond the person to whom they were addressed. This is good advice for anyone who writes emails, as everyone has had the mortifying experience of typing the wrong address and hitting *send*. What would have been a funny note to a friend is mortifying in the hands of Grandma or your boss. Similarly, I've had many a careless student forget to delete the informal email conversation among members of their group before sending an email to me. Let's just say they were less . . . ah . . . formal about how they referred to me than they would have been in person. Not good.

However, when you work in government settings, emails don't just have the potential to be seen by one or two other people through a careless mistake. Thanks to the Freedom of Information Act (FOIA), you should assume your emails will be out in the world for everyone to see. At its heart, FOIA means that when you produce something using government property (emails, in this case), the taxpayers have a right to see it.[1] So, when a curious journalist or angry private citizen asks for your emails, they get all of them. Similarly, if you've emailed a public official or employee, those emails can be made public through the FOIA request for their emails.

> *Dance like no one is watching, email like it will be quoted on the front page of the* Washington Post. (Charity Pennock, director of the Charlottesville Renewable Energy Alliance)

Most of the public gaffs that we see from email requested by FOIA are less about malfeasance and more about people not thinking about how their conversations might be interpreted out of context. And people who make a FOIA request for your email are unlikely to be generous about interpreting what you have written. For example, in the aftermath of Hurricane Katrina and the botched response by the Federal Emergency Management Agency (FEMA), Congress went looking for ways to show the agency was poorly run. FEMA director Michael Brown had his emails reviewed. He was widely quoted for this email:

From: Brown, Michael D.

Sent: Monday, August 29, 2005 8:51 AM

To: Bahamonde, Marty; Taylor, Cindy

CC: Widomski, Michael

Subject: Re: New Orleans update

If you look at my lovely FEMA attire you'll really vomit. I ama fashion god. [*sic*]

Read in context of the email stream and with a generous eye, he was probably simply trying to break the tension with his staff in a terrible situation. Instead, he was pilloried by the national press around the country as an out-of-touch narcissist. Fair? No. But email isn't fair.

---

[1] FOIA excludes certain kinds of information from being released, for example, classified information. FOIA differs by jurisdiction. For example, emails between legislators and staff are often exempt from FOIA. Similarly, while university emails can be FOIAed, some student records that are protected by the Family Educational Rights and Privacy Act (FERPA) will be removed from them.

Being on the Record Has Consequences

Because email is always on the record, officials can use it as a political tool. Email can be a way to protect yourself. When you put something in an email, there will always be a verifiable record of what you said. This can be helpful when you need to establish that a conversation occurred. For example, a former colleague, Kate, had an unscrupulous boss who was fond of making promises he never intended to keep. Once she caught on, Kate followed up every meeting with an email to him documenting what was said and asking him to make any corrections, if needed. The boss took the point and subsequently became better behaved around Kate than around others.

You can also use email to force action. If you used the public nature of email to ask a question, you can force people to behave as they would in public. If you ask, in an email, about a sexual harassment complaint, then you are very likely to get it addressed through the proper channels. That can be good in some settings and bad in others. If your situation is more delicate, then you might be better served to start a conversation offline, where people can be more direct and exercise more discretion.

Finally, some situations are so delicate that it's best to avoid email altogether. It's helpful to develop a sense of when it is the right time to walk down the hall or send an email simply asking someone to swing by for an in-person chat. For example, if you're working out a compromise around a thorny issue where every party loses something, then email isn't the right way to go. No one wants create a record detailing the things they offered to give up, especially if the compromise doesn't work out in the end. There is a reason why so many policy decisions are made in person behind closed doors.

Know which issues are right for email and which are not. You confuse the two at your peril.

Remember That Email Has No Context

While emails are a helpful way to communicate, they don't do a great job of communicating context. If you send an email with the subject line, "Come see me as soon as you can!" with nothing else in the body of the message, it is hard for other people to know how to interpret it. Are you upset? Do you have a new assignment for them that will change what they will be doing for the next month? Without the verbal and physical context that provides extra information, emails can be confusing. If they passed you in the hallway between meetings and you said excitedly, "Come see me as soon as you can!" and flashed a thumbs-up, they would probably worry a lot less than if you sent them an email with the same words.

Without the in-person context, email doesn't have the same emotional clues of verbal and nonverbal communication. That's one reason why emojis, ALL CAPS, and repeated punctuation are so often used in emails!!! People want to convey emotional context. Unfortunately, these are rarely appropriate for professional emails, so you have to think about how your audience might interpret your email and work to prevent misunderstandings through clear communication.

Never Email When Emotional (or Late at Night) (or Drunk)

As a corollary, never email when you are too angry or hurt to think straight. Because email is on the record, can't be retracted, and is often read without context, it's important to carefully gauge when to send a conflictual email, and when you're angry isn't one of those times. There's a reason why Gmail has a "mail goggles" feature that asks you to perform a series of math problems if you try to email between certain hours that you might not be using your best judgment. You can do a lot of damage if you email the wrong thing in the wrong tone at the wrong time.

Formality Matters

Email is a genre that tends toward the informal. Email chains often start with a well-constructed, half-page email we spend 15 minutes creating to start a thoughtful conversation. By the time the last email in the chain is sent it descends into one-line back-and-forths. This might work well with peers, but the seeming informality of email can be deceiving. A public official might dash off a one-sentence response to you, but that doesn't mean she is inviting you to reply in the same fashion. Stick with writing more formal emails, especially to elected officials.

Similarly, many people use automatic email signatures that can come across as informal. Just because you get an email signed "Valerie" doesn't mean that Senator Cooley is inviting you to address her on a first-name basis. A good rule of thumb is to continue to address authority figures with formal titles, even if they've directly corrected you once. The first time is often just politeness. If they correct you at least twice, then you can address them by their first name.

Use Good Email Etiquette[2]

Finally, there are a number of email etiquette principles that will help you email effectively. They all fall under the Golden Rule dictum of "do unto others as you would have them do unto you."

---

[2] For a quick, practical, and witty read on good, general email practices take a look at SEND: Why People Email So Badly and How to Do It Better (Shipley & Schwalbe, 2010).

Use Real Subject Lines

Policy makers are busy, and nothing annoys busy people more than looking at meaningless subject lines. It's hard to know which does more damage to your reputation as someone who respects other people's time: the subject line "<blank>" or the subject line "re:re:". Make it a habit to look at subject lines before you send an email to make sure the recipient has enough context to know what the email is about without opening it.

Introduce New People Copied on an Email

Often, when you're emailing about a complex policy problem, you are dealing with stakeholders from a number of different organizations. If you're not sure whether or not they know each other, take the time to introduce them, just like you would in an in-person conversation. Your online conversation will go better if everyone knows whom they are emailing.

Explain Attachments

Similarly, make sure to note and explain any attachments you've included. You may have attached a report, but without context, your reader won't know why. Don't make them open it to understand what it is. Give them information about the attachment so they can decide if it needs to be opened today. The same goes for links to news articles or other online sources. Tell your reader what you want them to get from what you send them.

Remember, You Aren't Texting

Public policy emails should be free of the emojis, abbreviations, and GIFs you use in your everyday texting with friends and family. Rest assured, the mayor won't be impressed that you were ROTFL about his jokes. Public policy is about making significant decisions that impact the long-term health, schooling, and economic viability of people and communities. These serious matters demand a seriousness of tone. It might feel old and stodgy, but you'll be diminished in the eyes of others if you don't take this rule seriously.

Schedule With a Tool

Email is a great tool for many tasks, but scheduling a meeting among multiple participants isn't one of them. Avoid the flurry of emails jamming everyone's inbox and use an online tool to find a time to meet. There are plenty of good free ones, and there is a good chance your institution has a subscription service to a professional one.

Don't "Reply All"

Finally, you should think twice before hitting that tempting "reply all" button. "Reply all" is tempting because it implies that you've kept everyone informed. However, it also means you've forced everyone else to give a little portion of their limited attention in a day to something about which they might not need to know. For example, when a colleague violates the previous rule and asks for when people can meet, the last thing I want is to hear about his schedule constraints. It would have been much more helpful simply to reply to the person scheduling the meeting, sparing me a flood of details through other folks' emails.

Pro-Tip

Managing the Flood of Emails

Whole volumes have been written on how to manage your inbox, and everyone seems to have a philosophy about how to deal with the constant flurry of emails arriving. Here are some of my personal tips for managing email:

1. *Email only at certain times of the day.* Admittedly, I'm a professor, so this is more practical for me than for other people, but I push emails off to times when I know I won't be able to be productive on other tasks. I do a lot of my email at night after the kids go to bed and in the early afternoon when I'm working in a postlunch haze. That means my phone doesn't notify me when an email comes in, nor does a little box appear in the corner of my screen. I decide when to email rather than simply responding to other people immediately after they email me.[3]

2. *Strive for inbox zero.* Early in my career I embraced the advice of the book *Getting Things Done*, which argues that you should have a system for sorting through emails, requests, and papers so that you can focus on what is important, not what is urgent (Allen, 2002). When it is time to work on my inbox, I try to deal with emails that take less than 2 minutes to respond to immediately. If I take the time to read it once, then I should reply while it's fresh, as the last thing I want to do is read

---

[3] I have the same philosophy with other electronic nudges like Twitter and Facebook notifications. I find the quality of my work and my conversations with others better when I'm fully present with them. Sherry Turkle's wonderful book *Reclaiming Conversation* renewed my vision for how I could live differently in relationship to my technology (Turkle, 2015).

piddly emails more than once. If an email takes longer to handle, I either keep it in my inbox if I can resolve it in a day or two or create a calendar reminder to deal with it a week or later in the future, when I'm better equipped to engage with the issue.

3. *You don't always have to read an email.* Email is a way for other people to put things on your agenda. Sometimes the best way to deal with an email is not to read it. I'm thinking specifically of mass emails. I'm not going to read the latest update from the grand vision of an administrator, nor am I going to read the latest newspaper article a friend sends me.[4] My boss and I set my priorities, not every person who emails me.

Twitter

Finally, the last genre to discuss here in the book is Twitter. As President Trump has shown us daily, Twitter is a powerful communications tool in the public policy arena. Government agencies and officials have official Twitter accounts that they use to communicate with the public, and advocates use Twitter to try to shape the debate around an issue.

Social media has become such an important tool that many large public policy organizations have written policies about how to use Twitter accounts, especially the handles controlled by the organization itself. For example, the Centers for Disease Control has several handles (e.g., @CDCgov, @CDC_eHealth, and @CDCespanol) that are owned by the CDC, and posts are created by employees (Centers for Disease Control and Prevention, n.d.). Many organizations also have a public information officer (PIO) who is in charge of monitoring these accounts (and knowing all the passwords!).

Organizations and individuals spend a lot of time thinking about how to use Twitter effectively because it has several functions in the policy world. Twitter is a tool for promoting the profile of an issue to having a real-time conversation with people across the globe about it.[5] Let's take a look at some of the common uses in the policy world.

---

[4] I'm also ruthless at unsubscribing from email marketing lists. I might have purchased your product, but I don't want you to tap me on the shoulder every week via email and tell me about another one when I want to be working or doing something more fun than reading email!

[5] For ideas about how to craft tweets that stick, see *Made to Stick: Why Some Ideas Survive and Others Die* (Heath & Heath, 2007).

Push Out Important Information Quickly

Twitter has become a standard way for policy makers to communicate with the public on real-time issues, from mundane school closings to terrifying real-time updates. For example, in January 2018, people across the state of Hawaii received the following message on their phones via the emergency alert system:

> Emergency Alert: BALLISTIC MISSLE THREAT INBOUND TO HAWAII. SEEK IMMEDIATE SHELTER. THIS IS NOT A DRILL.

Needless to say, this was terrifying to everyone who got it, especially during a time of heightened tensions with North Korea. State officials quickly realized that the warning was the result of human error and there wasn't actually a missile headed toward Hawaii. With emergency alert officials scrambling to figure out how to retract the message, the quickest way to respond was to tweet out that everyone was safe. These tweets were quickly retweeted by policy makers so more people could hear the good news. For example, Governor David Ige retweeted the Hawaii Emergency Management Association's tweet sounding the all clear.[6] This was not as good as not terrifying everyone in the first place, but it was better than not having Twitter as a communications tool.

Governor David Ige ✓
@GovHawaii

Follow

There is NO missile threat.

Hawaii EMA ✓ @Hawaii_EMA
NO missile threat to Hawaii.

2:24 PM - 13 Jan 2018 from Honolulu, HI

201 Retweets **216** Likes

63   201   216

Source: Twitter/@GovHawaii.

---

[6] In a less well known—but equally terrifying—error, a tsunami warning was issued in February 2018 for the Hampton Roads area of Virginia, home to 1.7 million people and the world's largest naval base. Government entities quickly used Twitter to push out the news that the warning was a technical error.

Have a Public Conversation

Also, Twitter is often used in public policy settings as a means to a conversation. Just like with celebrities, prominent public policy actors (op-ed writers, politicians, NGO leaders) have Twitter accounts and reams of followers. They post their takes on the news of the day and people respond with the wide variety you expect from social media, ranging from thoughtful comments to clear trolling. Conversations can take place among prominent Twitter users or in the comments following their tweets.

For example, former Fox News host Eric Bolling suffered one of the most difficult losses one can imagine when his only son died of an opioid overdose in 2017. His son's death was one of more than 60,000 opioid deaths in the United States that year. Bolling's personal tragedy led him to become an activist on the issue of opioid addiction, and he travels regularly to the White House to advise President Trump on the subject. While having an impact behind the scenes, Bolling also uses Twitter as a means to reach his 928,000+ followers and to engage them in conversation on this important policy issue.

Source: Twitter/@ericbolling.

More than just telling his followers his perspective on the epidemic, Bolling has inspired hundreds of them to engage in conversation with one another and with him about opioids, and more than 1,100 people retweeted the conversations to their networks. This kind of engagement can generate real value.

Providing Context to Current Events

Perhaps the most helpful part of Twitter (IMHO) is reading the real-time, short takes that people have in response to current news about a policy problem or the policy surrounding the problem. It can be really helpful to see the takes that other people from different perspectives have on the news. For example, in the tweet below, Nicholas Kristof, an op-ed writer for the *New York Times*, responds to news that President Trump will be focusing his efforts on an enforcement-oriented approach to the opioids crisis.

Nicholas Kristof ✔ @NickKristof · 10h

Exactly the wrong approach. One reason the opioid epidemic is so bad in the US is that only 10% of those addicted get treatment. We can't jail our way out of this crisis.

> **NPR Health News** ✔ @NPRHealth
> Trump Says He Will Focus On Opioid Law Enforcement, Not Treatment
> n.pr/2shuvJ1

💬 63   🔁 529   ♡ 1.3K   ✉

Source: Twitter/@NickKristof.

His tweet provides his perspective and gives his 2,170,000+ followers a chance to think about his real-time response to a real-time event. You may or may not agree with him, but he is using the platform Twitter provides to generate conversation on events he might not have time to write about in his op-ed column.

Point to Longer Articles and Resources

Finally, Twitter can be helpful in pointing people to resources about learning more about public policy issues. Agency personnel might tweet out a new report for the public to see. Academics might tweet out a new study they are releasing. Advocacy groups might tweet at a policy maker and include a link to an issue brief. For example, the American Enterprise Institute (AEI), an influential conservative think tank, posted this teaser for an article on paid family leave. It's an issue that is important to people on both sides of the aisle, and this is a chance to make them think about some important nuances of what makes for an effective policy to address it.

Advice on Writing for Twitter

The way that public policy writers use Twitter is still evolving, but there are some unique aspects of the genre that are still worth considering. Twitter, with its strict character limit, is clearly the most abbreviated of all of the genres covered in this book. As such, many of the formal writing rules and styles can be ignored or violated here. Emojis abound 👆 and

AEI ✔ @AEi · Feb 6

Unfortunately, the workers who are most in need of paid family leave, who lack the financial resources to take unpaid leave, are the least likely to have access through existing structures. @aparnamath

Time to give paid leave to the American workers who need it - AEI
With the combined responsibilities of the workplace and the family increasing, the case for providing paid time off from work for specific famil...
aei.org

♡ 9   ♡ 11   ✉

it's fine to use them to give 🖐 to good ideas. The character limit makes contractions a must & it's ok 2 use abbr 2 communicate. Use hashtags to promote #goodideas and enable people to engage in your conversation (#goodpolicywriting).

Simply participating on Twitter for a while will give you a good sense of what is appropriate in the policy area in which you live. While politicians sometimes use Twitter to attract attention, many policy writers use it simply to raise the profile of the good work they do through their research—more like a link to an issue brief than a 140-character op-ed. Look to the communities you engage with on Twitter for norms and keep in mind the advice from the email section above: You're always on the record, and never tweet when emotional. From there, enjoy writing as the newest form of #policywriting!

Conclusion

It might seem ironic for a professor to finish a book on writing on public policy with these concessions to a new genre and the accompanying GIFs and emojis, but my advice about writing in Twitter is actually exactly on point with the audience-centered principles at the center of this book: You have to put the needs and expectations of your audience first in order to be able to communicate with them. In the context of Twitter, the constraints of the genre mean that your audience expects you to write briefly and use the tools at your disposal. Continue to *think* and *communicate* as you write in this genre and you'll find writing for Twitter to be another effective tool to make progress on the most difficult challenges facing the communities in which you live.

The world needs you and your efforts. I hope this book has equipped you to serve the people you care for more effectively. Good luck and God bless.

CHECKLIST

Email

- Remember, you're on the record!
- Be appropriately formal.
- Use real subject lines.
- Introduce new people copied on an email.
- Explain attachments.
- Schedule with a tool.
- Think twice before hitting "reply all."

Twitter

- Remember, you're on the record!
- Be willing to be informal, while still being professional.
- Don't be a troll or engage with them.
- Understand how emojis, hashtags, and other Twitter tools work before you use them.
- Make sure your links work.

EXERCISES

1. Take a look at the last email you sent to a professional contact. Which principles laid out in this chapter did you follow? Which did you violate? Do you think any other principles should have been included?

2. Take a look at a recent email you received from a professional contact. Which principles laid out in this chapter did they follow? Which did they violate? Did this make them less effective?

3. Describe your current approach to handling the flood of email you receive every day. Are you satisfied with how your approach is working? Why or why not? What would you like to do differently?

4. Find a Twitter account of someone with whom you agree, disagree, or find boring. Which of the four ways of using Twitter do they use most often? Does it make them more effective? What are the norms that pop out to you from reading their tweets, either in terms of why they are tweeting or in terms of how they constructed the tweet (emojis, links, GIFs, etc.)?

5. Finally, what will you take away from this book as a whole? What did you learn from it? What do you hope you will do differently because of this book? How will it help you succeed in helping others in your career?

BIBLIOGRAPHY

Allen, D. (2002). *Getting things done: The art of stress-free productivity* (reprint ed.). New York: Penguin Books.

Centers for Disease Control and Prevention. (n.d.). *CDC guide to writing for social media*. Retrieved from http://www.cdc.gov/socialmedia/tools/guidelines/guidefor writing.html

Chui, M., Manyika, J., Bughin, J., Dobbs, R., Roxburgh, C., Sarrazin, H., Sands, G., & Westergren, M. (2012). *The social economy: Unlocking value and productivity through social technologies*. McKinsey Global Institute. Retrieved from http://www .mckinsey.com/insights/high_tech_telecoms_internet/the_social_economy

Heath, C., & Heath, D. (2007). *Made to stick: Why some ideas survive and others die* (1st ed.). New York: Random House.

Shipley, D., & Schwalbe, W. (2010). *SEND: Why people email so badly and how to do it better* (reprint ed.). New York: Vintage.

Turkle, S. (2015). *Reclaiming conversation: The power of talk in a digital age*. New York: Penguin Press.

Index

CPSIA information can be obtained
at www.ICGtesting.com
Printed in the USA
LVHW051949190122
708794LV00010B/389

9 781506 348780